What's Yours Is Mine

WHAT'S YOURS — IS — MINE

Against the Sharing Economy

TOM SLEE

O/R

OR Books

New York · London

Published for the book trade by OR Books in partnership with Counterpoint Press. Distributed to the trade by Publishers Group West.

For all rights information: rights@orbooks.com

First trade printing 2017

Cataloging-in-Publication data is available from the Library of Congress. A catalog record for this book is available from the British Library.

ISBN 978-1-944869-37-3

Text design by Bathcat Ltd. Typeset by AarkMany Media, Chennai, India.

Amongst the highly placed
It is considered low to talk about food.
The fact is: they have
Already eaten.

BERTOLT BRECHT, *From a German War Primer*

What's yours is mine,
what's mine is my own.

Traditional Yorkshire saying

To my mother, Audrey Slee

Preface to the Revised Edition

A lot has changed in the 20 months since I completed the original manuscript for this book.

Sharing Economy poster children Uber and Airbnb have continued to grow rapidly in terms of market capitalization, investment raised, revenue, controversy, media attention, and (in the case of Uber) financial losses. Both have followed through on their ambition to disrupt traditional industries as they continue to struggle for legitimacy. The companies seem to have validated the dramatic predictions that some people made about the Sharing Economy as a sea change in the way businesses worked.

But outside transit and travel, the picture is different. Beyond these twin pillars, the Sharing Economy looks more and more like a bubble, as companies offering delivery services, home services, and goods-for-rent through Internet and mobile platforms have struggled to grow and/or attain profitability. It turns out the Internet does not add much, after all, to the world of informal neighbor-to-neighbor sharing, and the tool libraries and other community initiatives have remained small, their success depending more on the strength of their underlying community than on the benefits brought by a software platform.

I don't know whether to be pleased or disappointed that the main thesis of the book has been borne out by events. The transition from the generosity of "What's Mine is Yours" to the self-interest of "What's Yours is Mine" is essentially complete, and the "sharing" in the Sharing Economy has been reduced to simple market exchange. The appeal of a bottom-up, personal, community-driven alternative to traditional corporations has fizzled; we are left with Uber, a company financed by high-net-worth investors via Morgan Stanley and by Saudi Arabia's Public Investment Fund, and Airbnb, by some measures the largest hotel company in the world.

But as Uber and Airbnb have grown, they still struggle to define a sustainable business model. Their success to date has been driven in part by the ease with which the platform model pushes the costs and risks onto the platform participants (drivers for example), and onto the neighborhoods and cities in which they operate. That success has led to pushback from cities around the world. During 2016 city governments have gained confidence in their dealings with these brash new arrivals, and no longer accept as a given that the Sharing Economy is an inevitable technological *fait-accompli*, a future that they must board if they are not to be left behind. The narrative of self-regulation no longer looks convincing.

Much of the book remains valid and is unchanged. So Chapters 1 and 2, which provide a sketch of the Sharing Economy at the peak of the hype, as well as Chapters 5 (on on-demand services) and 6 (on reputation and ratings) are also essentially unchanged.

Part of the book's argument is that the trajectory of the Sharing Economy follows a well-worn path for the Internet-focused technology industry. It's a path charted by other generous-sounding narratives build around community and openness, narratives that have found an uncritical and enthusiastic acceptance in the venture-capital funded hothouse that is Silicon Valley. These narratives are explored in Chapters 7 and 8 and, again, these remain as in the first printing.

Chapters 3 (Airbnb) and 4 (Uber) have been updated and extended. Disputes over business practices, accusations of platform-enabled racism, profitability (Uber), impact on affordable housing (Airbnb), conflicts with cities around the world (both), and more have left these companies rarely out of the news.

Finally, Chapter 9 takes a look at some of the debates and disputes around the Sharing Economy, such as employment practices and legal frameworks. I have added some of the more interesting proposals and developments to this chapter.

Any errors that remain are, of course, my responsibility.

Tom Slee
Waterloo, Canada
April 2017

Contents

1. The Sharing Economy

The Sharing Economy is a wave of new businesses that use the Internet to match customers with service providers for real-world exchanges such as short-term apartment rentals, car rides, or household tasks. At the leading edge of this wave are Uber and Airbnb, each showing eye-popping growth to bolster their claim that they are disrupting traditional transit and tourism industries. These two are followed by a flock of other companies vying to join them at the top of the Sharing Economy world.

Supporters sometimes describe the Sharing Economy as a new type of business and sometimes as a social movement. It's a familiar mix of commerce and cause in the digital world. Silicon Valley may have its share of the world's richest people, but it has always seen itself and presented itself as being about more than money: it's also about building a better future. The Internet is making the world better, not just by giving us better gadgets and more information, but by reshaping society, root and branch. We now have the technology to solve problems that have plagued humanity for centuries, making old institutions and old rules obsolete and replacing them with computation.

The buzz around the Sharing Economy began a few years ago, but it really started to enter the mainstream in 2013 and 2014. It makes promises that appeal to many people; they certainly appeal to me. Start with informal exchanges—giving a friend a car ride or borrowing a power drill, or running a few errands for neighbors—and use the connecting power of the Internet to scale them up, so that we as individuals can rely more on each other and less on faceless, distant corporations. Each exchange helps someone make a little money and helps someone save a little time: what's not to like? By taking part in the Sharing Economy we help to build our community instead of being passive and materialist consumers; we help to create a new era of openness, in which we can find a welcome and a helping hand wherever we go.

The Sharing Economy promises to help previously powerless individuals take more control of their lives by becoming "micro-entrepreneurs." We can be self-directed, dipping in and out of this new flexible mode of work, setting up our own businesses on Sharing Economy web sites; we can become an Airbnb host, a driver for Lyft, a handyperson for Handy, or an altruistic investor making loans on Lending Club. The movement seems to threaten those who are already powerful, like big hotel chains, fast food chains, and banks. It's an egalitarian vision built on peer-to-peer exchanges rather than hierarchical organizations, and it's brought about by the Internet's ability to bring people together: the Sharing Economy promises to "get Americans [and others] to trust each other."[1]

The Sharing Economy also promises to be a sustainable alternative to mainstream commerce, helping us to make better use of under-utilized resources—why does everyone need a power drill sitting on a basement shelf when we could share? We can buy less and so lighten our footprint on the planet—maybe use Uber rather than buy a car? We can choose access over ownership, and move away from a consumerism in which many of us feel trapped. We can be less materialistic, looking to experiences rather than possessions to give meaning to our lives.

Well, that was the promise.

Unfortunately, something different and altogether darker is happening: the Sharing Economy is extending a harsh and deregulated free market into previously protected areas of our lives. The leading companies are now corporate juggernauts themselves, and are taking a more and more intrusive role in the exchanges they support to make their money and to maintain their brand. As the Sharing Economy grows, it is reshaping cities without regard to those things that make them livable. Rather than bringing a new openness and personal trust to our interactions, it is bringing a new form of surveillance where service workers must live in fear of being snitched on, and while the company CEOs talk benevolently of their communities of users, the reality has a harder edge of centralized control. Sharing Economy marketplaces are generating new and ever-more-entitled forms of consumption. The language of "a little extra money" turns out to be the same as that used about women's jobs forty years ago, when they were not seen as "real" jobs that demanded a living wage, and so did not need to be treated the same, or paid as much, as men's jobs. Instead of freeing individuals to take control over their own lives, many Sharing Economy companies are making big money for their investors and executives, and making good jobs for their software engineers and marketers, by removing the protections and assurances won by decades of struggle, by creating riskier and more precarious forms of low-paid work for those who actually work in the Sharing Economy.

■

There is a contradiction built into the name "sharing economy." We think of sharing as a non-commercial, person-to-person, social interaction. It suggests exchanges that do not involve money, or that are at least motivated by generosity, by a desire to give or to help. "Economy" suggests market transactions—the self-interested exchange of money for goods or services. There has been a lot of debate about whether "sharing economy" is the right name to use to describe this new wave of businesses, and a raft of other names have been tried out—collaborative consumption, the mesh economy, peer-to-peer platforms, the gig economy, concierge services, or, increasingly, the "on-demand economy."

There is no doubt that the word "sharing" has been stretched beyond reasonable limits as the "sharing economy" has grown and changed, but we still need a name when we talk about the phenomenon. While it may not last more than another year or so, "sharing economy" is the name used right now in 2015. I will use the name, but to avoid repeated use of the word "alleged" or annoyingly frequent scare quotes I will capitalize it as the Sharing Economy.[2]

Definitions don't take us very far when talking about something as fluid and rapidly changing as the Sharing Economy, but we still need to draw some boundaries around the topic to talk about it coherently. Chapter 2 surveys the Sharing Economy landscape: it explores what kind of organizations are included, where they come from, what they do, and how they are funded. The chapter shows that there are at least two visions of the Sharing Economy: the first is the communitarian and co-operative vision focused on small-scale personal exchanges. The second is the disruptive, globe-straddling ambition of companies with billions of dollars to spend challenging democratically made laws around the world, acquiring competitors in search of scale, and (in Uber's case) researching new technologies to render its work force obsolete. If the former vision can be called "what's mine is yours," I think of the latter as "what's yours is mine."

It is impossible to talk much about the Sharing Economy without looking at its two acknowledged leaders: Uber and Airbnb. For many people, these two companies *are* the Sharing Economy, and they have given rise to a legion of imitators pitching venture capitalists with their efforts to be "the Uber of this" or "the Airbnb of that." Founded within a year of each other in the San Francisco area, both have grown by leaps and bounds ever since, bringing their business model to cities around the world. Uber's market valuation exceeds that of the world's largest car rental companies, Airbnb's matches those of the world's largest hotel chains, and despite being in seemingly prosaic industries (taxis, apartment rentals), the founders of each are now billionaires.

The technology of the two companies is often described in similar terms: each rely on software platforms, web sites, and mobile apps to match consumers with providers, and to take a slice of the proceeds. The software also handles payments, and each provides a reputation system that they claim solves the problems of screening so that strangers can trust each other.

But the two companies are also quite different. Airbnb is the poster-child for sharing: in its public statements and in its marketing it actively promotes a bucolic "shared city" where "local mom and pops flourish once again . . . that fosters community, where space isn't wasted, but shared with others." Uber, as its name suggests, is not interested in anything so soft and fuzzy as community: it projects an aspirational image of status ("Everyone's private driver") and its confrontational CEO Travis Kalanick is well known to be a fan of Ayn Rand and her ideology of rugged individualism.

Both companies have run into controversy in many of the cities where they operate, running afoul of city regulations and laws, and both have taken the approach of pushing for growth, aiming to present a fait accompli to slow moving and often understaffed city governments. Both believe that their innovations make existing rules obsolete and that their technology can solve the problems that city regulations were meant to solve, but better and with a lighter touch.

Chapter 3 is about Airbnb. It shows how the company's real business is different from the image it has cultivated, and how its growth is aggravating problems in the cities where it operates, particularly in its most popular destinations. Chapter 4 is about Uber: how its pursuit of a consumer-driven society is ushering in a new form of precarious work, and about its misleading claims that it is delivering both cheap rides for travelers and well-paid jobs for drivers.

Running errands and cleaning are among the other unglamorous jobs that have suddenly become the target of venture capital funding. The lives of those working in what are increasingly called "on-demand" services is the subject of Chapter 5, from early pioneer TaskRabbit ("neighbors helping neighbors") to the newer entrants who have long since given up on any idea of community in their drive to establish growing and profitable businesses. Other examples of Sharing Economy services are sprinkled throughout the book.

One of the limits to social engagement has always been trust. Our generous selves would love to pick up hitchhikers, but we worry that it would be unsafe to do so—if we can trust them—and so hitchhiking has almost vanished as a way for people to get around. Chapter 6 looks at one of the biggest claims made for the Sharing Economy: that it has used the Internet to solve the problem of trust between strangers by letting people rate each other on so-called "reputation systems." These descendants of the rating systems that Amazon and Netflix use to provide recommendations are becoming commonplace in our digital experience, and have been welcomed as almost magical in their ability to guide us to what we want. But magical they are not, and a look at how they work in practice shows that these systems fail in their stated goals, and are increasingly being used to establish a regime of mutual surveillance and even fear among those being rated.

You may have been a host or guest on Airbnb; you may have given or taken a ride on Uber; you may have ordered a meal from, or delivered one for, Postmates. This book is critical of the companies and of the broader Sharing Economy movement, but it is not my intent to make you feel guilty or defensive about taking part in Sharing Economy exchanges. The problems with the Sharing Economy do not lie with the individual participant looking for a novel vacation or a quick ride across town, any more than the broader problems of consumerism lie with the individual filling a car with gasoline or buying a new pair of shoes. The problems lie with the companies themselves, and with the financial interests using those companies to drive a broader agenda of deregulation in search of private wealth.

■

The Sharing Economy may be new, but it does have a history and a context, and we need to explore these to understand its agenda, and to understand how it is evolving. Chapters 7 and 8 explore the origins of the Sharing Economy in Internet culture: the values and practices that permeate Silicon Valley companies and the wider world of technology enthusiasts, from open source programmers to Bitcoin advocates to the "maker movement" and beyond.

Any short description will undoubtedly be an oversimplification, and of course there are disagreements and disputes among its adherents, but a coherent Internet culture does exist. It embraces values of rebellion, drawing from a loose set of attitudes sometimes called the hacker ethic. Facebook's headquarters are at "One Hacker Way" and it has the word HACK laid out in 12-meter letters in the stone. The company's mantra until last year was "move fast and break things," and Mark Zuckerberg recently explained to potential investors: "Hackers believe that something can always be better, and that nothing is ever complete. They just have to go fix it—often in the face of people who say it's impossible or are content with the status quo."

Internet culture also believes that the Internet itself is a key to building a better world. The invention of the Internet marks a break with the past, and an opportunity to open many old political and social debates. Companies see themselves as enlightened participants in these debates, with a social mandate as well as a business mandate; Google's "Don't be evil" mantra encapsulates their belief that the company has a moral mission as well as a technological one.

Internet culture is also supremely ambitious and self-confident. It's a confidence captured in venture capitalist Marc Andreessen's saying that "software is eating the world." In its outer reaches it is an ambition manifested in ideas of Seasteading (a movement to build self-governing floating cities, started by PayPal founder Peter Thiel) and the Singularity (a belief in "the dawning of a new civilization that will enable us to transcend our biological limitations and amplify our creativity," originating with the ideas of inventor and now Google employee Ray Kurzweil).

Just as Hollywood is both a physical location and a global industry with a distinctive set of traditions, beliefs, and practices, so Silicon Valley is more than a place—it is shorthand for the world of digital technology, specifically Internet technology. Silicon Valley includes big companies like Apple, Google, Facebook, Amazon, and Microsoft, and it includes a never-ending stream of ambitious startups, not all physically located in Silicon Valley proper, but all driven by and products of the broader Internet culture.

The Sharing Economy takes its inspiration from one particular tenet of that culture: a belief in the virtues of openness. Openness and sharing go hand in hand: to make something open is to stop it being a commodity, to take it out of the realm of private property and make it shareable among members of a community. So open-source software, in which computer code is built by a network of peers and shared for free, is an inspiration for sharing our physical possessions and our labor. Wikipedia shows that software platforms can collect together the efforts of millions of collaborators to make something that is new and global and different, and it inspired the building of web sites such as Airbnb's. Starting with Napster, file-sharing sites challenged industries that are based on copyright and private ownership, such as music, movie-making, and professional photography. Social media is built on a willingness of people to be open, to share aspects of themselves with others. The Open Data Movement looks to make governments open, using digital technology to drive transparency and innovation.

Chapter 7 takes a look at the politics of openness, but the message of the chapter is not as sunny as Sharing Economy advocates would like. Economically, openness has two roles: it is an alternative to commerce (music sharing was an alternative to record stores), but it also generates new forms of commerce (music sharing built YouTube), and those new forms of commerce come with problems of their own. Industries built on openness have delivered some remarkable things, but they have repeatedly failed to deliver on their promises of democratization and equality, and the Sharing Economy is busy running down the path paved by these previous industries.

As Silicon Valley has grown wealthier and more powerful, the beliefs that you can do well by doing good and that markets can in fact be used to "scale up" efforts for social change, have become mainstream within Internet culture. It's a viewpoint sometimes called the Californian Ideology.[3] From global poverty to civil liberties to education and healthcare, Internet culture sees the combination of technology and the entrepreneurial mindset as the key to solving our biggest problems. But markets, sharing, and social good are uneasy partners, and the relationships between them are the subject of Chapter 8. The Internet is not so complete a break with the past as some would like to believe, and a look at our civic lives and at how cities operate shows that commercial incentives can often crowd out non-commercial forms of sharing. New businesses may be built around sharing and openness, but commercial instincts will tend to drive out altruistic behavior, and the generous impulses that inspired the Sharing Economy will be crushed by monetary incentives.

■

The Sharing Economy is young and it is changing rapidly. It will be shaped by our behavior as consumers, but also by our behavior as citizens and our behavior as workers. Sharing Economy companies claim we should trust them and their technologies to take over functions provided by governments: guaranteeing a safe consumer experience, ensuring that employment is fair and dignified, and shaping cities to be livable and sustainable. We should not do so.

I wrote this book because the Sharing Economy agenda appeals to ideals with which I and many others identify; ideals such as equality, sustainability, and community. The Sharing Economy continues to have the support and allegiance of many progressive-minded people—particularly young people who identify strongly with the technologies they use—who are having their best instincts manipulated and who will be betrayed. The Sharing Economy is invoking those ideals to build massive private fortunes, to erode real communities, to encourage a more entitled form of consumerism, and to create a future that is more precarious and more unequal than ever.

There are others who see no contradiction between a social movement and private for-profit firms: these are the believers in "Benefit Corporations" and other forms of enlightened capitalism, who are thick on the ground in the San Francisco Bay area where the Sharing Economy has its home. I hope to convince some of these that the Sharing Economy is failing to deliver on their hopes.

Many others are happy to promote a vision of inequality and deregulation for its own sake, in which money takes over the role of democratic institutions; this book does not have much to say to those who have that outlook.

I work in the technology industry and in my daily life I spend a lot of time with computers. I do not doubt that new technologies can play an important part in building a better future, but they do not provide a shortcut to solving complex social problems or to resolving longstanding sources of social conflict. If the Sharing Economy proponents who do believe in equality and sustainability want to build something useful, they need to drop the hubris of Internet culture and learn some lessons from those in other fields who have been engaged in sharing for years. Just as there are no shortcuts to solving complex social problems, so there is no simple Big Idea to countering the worst of the Sharing Economy. A starting point is that we recognize it for what it is.

2. The Sharing Economy Landscape

One way to explore the makeup of the Sharing Economy is to look at an organization called Peers. Formed in 2013, Peers described itself as "a grassroots, member-driven organization that supports the Sharing Economy movement." When Airbnb ran into business permit problems in Grand Rapids, Michigan or when a neighborhood council threatened to ban Airbnb in Silver Lake, California, it was Peers that rallied Airbnb hosts to lobby councilors on the company's behalf. When Seattle City Council decided that Lyft and Uber were breaking taxi regulations, it was Peers that mobilized supporters to sign petitions. And these efforts were not in vain: they succeeded in getting councils to back down, and in one of the organization's most important victories they got the state of California to recognize a new category of transit organization called "Transportation Network Companies," which created a framework within which Lyft, Uber, Sidecar, and others could operate legally, and which has been imitated in several other states since.

In the summer of 2014, Peers listed 75 partner organizations on its web site, and the list gives a snapshot of the Sharing Economy landscape as it hit the mainstream. Spanish company Gudog is "a platform that brings together dog owners and trustworthy dog sitters"; with BoatBound you can "find the perfect boat with or without a captain"; if you prefer eating to boating, you can go to Cookening, a web site where "your host cooks and shares a meal with you, at his or her place." Cookening is a bit like EatWith, whose "hosts share a talent for making amazing meals and a love for welcoming people into their homes to share them," and Cookisto charts a similar path, providing a web site through which "neighbors share delicious homemade meals." If you need to do some handiwork around your house but lack the tools, then you might want to go to NeighborGoods ("share goods with your neighbors and friends"), 1000 Tools ("the rental marketplace for tools"), or, if you are in Australia, Open Shed ("why buy when you can share?"). If you don't have the skills yourself, you could call on TaskRabbit to provide a helper; if you need an office space to work, try PivotDesk; if you need to raise funds, go to CrowdTilt; if you need your house cleaned, go to Homejoy's web site; if you need a place to park your car, try ParkAtMyHouse; if you want to rent a bike or surfboard, reach out to Spinlister. There are Sharing Economy organizations sprouting up for all kinds of activities.

Getting around is the most prevalent offering, represented by ride-sharing companies (Lyft, Sidecar), car sharing (RelayRides), bike sharing (Spinlister, Divvy), and more. Sharing meals and sharing household goods are popular, and personal services such as house cleaning (Homejoy, Proprly) and errands (TaskRabbit, PiggyBee) all have a presence too. Almost all of these organizations have started in the last few years.

Peers partners come from around the world. California and New York are the most common origins, but there are partners from several European countries (PiggyBee is Belgian, Blablacar is French, Carpooling is German, Swapsee is Spanish, ParkAtMyHouse is British), from Australasia (Zookal, Airtasker), as well as from Israel (EatWith, CasaVersa), South Africa, and Turkey.

This diversity, this range of small and neighborhood-focused organizations, is why the Sharing Economy has appealed to the ecologically minded and to those who identify with artisans. It's why author Rachel Botsman can describe the Sharing Economy this way in a TED talk:

> At its core, it's about empowerment. It's about empowering people to make meaningful connections, connections that are enabling us to rediscover a humanness that we've lost somewhere along the way, by engaging in marketplaces like Airbnb, like Kickstarter, like Etsy, that are built on personal relationships versus empty transaction.[1]

It's also why stories in the mainstream press tended to start off with the quirky and personal. Here is the *Wall Street Journal*:

The hottest technology trend is apps that let anyone share anything, which is why Grace Lichaa recently found a group of strangers eating her home-cooked macaroni.

About a dozen people she met through the Internet arrived, mostly on time, at her Washington, D.C., house in November for three flavors of macaroni and cheese: garlic-crusted, goat cheese tomato, and curried. Ms. Lichaa, 32 years old, advertised seats for the "mac attack" on a site called EatFeastly.com for $19.80 each.[2]

And here is *Wired* magazine, in the same vein:

In about 40 minutes, Cindy Manit will let a complete stranger into her car. An app on her windshield-mounted iPhone will summon her to a corner in San Francisco's South of Market neighborhood, where a russet-haired woman in an orange raincoat and coffee-colored boots will slip into the front seat of her immaculate 2006 Mazda3 hatchback and ask for a ride to the airport.[3]

Peers is only one lens through which to view the makeup of the Sharing Economy. In 2013 Rachel Botsman presented a classification of Sharing Economy services,[4] and in a 2015 report, consultant Jeremiah Owyang presented his own profile.[5] In addition to the examples given above, Botsman and Owyang each highlight some sectors that are less well-represented among the Peers membership.

One prominent sector is finance. Peer-to-peer lending companies such as Lending Club and Prosper claim to replace credit cards and banks with lower-interest person-to-person loans. Lending Club became a publicly owned company in December 2014 and the volume of peer-to-peer loans is growing rapidly: as of May 2015 the five biggest companies have issued nearly a million loans between them and are generating more at the rate of well over $10 billion a year.[6]

Another booming sector is shared working spaces, promoting "access over ownership" for new businesses and independent creators. WeWork, the leader in this space, has raised over $500 million to help it expand.

Wired magazine explicitly compares WeWork to Uber and Airbnb after the company's latest funding round valued it at $5 billion:

> It's a steep price for what is essentially an office leasing company. But WeWork's business model, which combines real estate with technology, plays into the "sharing economy" trend that has captivated investors in recent years, thanks to hit companies like Uber and Airbnb. Both companies infused established industries (car services and vacation rentals) with a high tech touch, and as a result, both companies have garnered valuations far beyond their established predecessors (taxi and limo services and hotels). And so it goes with WeWork.[7]

Botsman and Owyang both extend the definition of the sharing economy to include companies largely outside the scope of this book. Coursera and others are challenging university education by providing massively open online courses (MOOCs), online marketplaces for products—such as eBay and Etsy—predate the rise of the Sharing Economy and its focus on "real-world" exchanges, and crowdfunding platforms such as Kickstarter can be seen as an extension of the peer-to-peer finance platforms.

■

The Sharing Economy landscape is defined not only by what it includes, but by what kind of sharing organizations are missing. Sociologist Juliet Schor sums up the situation:

> There is great diversity among activities as well as baffling boundaries drawn by participants. TaskRabbit, an "errands" site, is often included, but Mechanical Turk (Amazon's online labor market) is not. Airbnb is practically synonymous with the sharing economy, but traditional bed and breakfasts are left out. Lyft, a ride service company, claims to be in, but Uber, another ride service company, does not. Shouldn't public libraries and parks count? When I posed these questions to a few sharing innovators, they were

pragmatic, rather than analytical: self-definition by the platforms and the press defines who is in and who is out.[8]

(Uber initially resisted being identified with the Sharing Economy, but since starting its UberX program it has increasingly adopted the Sharing Economy language. While some observers resisted including Uber in the ranks of Sharing Economy companies, it now clearly belongs—it was the principal beneficiary of Peers' efforts around "ridesharing," and especially the establishment of the Transportation Network Company classification in California.)

The normal way in which communities provide shared goods is through government, from municipal swimming pools and soccer fields to public transit to libraries and much more, but there are no government groups in the list. There is no representation among Peers partners from the world of food co-ops, worker co-ops, lending libraries, allotment groups, or other groups involved in non-digital community-sharing initiatives. Zipcar is included (shared access to a vehicle), but the Youth Hostel Association is not (shared access to accommodation). There are many organizations that seem to fit into the Sharing Economy mandate, taken literally, but that have no link to Peers, whether they be equipment rental shops, secondhand stores, boat rentals, or even the big car-rental companies.

But the boundaries of the Sharing Economy are not arbitrary. Almost all the members of Peers, and all the groups mentioned by Botsman and Owyang, are technology-focused organizations, and this is central to the Sharing Economy story. If Sharing Economy companies define the name, then it is clear that the Internet is a central part of their self-identification.

It is the commercial embodiment of author Steven Johnson's idea of the "peer progressive." In his recent book *Future Perfect*, Johnson says: "When a need arises in society that goes unmet, our first impulse should be to build a peer network to solve that problem." To build a "peer network" means, first and foremost, to build an Internet software platform: a web site and/or mobile application on which consumers and service providers can create a presence and exchange goods and services.[9]

Looked at from other perspectives, the Sharing Economy is not as diverse as it first appears.

Strangely, considering the language of altruism and generosity that is so often used to describe it, the Sharing Economy is overwhelmingly made up of commercial organizations rather than non-profits. Out of Peers' 70 partners, over 60 are for-profit companies, and over 85% of the funding for Peers partners went to California companies. Despite the sprinkling of partners from around the globe, the money shows that the Sharing Economy is predominantly a Silicon Valley phenomenon. (This is one reason why, although I am Canadian and British, this book focuses on American events and debates.)

Three kinds of service dominate: hospitality (43%), transport (28%), and education (17%). In the world of hospitality most of that funding has gone to one company: Airbnb, which in summer 2014 had raised $800 million since 2009, with the majority coming in the previous twelve months. In the world of transport, the leading fundraiser was Lyft, which had raised just over $300 million, most of that in April 2014. For all the talk of neighbors swapping power drills, these are the kind of companies that are making waves and leading the Sharing Economy.

Since summer 2014 the picture has become even more exaggerated. As of August 2015 Airbnb has taken its fundraising to a massive $2.3 billion, Lyft had raised $1 billion, and its competitor Uber (not a Peers partner) had raised no less than $7 billion.[10]

What this all comes down to is that, while the Sharing Economy is often presented as a diverse set of commercial and non-commercial initiatives around the world (from tool-exchange co-ops to pet-sitting and so on), this presentation is a bit misleading. The Sharing Economy is almost entirely a small number of technology firms backed by large amounts of venture capital.

∎

The history of Peers itself reflects the tension between the disparate and geographically scattered organizations on its partner list and the reality of a few, well-funded Silicon Valley companies. At its founding, the organization was led by Natalie Foster, who had a background as a community organizer and who had worked with the Obama administration and the Sierra Club, and other leading members had community-organizer backgrounds. When Peers described itself as a grassroots, member-driven organization that supports the Sharing Economy movement, there were people who believed in that description.

But the picture is more complex. The formation of Peers was announced by another co-founder, Douglas Atkin. His words, at the LeWeb conference in 2013, have a communitarian ring:

> I'd like to talk about a movement for the sharing economy. By "a movement" I mean exactly that. I mean huge numbers of people, with a shared identity, mobilized to take action to do two things: to grow the peer sharing economy, and to fight for their collective interests against unfair and unreasonable obstacles.[11]

But in addition to being Board Chairman at Peers, Douglas Atkin is Global Head of Community and Mobilization at Airbnb. Airbnb is not the only company involved in Peers: much of the organization's funding came from "mission-aligned independent donors" and foundations, but those independent donors included investors and executives of Sharing Economy startups. Peers leader Natalie Foster traced the idea for the organization back to seed money from Airbnb that started a "conversation among stakeholders" at Purpose, an organization that creates "21st century movements."[12] Douglas Atkin was also a co-founder of Purpose.

So Peers itself reflects this mix of communitarian intent and corporate self-interest. Atkin, in particular, is well aware of the power that can come from identifying a business with a movement. He set out his philosophy in a 2004 book called *The Culting of Brands: Turn Your Customers into True Believers*. His approach consists first of determining and declaring your brand's sense of difference—what sets it apart from the rest of the world—and then providing ways for members to identify with the "cult," while also identifying an opponent to demonize.[13] As Atkin spoke at LeWeb, he slipped back and forth between the language of business and the language of movement. In one part of his speech, participants are taking part in a political action:

> So what we're talking about here is not just people sharing their skills, or their apartment, or their car, but also their collective power to expand the Sharing Economy together, and to stand up against entrenched interests who stand unfairly in their way. So "people power" if you like, or more accurately "peer power."

But a moment later, he is more interested in building businesses:

> I attended a meeting of Sharing Economy participants . . .
> they were developing ideas—brilliant ideas actually—to
> share customers with each other, across verticals. One
> person even suggested that there could be a peer economy
> currency—maybe Bitcoin. Or even points to encourage
> people to cross verticals and recruit new people into this
> new economy.

So it is not surprising that almost all the campaigns at Peers were focused on the well-funded sectors of the Sharing Economy represented by Airbnb and Lyft. The highest-profile campaigns, such as the 2014 ride-sharing initiative in Seattle, operated side-by-side with well-funded efforts driven by Lyft and Uber themselves. Whatever the intent of the more community-focused Peers activists, the group functioned in part as a front for Silicon Valley lobbying.

■

The funding behind the larger Sharing Economy companies highlights the contradictory currents that drive it. Billionaire and Amazon CEO Jeff Bezos has invested in both Airbnb and Uber; leading venture capital firm Andreessen Horowitz has invested in Airbnb, Lyft, and delivery service Instacart; Founders Fund, a firm set up and led by billionaire and PayPal founder Peter Thiel, has invested in Airbnb, Lyft, and TaskRabbit. Goldman Sachs is another investor in Uber as well as WeWork, which has also been funded by JP Morgan. Lending Club sends emails emphasizing that "Instead of paying interest to a credit card company or on a traditional bank loan, you get your loan through ordinary people like YOU who want to invest in YOUR success,"[14] but its board includes John Mack (ex–Morgan Stanley) and Larry Summers (former Treasury secretary). This kind of wealth and, in some cases, outspoken Libertarian politics, is a long way from the picture of a grassroots movement invoked by Douglas Atkin.

The Sharing Economy is a movement: it is a movement for deregulation. Major financial institutions and influential venture capital funds are seizing an opportunity to challenge rules made by democratic city governments around the world, and to reshape cities in their own interests. It's not about building an alternative to a corporate-driven market economy, it's about extending the deregulated free market into new areas of our lives. An enthusiasm for "the end of ownership," the title of one Andreessen Horowitz blog post on the Sharing Economy, is difficult to take seriously when it comes from those who actually own the companies involved. And when Atkin dreams of "citizens band[ing] together to grow and protect their interests in the Sharing Economy rather than companies wielding their power," one has to wonder where his own company stands.

Toward the end of his speech, Atkin made a pitch for help:

> So I'm here to tell you about some plans which will enable people to create a member-driven movement for the sharing economy [Peers]. If you like, a new kind of union for a new kind of economy. And I'm also here to ask for your support. So if you're a platform: help your users create this organization and join it. If you're a thought-leader, blogger, or conference speaker: champion it. And if you've got some ready cash, please help fund it.

The chutzpah of asking his audience to dip into their pockets to fund an organization put together by billionaire-funded companies is remarkable. One of the motivations behind writing this book is to push back against people such as Douglas Atkin appropriating the language of collective action and progressive politics for private financial gain.

∎

You may have noticed that I use the past tense when discussing Peers. That's because, in October 2014, Peers changed its leadership and its mission. Natalie Foster was replaced as Executive Director by Shelby Clark, the founder of Sharing Economy company RelayRides. In December 2014, Clark announced that Peers would split into two organizations: the Peers corporation and the Peers Foundation.[15]

The Peers Foundation is "still defining its future" but the Peers corporation, still using the .org domain usually associated with non-profits, is no longer presenting itself as a grass-roots activist organization. Instead, it is a for-profit service provider for people who work in the Sharing Economy, helping them to find insurance and tax advice.

Airbnb itself has not lost sight of the benefits of a social movement for its business. Following the success of its 2015 campaign against Proposition F (to limit homesharing) in San Francisco, it set up the Airbnb Host Movement, and in the next year organized hosts in 100 cities into Home Sharing Clubs.[16]

The tension between activist, communitarian, social movement, and business venture was resolved, and the commercial basis of the Sharing Economy has become clearer than ever.

3. A Place to Stay with Airbnb

If there is one company that exemplifies the Sharing Economy, it is surely Airbnb. As we have already seen, it was involved in founding Peers through its executive Douglas Atkin. Rachel Botsman and Roo Rogers' *What's Mine Is Yours*[1] was an important book for the Sharing Economy, setting out a vision that has helped to define the movement. The book opens with the story of Airbnb's beginnings, and Botsman also looks to Airbnb to set the tone for her TED talk on sharing. When leading public commentators like *New York Times* columnists David Brooks and Thomas Friedman write about the Sharing Economy, they look to Airbnb CEO Brian Chesky. And Chesky speaks out about the values of sharing; in March 2014 he wrote a photo-heavy manifesto-like short essay called "Shared City," which started like this:

> Imagine if you could build a city that is shared. Where people become micro-entrepreneurs, and local mom and pops flourish once again. Imagine a city that fosters community, where space isn't wasted, but shared with others. A city that produces more, but without more waste. While this may seem radical, it's not a new idea. Cities are the original sharing platforms.[2]

Airbnb traces this vision back to its roots. "If you want to understand Airbnb, you have to understand our beginnings," says the company on its blog.[3] Many Sharing Economy companies seem to have started out the same way: some talented young people come across a problem in their own life, they put up a web site to help solve it, and then they look to turn it into a business. With the help of Silicon Valley venture capitalists, they build a successful and growing company.

In Airbnb's case, the problem was for some young former design students to pay the sky-high rents of San Francisco. In 2007, Brian Chesky and Joe Gebbia were looking for ways to make their end-of-month payments when a design industry conference came to town. They bought some inflatable airbeds and offered accommodations to attendees who would be interested in a cheap place to stay. They were inundated with requests and realized there may be a market for this kind of thing, and so "Airbed & Breakfast" was born.

Since then, the story has been one of hard work and growth. Running up the limit on multiple credit cards to finance the very beginnings, they got an early investment from Paul Graham's Y-Combinator fund. Struggling to get the site to take off, they went out to their biggest city (New York) and got the hosts to have professional photos taken of their rooms to make them more appealing; the bookings increased, and professional photography continues to be the most effective way for a host to attract guests. Other maneuvers included a breakfast-cereal pitch around the Democratic convention in Chicago and a widely criticized email campaign via Craigslist.

After the early tribulations, the now-trio of Chesky, Gebbia, and Nathan Blecharczyk found themselves at the head of a phenomenon. In 2011 Airbnb had 50,000 listings; in 2012 that number more than doubled to 120,000; by the end of 2013 it was 550,000; by mid-2015, Airbnb claimed 1.2 million listings and in April 2017 over 3 million. For comparison, the largest hotel company in the world by number of rooms is the InterContinental Group with 700,000 rooms.

The number of visits booked through the site has followed a similar trajectory: before 2013 there were a total of 4 million visits, by the end of 2013 the number reached 10 million, by early 2015 it claims 25 million visitors, and industry analyst Vicki Stern estimated it was running at 37 million overnight stays in a year.[4] While this number is about 20% of the number of guests claimed by the leading hotel companies, growth is not slowing down.

Financially too, Airbnb has become a major actor: the company is still private but continues to attract investors. Its $4.4 billion of funding corresponds to an estimated market valuation of $30 billion, comparable to hotel industry giants such as Marriott International ($35 billion) and Hilton

($20 billion). Its three founders no longer struggle to pay the rent: each of them is now a billionaire.

By the time you read this book, all those numbers will be bigger.

Sharing Economy supporters see the Airbnb story as an inspiration, and it is easy to see why. It's a web site for "regular, local people who make a little extra money by sharing their homes with respectful guests from around the world"[5] that has grown to challenge the largest global hotel chains. It has shown that a personal visit—human-level contact—is a viable alternative to the impersonal and uniform mass-produced anonymity of the corporate tourist industry. On Airbnb you can rent a tree house, a castle, a room in a clock tower, or a houseboat. Who wouldn't prefer this to yet another identikit hotel room? In an interview, Brian Chesky says, "We really, really care about this deeper idea of bringing the world together."[6]

Airbnb emphasizes that many of its hosts are artistic, and not wealthy: in Barcelona "75 percent of Airbnb hosts earn at or below Catalonia's average household income."[7] Airbnb's web site and its advertising are both built around stories of personal connection: of welcoming hosts, of meals taken together, of friendships formed. It would seem that only the most cynical, jaded person could see Airbnb's success as anything other than a good thing.

But there are two sides to Airbnb's growth, and they are revealed in the stories that float around the company. Airbnb's publicity relies heavily on inspirational personal stories. I do not know whether those telling the inspirational stories are being sincere or cynical—how could I?—and to some extent it doesn't matter. Perhaps Brian Chesky knows that the story of the host with an illness who wrote him a letter to thank Airbnb for saving her life always goes over well and so he tells it repeatedly, or perhaps it has some real significance for him, and he really does believe that his mission with Airbnb is to make it possible for thousands—millions—of such people to find a little independence in this difficult world.

But I do believe it is possible—even essential—to be skeptical about what I think of as Inspirational Technology Tales. When coupled to an agenda with a lot of money behind it, we owe it to ourselves to ask what it is we are being sold. Airbnb in particular relies on the personal narrative as part of its message—its corporate message—plastering posters of its "regular people" hosts around New York City as part of its campaign to achieve legitimacy in its second-biggest market.

And so I have developed a habit of stopping whenever I see an Inspirational Technology Tale and asking myself if there are different stories to be told, one that has a different message. And invariably there is. So here is a story from the Airbnb web site:

> When the economic crash hit, Tama's livelihood as a painter and real estate broker was threatened. A serious health condition was only increasing her expenses, with prescription costs at times topping $1000 per month. Receiving guests not only introduced her to new friends— it allowed her to eat, pay her bills, and stay in her home.[8]

Airbnb has clearly been good for Tama. But here is another story, which appears in the *San Francisco Chronicle*:

> Chris lost his home so that his landlord could make more money by renting out apartments on Airbnb. Chris says: "They forced me out of a home I loved. It was incredibly difficult to find a place, especially because I have a really old dog. I ended up paying over double what I was paying there." Chris is now suing his landlord and his attorney says: "Airbnb is contributing to the displacement of long-term tenants in San Francisco . . . . It has made it so easy to go into the short-term rental business; it is ubiquitous."[9]

If we are to think about Airbnb, we have to keep Chris' story in mind as well as Tama's. Here is another story that Airbnb does not include on its web site:

> Ken owns a few buildings in Nolita [in New York City]. He runs a non-profit that teaches people how to ride bicycles. Now he's hiring private investigators to see what his tenants are doing. Ken doesn't like it: "It's so not me. It's like how did I become that guy?" But apartment 3 had become a kind of hotel, charging $250 a night and he suspects the tenant made half a million dollars before he evicted her. He says of Airbnb that "They see how lucrative her

business was . . . And they refuse to take it down. So they're not good guys."[10]

Airbnb does not mention Ken, or his tenant, but it does claim New York host Shell as part of its community:

> When New York City was hit by one of the worst hurricanes in history, Shell, a long time host on Airbnb, realized that the loss for some people was devastating. As the waters rose and people had to evacuate their homes, many of them couldn't return for days, if at all. Shell decided to go online and list her space for free for those who were in need.[11]

Shell's story became more complex when it turned out that she was renting out several leased properties "in direct violation of her lease." Her landlord said that "Friends [staying over] are one thing. Groups of social-networking strangers is a completely different ball of wax" and that Airbnb washed its hands of his problem, saying "Airbnb is an online platform and does not own, operate, manage or control accommodations, nor do we verify private contract terms or arbitrate complaints from third parties."[12]

The stories that Airbnb leaves out start to paint a different picture, which exists alongside the stories it promotes: a picture of neighbors, landlords, and tenants left frustrated and angry by Airbnb's business.

The overall debate around Airbnb is also framed as a narrative. So Rachel Botsman's story of Airbnb is of a clash between the impersonal corporate world of global hotel chains and the personal, quirky world of individuals sharing the home in which they live.

Again, I have tried to develop the habit of stopping to reflect on how this narrative matches my own experience and what I know about the world. And in the case of Airbnb, the conclusion is that it does not match very well.

I grew up in the UK during the 1960s and 70s, one of four children of two teachers. We used to take a holiday each year, and the first holiday I remember was in 1963 when we, together with another family, went to Aberdovey in Wales. There, we stayed for a week in a railway carriage that had been converted into a place to stay—rather like a stationary caravan or trailer, but more interesting for young children. I was too young to remember much about that holiday except for the repulsed fascination I felt for the rows of jellyfish washed up on the beach (alive or dead? I don't know), but it was neither an Airbnb nor a hotel.

The rest of my childhood holidays were mainly booked through a Farm Holiday Guide. We would stay in self-catering or B&B-style rooms, often on a farm. It made a little extra money for our hosts and gave us a great holiday. We returned frequently to Miss Whitaker's home: she was a dinner-lady in the village of Ulpha in the picturesque Lake District, and she opened up her home for visitors during the school holidays. The River Duddon bubbled past the bottom of her garden; she had a dog named Jan that we used to play with—the first dog I felt comfortable around—and on the frequent rainy days I got to meet Hercule Poirot and Miss Marple from the books on her bookshelves.

As I grew up, I spent holidays with friends in other venues that have been around for a long time: commercial and youth hostels, trailer parks, and camp sites.

We were a normal family having normal holidays: our experiences were multiplied millions of times over. In North America, the traditions are a bit different but the rented holiday home or cottage is an experience familiar to millions. Airbnb's biggest cities are all major tourist centers, and Airbnb now does more business in Europe than in the US. Maybe, instead of an explosion of sharing, part of the Airbnb phenomenon is simply an existing activity moving onto a single web site from a million noticeboards and booklets.

Airbnb has its precedents in the digital world too. Couchsurfing started as a non-profit web site (couchsurfing.org, not couchsurfing.com) with a very active and involved community of members. There were get-togethers in many cities and Couchsurfing members even helped to build the web site itself. Couchsurfing had a lot in common with Airbnb, but also some big differences: members would host each other as guests, and often spend time with them during their visit, but unlike Airbnb one of the rules of Couchsurfing was that no money was exchanged. The story of Couchsurfing is an intriguing one, and we shall return to it later.

The other digital precedents to Airbnb were the commercial vacation rental sites, some of which are still healthy and growing. HomeAway and VRBO are still as big as Airbnb by many measures, but they have not had the same publicity, and Airbnb's rapid growth threatens them. The people offering a place to stay on HomeAway tend to be professional property managers who look after a number of vacation rental properties. Unlike Airbnb, these sites have existed largely without conflict with regulators for years, but in December 2015 Expedia bought HomeAway and VRBO seeking to build a competitor that adopts much of Airbnb's business model.

Counting the value of these disparate types of accommodation is probably impossible, but it's clear that the "Airbnb versus Hotels" story is a long way from a true history. The narrative of incumbent corporate hotel megachain versus scrappy young, idealistic startup turns out to be a cartoon version of history. The market for short-term rentals and vacation rentals is more complex than that.

ECONOMICAL WITH THE TRUTH

Airbnb has been controversial around the world. The highest-profile dispute has been in New York City, but it has also run into problems in all its major markets, including Amsterdam, Los Angeles, Berlin, Barcelona, and Paris. The company claims the opposition to them is the reaction of slow-moving bureaucracies in hock to the established interests of the hotel industry, but the variety of locations that have had problems with Airbnb suggests something else is going on.

To understand what kind of business Airbnb really is, we have to go beyond what political scientist Henry Farrell calls "dueling anecdotes," and take a look at some numbers. In 2013, just as Airbnb was starting to get mainstream publicity, I was frustrated by the lack of solid data behind the debate, so I wrote a program that would go to the Airbnb web site and collect as much information as I could about all the Airbnb listings for a given city. It's far from perfect, and there are many questions that cannot be accurately answered by data from the web site, but it has been a useful tool for me to understand the true shape of Airbnb's business.

Unexpectedly, soon after I started collecting data, Airbnb got into a dispute with the Attorney General of New York, Eric Schneiderman. The number of Airbnb listings in the city was growing and the Attorney General's office suspected that many hosts were violating a New York City law that bans renting out an apartment in a multiple-dwelling building for periods of less than thirty days. Schneiderman wanted the names and addresses of all 15,000 Airbnb hosts in the city, Airbnb refused, talks broke down, and the company accused the Attorney General of a "fishing expedition."[13] In the wake of the Snowden revelations the Attorney General's demand was seen as another intrusive data-collection sweep by a government, and both the Electronic Frontier Foundation and the Internet Association ("representing the leading internet companies") stepped in on the side of Airbnb to "fight this tooth and nail."[14] Meanwhile, Peers collected over 200,000 signatures on a petition to "save sharing in New York," and Airbnb released a study touting the economic benefits it brings to the city and promoted videos in support of their position. Tensions were running high.

Sharing Economy advocates presented the dispute as a conflict between well-heeled incumbents and regular New Yorkers making a little extra money to get by in a tough world; they argued that the laws were written for a pre-Internet landscape, and need to be updated to allow new industries to grow. Airbnb claims that "We all agree that illegal hotels are bad for New York, but that is not our community. Our community is made up of thousands of amazing people with kind hearts."[15] The company published a report insisting that its hosts were almost all "regular New Yorkers, occasionally renting out the home in which they live,"[16] and that many of them were using that extra money to help them stay in their homes; they told stories that emphasized the person-to-person sharing of a living space.

On the other side, the dispute has drawn in not only the hotel industry but also, in a rare alliance, landlord and tenant groups, as well as affordable housing advocates and neighborhood associations.[17] The Attorney General claims that illegal hotels are abusing Airbnb's site, and New York State Senator Liz Krueger complains that Airbnb is "actively recruiting tenants to list their apartments on their web sites even though they are well aware they are putting residents at risk of eviction" by breaking tenancy or co-operative housing agreements as well as violating the thirty-day law. Some "online businesses have become highly profitable by ignoring state and local laws and ignoring the damage their business model has done to communities."[18]

So what does the data have to say about the dispute? My program picked up 15,000 listings, matching the number Airbnb claimed to have in New York City (that number has now reached 38,000). And the data showed that, while not lying, Airbnb was being economical with the truth.

Airbnb's claim that "87% of our hosts rent out the home in which they live" is important to the company because it has repeatedly argued that existing rules designed for professionally run accommodations do not address their new market of regular people, offering accommodation on a more informal basis. At first glance my data actually supported Airbnb's claim: it showed that 87% of hosts do indeed have a single listing, which matches Airbnb's number exactly. However, there are several ways to look at the data, and unsurprisingly Airbnb has chosen the way that fits best with the image they seek to create. From 2013 through 2015, those 13% of hosts with more than one listing make up a substantial part of the Airbnb business, renting out no less than 40% of all Airbnb listings, and accounting for over 43% of the Airbnb visits to the city. These figures changed only when New York City took serious action against multiple-listing hosts on Airbnb. So almost half of Airbnb's business comes from hosts with multiple listings. Airbnb is being economical with the truth. The company presents its business as one of informal, personal exchange, but Airbnb also makes a lot of money from hosts with multiple listings, people who are using the site as a way to build a business by avoiding the rules around bed & breakfasts and short-term rentals.

Every listing in Airbnb is classified as one of three types. One type is a "Shared Room": this corresponds to the original "Airbed & Breakfast" story of the company founders renting out airbeds. Then there is "Private Room," which is what most of us think of when we hear "sharing the home in which we live" with a guest. And finally, there is "Entire Home/Apt," which means that the host is not present in the house when the guests are there.

The data showed that the majority of listings in New York (60%) were Entire Home rentals, and only 3% were the Shared Room rentals that represent the story of the company. In terms of revenue, the figures are even more dramatic, because entire homes usually rent for more than private rooms, which rent for more than shared rooms. Three out of every four dollars that Airbnb makes come from Entire Home rentals, and only 1% from Shared Room listings. Given that most of the Airbnb activity takes place in Manhattan and Brooklyn where multiple-dwelling buildings predominate, it seems likely that a majority of Airbnb listings, and over two-thirds of its income, came from Entire Home rentals that were breaking New York's short-term rental law.

Airbnb has built a replica of the original apartment's living room in its headquarters (along with a replica of the war room from *Dr. Strangelove*)[19] but that living room no longer represents the company's business. The

Private Room rentals, represented on the company web site by pictures of hosts welcoming guests to their dinner table, have also been relegated to a minority. Most of Airbnb's money comes from exchanges where the host and guest may never meet except to exchange a key. And if the host takes advantage of one of the cluster of management services that are growing up around Airbnb listings, even that meeting may never happen.

■

The dispute between the Attorney General and Airbnb was resolved in 2014. Airbnb maintained that it ejected a small number of "bad apples" from its platform, and then it handed over select data to the Attorney General. Unlike the attempts of myself and others to collect data from the public site, the Attorney General's office had access to Airbnb's own internal data: almost half a million transactions for stays between January 2010 and June 2014.

In a report released in October 2014, the AG's office confirmed the broad outlines of Airbnb's business that my survey showed, and added to it.[20] It confirmed that well over half of Airbnb listings were breaking the short-term rental law for multiple-dwelling buildings, and showed that the skew of rentals to hosts with multiple listings is even more severe than the web site data suggested: the report found that the 6% of hosts with more than two listings made up 36% of Airbnb's revenue.

Airbnb continues to drive its narrative of low-intensity tourism by emphasizing that its *listings* are scattered around New York's neighborhoods, claiming that "82% of Airbnb properties are located outside of Mid-Manhattan, compared to 30–40% of hotels located outside of Mid-Manhattan" and that "Airbnb visitors stay throughout New York's diverse neighborhoods, in all 5 boroughs."[21] But again, this is one highly selective way of looking at the data: the Attorney General's report found that Airbnb *visits* are not nearly so scattered around the city as the cherry-picked statements suggest: Manhattan and Brooklyn made up no less than 97% of the company's New York revenue.

Airbnb emphasizes the occasional nature of many hosts' offerings, but again this is one way of looking at the data, and there is another side to the story. The Attorney General's report showed that "the share of revenue hosts received from units booked for more than half the year has increased, rising from 18% of private short term rental revenue in New York City in 2010 to 38% of such revenue in 2013. Units booked on Airbnb as private short term rentals for half the year and more—and thereby largely removed from long-term housing—generated 38% of all fees Airbnb received in 2013."

Since 2014, the pattern has continued. Airbnb's business has a large component that is professionalized—either listings that are owned for the primary purpose of renting or hosts who own multiple listings—and concentrated in already tourist-intensive parts of the city. Airbnb's response to each report based on actual data is to claim vaguely that the data is out of date, or inaccurate, but they refuse to come out with any real data of their own to make a counter-case. They release occasional city reports that, they claim, puts the numbers behind their narrative, but these reports lack any substance: their report on Airbnb in New York City ran to a grand total of of 300 words—fewer than the words on this page—and included no methodology statements to back up their claims.[22]

Looking at 2015, Airbnb has claimed that in Manhattan the typical (median) listing is rented out only 11% of the time, but a recent independent paper concluded that "all listings with up to this value account together for less than 5% of the revenue" and that over half the company's revenue comes from listings booked for over half the year.

The shape of Airbnb's business in New York is reproduced, with variations, elsewhere. I have carried out surveys of the listings in all of Airbnb's biggest cities, and the data shows that the biggest and simplest deviations from the Airbnb narrative found in New York persist. Despite the continued repetition of the Airbnb origin story, the Shared Room now plays a minuscule part in the Airbnb business around the world. Even the Private Room listings that fit with what most of us think of as "sharing" are a minority slice of the Airbnb business. Everywhere, Entire Home rentals are the main source of revenue for Airbnb. In Paris, the company's biggest city, entire homes make up nearly 90% of Airbnb's business, and in major centers such as Berlin, Amsterdam, and Lisbon they make up over 70%.

Finally, despite the emphasis on regular people sharing the homes in which they live, hosts with multiple listings do make up a substantial part of the company's business. The makeup differs from city to city. In Paris the number of visits to hosts with multiple listings is relatively small (27%). In San Francisco and Berlin multiple-listing hosts account for over 40% of the visits, and in London and Los Angeles they account for half the visits. In Barcelona, Lisbon, and Rome the majority of visits are to multiple-listing hosts, and in Istanbul, which has over 7,000 Airbnb listings, no less than 80% of visits are to hosts with multiple listings.

AIRBNB AND THE CITIES

The legality of Airbnb's business in New York City is important, but it is not my main concern; I want to focus on the broader picture of how Airbnb affects cities in its most popular and lucrative markets.

The Sharing Economy appeals to exchanges that are informal and person-to-person, and that largely sit outside the area of commercial regulation for a reason. If I give a bowl of sugar to my neighbor, food safety inspections do not come into play. Regulations that affect Airbnb are, by and large, municipal regulations, and in many cities bylaw enforcement is carried out by a small team of people acting on a complaint-driven basis. There is a gray area of tolerance built into these regulations, and many cities see enforcement as a last resort, hoping that minor disputes between neighbors can be sorted out directly without involving the authorities. Complaint-based enforcement goes together with blurred boundaries between non-commercial and commercial activities to provide a space for a "gray area" of informal commerce that is part of daily life in most cities.

The goal of Airbnb, as of many Sharing Economy companies, is to take this gray area and scale it up. But scale changes things, informal dispute resolution becomes impossible, and activities that were previously benign become problematic. For those of us living on streets with driveways: most of us have no problem with occasional yard sales; if a neighbor starts to run a yard sale every weekend we might get irritated with the cars parked in the street; if half a dozen people on the street are constantly having yard sales, then it starts to disrupt the community and maybe the city should enforce its zoning laws.

The same issues of scale apply to visitors. Most of us would not mind if one of our neighbors occasionally has a guest stay over. If all our neighbors are consistently having new and different people stay in their apartments or houses, it becomes a problem.

Scale is central to the conflicts around Airbnb. The company emphasizes its commitment to cities and community, but it doesn't seem to understand how real communities work, and the balances that must be struck between different interests.

It is tempting to think that Airbnb is simply replacing rigid rules with informality and trust, but that is far from the case. The company makes it easy to add a property to its site, but when you sign up for Airbnb as a host or a guest you agree to four separate terms of service that total 30,000 words: almost half the length of this book. The company knows rules when it suits them.

Our housing and residences are surrounded by rules because we are part of a community and need to get along. Not all these rules are good ones, but co-operative housing organizations place limits on what members can do, landlord–tenant agreements place limits on what tenants can do, city rules put limits on what landlords can do, and rent-controlled apartments are made available with a set of conditions about how they are used.

Airbnb has no interest in these rules. Instead, despite its talk of community, the only logic it seems to understand is that of the free market: the right of property owners to do what they want with their property. Tenants in shared buildings don't like it when their neighbors all start renting out and a new wave of strangers appears in the building every weekend, but this is not Airbnb's responsibility. Some tenants claim to have been driven out of their apartments so their landlord can make more money by renting out at higher rates on a short-term basis, but Airbnb has no useful response to this except to assert it doesn't happen very much.

Much of the press around Airbnb presents it as a dispute between an innovative technology startup disrupting an older, established hotel industry, but the major hotel chains are among the last to be affected by the Airbnb phenomenon, and much remains to be seen about how that particular relationship will play out. For example, Airbnb's head of global hospitality (now advisor), Chip Conley, comes from the hotel industry and recently said this:

> One of my chief roles here at Airbnb has been to create a more collaborative relationship with the global hotel industry. I'm proud of the fact that some of these hotel global chain CEOs have spoken in a more neutral or even a positive way when asked about Airbnb. There's been two studies—one we commissioned in New York City and one performed independently in Texas by a Boston University professor—that have shown that Airbnb's impact on hotels is relatively negligible.[23]

When it comes to the disputes around the company, the Airbnb versus Big Hotels narrative is a red herring. In mid-2015 Hyatt Hotels invested in a small Airbnb competitor called OneFineStay, and we can expect to see more collaboration between the chain hotels and the Airbnb market, as

Airbnb seeks to expand into business travel and as hotels see an opportunity to make more money from travelers.

Instead, those who have been affected are the smaller independent hotels and the bed & breakfasts, who complain that they have to register with their city, have the expense of passing fire inspections and health and safety inspections, and have to pay tourist taxes, so cannot compete with the unregulated apartment down the street that has none of these expenses. Ironically, it is the "human scale" part of the tourism industry that Airbnb is damaging.

City governments are concerned about tax revenue, zoning rules, and consumer protection (who pays when things go wrong?). Civic activists are concerned about the effect of the booming short-term rental market on the price of accommodations and the stock of affordable housing. Will it drive up rents? Will popular but affordable neighborhoods get gentrified? The debates are fiercest in tourist destinations, which are Airbnb's biggest locations, and Airbnb must be seen against the backdrop of a continually and rapidly growing tourist industry. Worldwide, the number of international tourists has doubled in the past two decades alone,[24] growth in the leading destinations outstrips even that number, and the flood of tourists creates inevitable tensions. For example, Barcelona has experienced a massive increase in tourism:

> The number of tourists visiting has jumped drastically in
> recent years, from 1.7 million in 1990 to more than 7.4 million in 2012. As residents attempt to go about their lives in
> a city where tourists often far outnumber the 1.6 million
> residents, the number of complaints about noise, nudity,
> public drunkenness and littering has rocketed.[25]

Faced with these changes, cities need to balance the interests of tourism with other interests of the city, including livability for the residents. Each city's needs are different, because the stresses and challenges facing each city is different.

In the cities where it is a major presence, Airbnb has given tourism growth an extra twist. The company is only too happy to take credit for the economic contribution its trade has made to cities around the world—but it is less happy to discuss its other impacts on residents. Repeatedly, Airbnb has proven itself an untrustworthy partner in building livable cities.

The experience of Amsterdam shows many of the issues. Back in 2012 Airbnb faced one big problem in Amsterdam, which was legality: to rent out homes to tourists, Amsterdam residents were required to register with the city, keep business records, limit the number of guests to a maximum of four people, and rent no more than 40% of the floor area of the house.[26] At the time, Airbnb had about 4,000 listings, and the city was concerned about 2,000 illegal rentals.

Like many cities, Amsterdam's bylaw enforcement is largely complaint-based, and is not heavily staffed. There is no way that the city could check up on 4,000 listings even if it knew the addresses. So in June 2013 the city decided that so long as there are no complaints, no fire safety issues, and so long as the owner still lives in the house, it would allow short-term tourist rentals.[27] Airbnb welcomed the decision, saying that it shows "a line can indeed be drawn between unwanted illegal hotels on the one hand, and the amazing economic benefits created when regular residents are allowed the freedom to rent out their own homes once in a while."[28]

The decision was formalized in January 2014, when Amsterdam city council decided to permit short-term rentals for a maximum of 60 days per year, so long as they can be done "safely and honestly without causing nuisance."[29] Again, the decision was welcomed by Airbnb as making it "easy for local residents to share the home in which they live, while simultaneously cracking down on illegal hotels that abuse the system."[30] It looked like everyone was happy.

But that's not where the story ends. By August 2014, it was clear that many Airbnb hosts were flouting the city council's rules. Council research showed that of the 7,000 Airbnb properties in Amsterdam, over 900 were renting to more people than the limit, and over 500 were renting out for more than the allowed time; there were "a large number of professional landlords with multiple properties using the service," and "private investors are buying up attractive properties to rent out."[31]

By October, the city's twenty-two full-time inspectors were overrun with complaints from neighbors, and Airbnb was not helping: "They have the rental details and could help us but they are reluctant to do so" said Laurens Ivens of the city council. Despite its claim to welcome a line between illegal hotels and regular residents, the company was not interested in actually helping to enforce that line or in limiting the revenue it made from Amsterdam by being more rigorous about its "community."

It was also clear that many hosts were not paying tourism taxes, and that many were not even aware of the rules they were supposed to follow. In December, an agreement was reached between the city and Airbnb for Airbnb to collect those taxes on behalf of its hosts. The *Wall Street Journal* reported that "As part of the deal, Airbnb would also actively promote rules and regulations that apply to people renting their house to tourists in Amsterdam."[32]

Unfortunately, Airbnb's agreement did not extend to helping the city council enforce the rules that it had welcomed. City officials had no way to verify who is paying the tax that Airbnb is collecting, or whether the amounts are correct. As usual, Airbnb declined responsibility: Airbnb executive Patrick Robinson told a Dutch newspaper that it is up to hosts to make sure they obey the rules: "It is not our responsibility."[33]

Even though Amsterdam was the first city to reach an agreement with Airbnb, and is often mentioned by the company as a positive example of co-operation, the tension continues. From November 2015 to November 2016 the number of Airbnb listings in Amsterdam grew from 10,000 to 17,000, and "In the most popular neighbourhoods, as many as one in six homeowners rent out a room or flat on Airbnb."[34] While Airbnb is not the primary driver of gentrification in the tourist areas of Amsterdam, but it contributes to the problems of affordability and family housing worse. Over winter of 2016-2017 the city "levied fines of €526,500 on home owners who are illegally renting out their properties on holiday rental sites like Airbnb."[35]

■

Other cities have watched in frustration as Airbnb profits from tourism, disowns any responsibility for managing the activities that provide its revenue, and refuses to provide the information needed for cities to enforce their own rules.

Following an explosion of tourist rentals in the city, and complaints by residents, Barcelona cancelled vacation housing licenses in the neighborhood of Eixample in April 2014. As in Amsterdam, the city has limited resources to locate and clamp down on hosts who are renting without a license. As in Amsterdam, Airbnb could help with the problem but doesn't, preferring to paint a rosy picture of their own presence using their normal language of "home sharing": "77 percent of Airbnb hosts in Catalonia have only one listing and 53 percent say hosting helped them stay in their homes."[36] Airbnb hosts are "local people who make a little extra money by sharing their homes with respectful guests from around the world."[37] Also as usual, while data I collected from the Airbnb site agrees with this statement (showing, for example, 74% of hosts with a single listing), Airbnb is not telling the whole truth. The company's business is concentrated in the tourist centers: two-thirds of visits are in two of the city's dozen neighborhoods. Listings belonging to professional hosts make up over half of all listings in the city. Over half of Airbnb's Barcelona income comes from professional hosts.

Airbnb's impact in Barcelona is multifaceted, but at least part of it is destructive: it erodes the quality of life for those living in high-intensity tourist neighborhoods, it prevents the city from being able to balance tourism with other aspects of city life, and it impedes attempts by the city to establish safety and other standards.

Deputy mayor Janet Sanz voices a fear heard from many European tourist destinations when she says: "We don't want Barcelona turning into a new Venice", and in November 2016 the city fined Airbnb 600,000 euros for advertising illegal rentals.[38]

Paris shows the same pattern as Amsterdam and Barcelona. The city is Airbnb's biggest market, with over 60,000 listings—so many that in summer 2014 the popular Marais district saw 66,320 Airbnb visitors, which is slightly more than the 64,795 who actually live there.[39,40]

The impact on the city is significant. Here is Ian Brossat, the city's Director of Housing: "There is already a serious shortage of flats in Paris, especially studios and two-room apartments where couples might start a life together. Now we have this growing problem of holiday lets, with investors moving in and buying up as much as they can. It has become a business, and the result is fewer properties on the market for ordinary Parisians, and higher prices for what is available."[41]

In Paris you can rent out your primary residence for short periods to holiday-makers, but the Paris government believes that as many as two-thirds of properties being rented on very short lets are not primary residences. As usual, Airbnb had platitudes but no data to counter this claim. In February 2015 Airbnb made an agreement with the mayor of Paris to enforce the law, but by May 2015 relations seemed to have taken a turn for the worse again as the city ran spot checks on 2,000 listings in the Marais. Lead officer François Plottin said "The center of our city is becoming deserted. More and more, it's just tourists."[42]

In early 2017 a study showed that the population of some of the more popular tourist areas of the city was actually falling, and the mayor's office attributed the fall to "lower birthrates, but also to an increase in second homes, particularly those rented out seasonally to tourists. Meanwhile, 1st arrondissement mayor Jean-François Legaret told Le Parisien that Airbnb 'has been a catastrophe for central Paris.'"[43]

The company's claim to let you "live like a local" loses its meaning when there are no more locals; its claim to promote a Shared City sounds increasingly like a cover for an American company that is not interested in understanding that other countries and cities are different, and have the right to make their own rules for their own reasons.

In a 2016 advertising campaign Airbnb exhorts you not to be a tourist:

> "Don't go to Paris, don't tour Paris, and please don't do Paris." But then the punchline: "Live in Paris…even if it's just for a night." Airbnb executive Jonathan Mildenhall told Adweek that the campaign reflects a growing "demand for experiences that are not like the typical tourist experiences, that actually more reflect what it's like to live in local places."[44]

Sadly, Airbnb is contributing to the erosion of the very experiences it celebrates.

■

If there is any city where Airbnb should be at home it might be Portland, Oregon. In March 2014 this was where Airbnb announced its "Shared Cities" initiative. Portland was the first city to partner with Airbnb on a number of initiatives designed to help the company fit into the urban fabric, and the company also announced that it was building its first office outside San Francisco. Airbnb got legal approval from Portland to legitimize its business: hosts would get a safety inspection, notify the neighbors, and get a $180 permit; Airbnb would pay lodging taxes on behalf of the hosts. "We have to strike a balance between how we accommodate commerce, including this new kind, and our great neighborhoods," said Mayor Charlie Hales, adding, "I think we got it right this time."[45]

But again, the relationship deteriorated quickly. As the deadline for getting a permit approached, only 166 hosts of about 1,600 had got one.[46] The city demanded the addresses and city permits of the hosts from Airbnb; Airbnb Director of Public Policy David Owen refused, saying the data was private. City Commissioner Nick Fish challenged Owen, saying that Airbnb was claiming "an exemption from all the other laws and rules of society, because we're somehow 'on the Internet.' We welcomed you to Portland, we're pleased that you've harnessed the Internet. But sir, we have to make sure that the guests in one of your hosts' places—and you do not inspect your hosts' places—we have to make sure that guest is safe."[47]

Again, the dispute has continued. At the time of writing the most recent development is that, faced with a determined city council, Airbnb has agreed to implement a "one host, one listing" policy.[48] Early data I have collected suggests the policy is having an effect.

■

The repetitive trajectory of Airbnb's growth in tourist centers is particularly sad because there is a clear potential for new forms of informal and low-intensity short-term and tourist accommodations, like older-style hostel offerings and digital initiatives such as Couchsurfing. But Airbnb's investors have put a lot of money into the company and they expect a return, so Airbnb needs to grow. To satisfy its investors, Airbnb has no choice but to seek to become a global company, operating at scale in as many cities as it can find. And with that goal, any of the benefits of informal sharing are being pushed to one side. The company still speaks of sharing, still uses those heartwarming stories, but as it professionalizes its hosts and seeks to deliver a consistent brand experience, it's playing an increasingly destructive role in global travel, preventing cities from striking the balance they need to find between tourism and the other needs of a healthy city. There are many actions it could take to stay closer to the city-friendly image it projects—it could limit the number of properties a host lists on the site, limit the number of days a host can rent a property, or limit the density of listings in a neighborhood, for example—but it chooses not to do so.

As the cases above show, during 2016, cities increasingly found the confidence to push back against Airbnb and demand some kind of accountability from the company: limits to the density of listings, caps on the number of listings a host can provide, or caps on the number of days a listing can be rented out over the course of a year. This topic is returned to in the final chapter of the book.

■

To finish this chapter, here's another story, this one of Airbnb in Rome.

I live in Canada, but my family of origin lives in the UK, and while I was visiting them last year my sister and I got to take a trip to Rome for a few days. It was a great trip (we stayed in a rented apartment, in case you were wondering, but not rented through Airbnb), and one of our favorite parts of it was spending an afternoon in the Trastevere district. While Trastevere doesn't have the big sights, it has many cobbled streets, charming restaurants, a beautiful square, and one of the oldest cathedrals in the city. It's a more artisan, bohemian atmosphere than some of the other areas of the city, and that's part of its appeal.

So like many other visitors we loved Trastevere, and like other tourists we brought money with us, and spent some of it there, so in a way our visit was good for the city too. But of course our presence is a mixed blessing: too much tourism can erode the very things that make Trastevere so atmospheric and special—especially when those things are the "authentic" life of the locals—raising the cost of living, and putting pressure on property prices. In the end, as tourists you have to hope that the city of Rome and the neighborhood itself find ways to balance the various pressures acting on the place where they live.

Not surprisingly, Trastevere does have conflicts over gentrification and the impact of tourism. Here's a story from last September.[49] In 1956 a cinema opened in Trastevere called Cinema America, and it was a feature of the area until it closed, sometime around 2000. In 2004 it was bought by a new set of owners who decided to tear it down and replace it with a parking lot and some apartments. There was local opposition to the plan, and stalemate until in November 2012 a group of young people occupied the cinema. By all accounts, they turned it into a focal point for the community and also attracted some big names of Italian cinema and the arts. In September 2014 the occupiers were evicted by the police, but they have apparently set up elsewhere in the neighborhood and the campaign continues.

What does all this have to do with Airbnb? Well, this . . .

Figure 1 shows a map of the 8,000 Airbnb rentals in Rome as of May 2014. You can see that the rentals are densest and most expensive in the middle of the city, and that's also where the most expensive listings are.

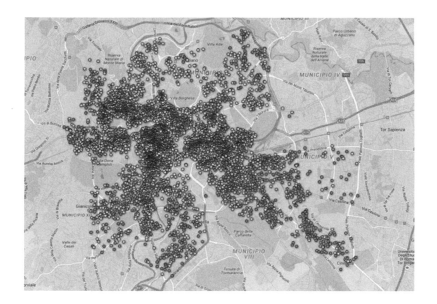

Figure 1. Airbnb listings in Rome.
Map data ©2014 Google

Using the number of reviews as a proxy for the relative number of visits allows an estimate of which listings are the most valuable to Airbnb. Here is (by this estimate) the most valuable listing in Rome—the one with perhaps the highest rental income of any in the city. It's the dot in Figure 2.

If you look just south of this listing, you can see "Basilica di Santa Maria in Trastevere." This listing is, you will not be surprised to know, right in Trastevere. It's a beautiful looking place—although not exactly cheap at over $600 per night. The listing text says that it has been "Selected by the airbnb staff who stayed and filmed here for the upcoming airbnb hosting in Rome video" so its charms have been noticed by the company too.

Airbnb, of course, says that its hosts "are regular people who occasionally rent out their homes and use the income they earn to pay the bills." So who is the host for this particularly successful rental?

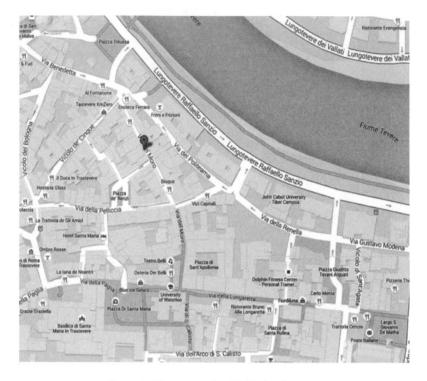

Figure 2. The most valuable listing in Rome
Map data ©2014 Google

Well, it turns out that Martin is not so much a regular Trastevere resident. He does have family roots in Rome, but is a Harvard-educated technology entrepreneur who lives in Austin, Texas and who is "rent[ing] out the places I bought with the proceeds from my last software company." He is now CEO of Vreasy, a "novel software platform" which is "a growing force in the tourism and travel market."

Martin is listed as an Airbnb "superhost." In addition to the Historic Nobleman's Loft his listing page shows (in April 2015) a total of six listings on the site—one more in Rome (an "Ultimate Panoramic Roman Penthouse"), one near Monaco, two in Barcelona, and one "Seaplane cabin" that he will fly to any legal European lake so that you can use it as a hotel.

Now I don't know Martin and have made no effort to talk to him, because this is not really about Martin; it's about Airbnb, and the gap between the idealized "regular people" they present and the reality of multiple-property owners. It's the gap between their message of caring for neighborhoods and the reality of gentrification driven by uncontrolled tourism, which they are playing a big part in accelerating. Airbnb's true business in Trastevere is eroding the very qualities that make the district appealing, and it's exactly the kind of business that the locals of Trastevere are protesting.

Figure 1 showed the 8,000 listings in Rome in May 2014. Three years later, the number is over 25,000, with about two thirds of visits going to hosts with multiple listings on the site. Martin's villa is no longer the top listing in Rome, but the pressure of tourism on communities in the city, and Airbnb's central role in promoting tourism without responsibility, are greater than ever.

4. On the Move with Uber

There is one sector of the Sharing Economy that is bigger than accommodation, and that's transit, and specifically ridesharing. Just as Airbnb dominates the accommodation market, so Uber dominates ridesharing, but Uber did not create its market in the way Airbnb did. The story of ridesharing is of a set of companies learning from and competing with each other until one emerged victorious.

But before ridesharing came carsharing. *Carsharing* is people getting time-limited access to a car, while *ridesharing* is a person being a passenger in a car driven by someone else.

Just as "sharing economy" is no longer a realistic description, so ridesharing is not accurate, to the point that the Associated Press stylebook explicitly says not to use it to describe Uber. Some have taken to calling this model "ridesourcing";[1] the AP stylebook suggests ride-hailing or ride-booking services. Nevertheless, the phrase "ridesharing," inaccurate as it may be, is still more widely used and I will use it, without the scare quotes.

But let's start with carsharing.

ZIPCAR

Carsharing co-operatives have been around for a long time, some run as non-profits and some as commercial companies. There is a continuous history of activities starting in the 1970's, and in Kitchener-Waterloo where I live, Community CarShare was founded in 1998 and is still running.

But in 2000 when Antje Danielson and Robin Chase started ZipCar, they brought a new ambition to the space. Just as the story of Airbnb is featured in

Rachel Botsman and Roo Rogers' *What's Mine Is Yours*, Zipcar takes the pole position in Lisa Gansky's 2010 book *The Mesh: Why the Future of Business is Sharing*.[2] Zipcar was never a peer-to-peer company, as the cars were all owned by the company, but it was a form of shared or collaborative consumption based on digital technology: Gansky quotes Chase as saying, once Danielson described a Berlin car-sharing service to her, "A lightbulb went off in my head. I thought: *This was what the Internet was made for*." Perhaps even more than Airbnb, Zipcar became the original Sharing Economy company.

And Zipcar did grow: from its beginnings in Boston (2001) to New York (2003), and then to San Francisco in 2005, Toronto in 2006, and London later that same year, reaching about a quarter of a million members by 2008. Zipcar continued to expand. It provided an iPhone app to help you book a car, it took investments from Benchmark Capital and General Electric's Commercial Finance Fleet Services, it merged with competitor Flexcar, it created a partnership with Spanish car rental company Avancar, it acquired UK service Streetcar.

The appeal of the company was economic, social, and environmental: it provided affordable driving options (access over ownership), it fostered an alternative, community feel (you are a member, rather than a customer), and it promoted a green image (a more efficient use of resources than individual ownership). It's a combination that continues to draw people to the Sharing Economy.

Sadly, the appeal to community turned out to be more hope than reality. In 2012, researchers Fleura Bardhi and Giana Eckhardt interviewed a set of Zipcar users in Boston, rode with them, and found that Zipcar users are motivated by self-interest and utilitarianism rather than by any altruistic community motives.[3] The researchers expected a community to emerge around the Zipcar brand, but found that users resisted the company's efforts to create a community beyond the straightforward fact of market exchange. Zipcar users were prepared to "look out for their own interests at the expense of the object [the car] as well as the other users," so that "surveillance and command controls are welcomed" to stop other users from treating the shared cars badly. In an interview the authors say, "Zipcar uses a strict style of governance to maintain compliance with the rules of car sharing to make sure cars aren't brought back late, the gas tank is filled, etc. Consumers like and even want more of this surveillance, as they feel it is the only way the system can work effectively, since they don't trust each other to obey the rules without Zipcar's heavy handed enforcement."[4]

Bardhi and Eckhardt also expected Zipcar users to be motivated by political consumerism, especially as it relates to anti-car, environmental concerns, but they found no evidence of these motivations either.

The Zipcar experience was clearly a lot more of a normal, mainstream consumer exchange than advocates were claiming, so perhaps it should have been no surprise when, in January 2013, Zipcar was bought by rental company Avis.[5] With that purchase there is no longer a suggestion that the relationship between Zipcar users and the company is anything other than a straightforward commercial exchange (with the usual company brand promotion), and there is no suggestion of any relationship at all between Zipcar users and each other.

The brand continues to promote its environmental message, saying on one of its university pages that: "Every day we are working towards a place with less dependence on personally-owned vehicles. Why? Because it matters . . . Each and every Zipcar takes 15 personally-owned vehicles off the road."[6] But there is little substance behind the claim. Sociologist Jathan Sadowski traced it to a report from the Transportation Research Board dated 2005 (the early days of Zipcar), which covered all kinds of car-sharing (profit and non-profit), and the main cause of the result is families foregoing the purchase of a car and choosing to car-share instead.[7] The Transportation Research Board did not make a big deal of this as an environmental benefit (there is nothing to suggest that the total number of car-miles driven decreases after all, just that car ownership decreases).

Zipcar's claim of an environmental benefit depends on the baseline comparison. It is plausible that a Zipcar has less environmental impact than fifteen personal cars. It is equally plausible that a Zipcar has more environmental impact than more widespread use of public transit. So it is cheeky, to say the least, that Zipcar is using the "15-car" figure as part of an effort to encourage university students to take up car-sharing: efforts that are likely to add to the number of cars on the road rather than reduce it. Zipcar's universities page promises "a different degree of freedom . . . the convenience of car ownership without the hassles of having a car on campus"; the freedom and convenience are in comparison to the use of public transit.

So community has gone, and environmental benefit is promoted only when convenient for the company. What's left is a company that, as Juliet

Schor writes, was "Once the face of the Sharing Economy, [and] is now a sub-brand of Avis."[8] Meanwhile, less ambitious car-sharing initiatives such as my local car-sharing co-op continue to operate much as they did a decade ago.

The Zipcar story is similar to that of Airbnb: an original motivation based around community and around an interaction that is not primarily economic, the hunger for growth, the rapid expansion, the erosion of the original model, the end game of a large company—successful in economic terms—that has completely failed to challenge current economic models and that fails to deliver on sustainability or community ideals. Despite the anti-consumerist talk of the advocates, these scaled-up Sharing Economy companies are just as consumerist as those they have disrupted.

LYFT

Zipcar and Airbnb are not alone. Lyft is another company that has traded on the goodwill generated by its founding ideals of community and sharing, before the promise of community and person-to-person exchange became lost in the pursuit of growth and profit.

In 2007 Logan Green and John Zimmer launched a ridesharing program at Cornell University called Zimride. The program took the traditional student ridesharing board and put it on to the Web, requiring that users sign on with their Facebook login. The Facebook decision meant that people could have some basic level of trust in their fellow traveler: at least they would have a name and a way to locate them.

Zimride was a big success at Cornell, signing up a fifth of all the students on campus. It took venture capital funding, moved to the San Francisco Bay area, and expanded to new campuses. But there were limits to the number of inter-city rides that students would take, and Zimride had bigger ambitions.

In 2012, Zimride launched Lyft, an app that paired riders and passengers for short-distance rides (within a city, rather than between cities).[9] The idea sounds like a carpool ride-matching service, but Lyft made another decision to scale up their offering: it made it possible for drivers to earn enough on a ride that they would undertake journeys that they would not otherwise take. Instead of picking up someone who is going their way and sharing the expenses of the journey (as in carpooling), Lyft drivers would find out where your rider wanted to go and take them there (for money).

At first, Lyft maintained its community feel. Lyft cars were identified by a large and kind-of-corny big pink moustache. Riders were expected to sit up front, and rides would start with a fist-bump: quite a different practice compared to traditional North American taxi rides. Drivers did not charge a fee, but riders could make (and, basically, were expected to make) a voluntary donation in lieu of a standardized fare, with Lyft suggesting a donation amount. Marketing promoted its drivers as regular people rather than professionals ("Your friend with a car"), and emphasized the community nature of the experience.

Lyft focused on growth. In June 2013 they raised $60 million from Silicon Valley venture capitalists led by Andreessen Horowitz. In discussing the deal, Scott Weiss of Andreessen Horowitz said, "Lyft is a real community—with both the drivers and riders being inherently social—making real friendships and saving money." Lyft's John Zimmer had a clearer idea of the goals of the investment, saying "Andreessen Horowitz is ideal for us because they've built big businesses . . . They're very accomplished operators and they understand how to scale a business."[10]

In the early days of the purchase, the media was confused about the business Lyft was in. *Time*, for example, wrote that "Today, millions of people are driving around in cars with empty seats while millions of others lack affordable auto transportation options. Lyft aims to bridge that gap."[11] Lyft themselves encouraged the conflation of their business model with non-commercial activities like carpooling: when the service was first launched in 2012 journalist Liz Gannes asked John Zimmer about insurance and regulation, and he replied "our understanding is that when it's ride-sharing, you can use your personal insurance policy. As for regulation, a lot of state laws are supportive of carpooling and ride-sharing and want to make that work."[12]

But of course most Lyft drivers were not giving a lift to people who happened to be going in the same direction, and they were not saving money, they were driving to make money. Things became quickly clearer: in July 2013 the company sold off the original Zimride business to Enterprise Rent-A-Car to focus on Lyft.[13] Every now and then passengers would not make the suggested donation, and bad feelings and bitterness would ensue, so in late 2013 Lyft ditched its voluntary donation system and replaced it with a fare system.

During 2014 the trends continued: in April the company raised a further $250 million to boost its growth; any green message was damaged in May when the company launched an SUV service in San Francisco, and in December Lyft made it clear that the fist-bump, the practice of sitting up front, and the pink "carstache" were now optional.[14] In March 2015 the company raised another $530 million and in May another $150 million to take its total funding up to $1 billion. For 2015 the company planned to grow from 2.5 million rides per month to over 12 million. In 2016 Lyft provided 160 million rides and in early 2017 its total funding had reached $2.6 billion.[15] Like Zipcar and Airbnb, any sharing aspects of its business were shed as the company's finances moved to new heights.

The oddly named French company BlaBlaCar has stayed closer to Lyft's original idea of becoming the digital equivalent of the student bulletin board, providing a matching service for long-distance travel that is more like hitchhiking than riding in a cab. BlaBlaCar drivers cannot make a profit on their drive: the recommended fare is less than the cost of driving from A to B. Drivers can say, honestly, that giving a ride helps offset their costs but does not provide an income, so they do not require commercial insurance and they do not have to deal with income tax requirements.

For some time, BlaBlaCar avoided the temptation of venture capital funding. In July 2014 it raised $100 million and it has used this to expand into other countries and buy competitors, notably German ridesharing company Carpooling. By early 2017 BlaBlaCar had raised $333 million. Perhaps the pressure of having to establish a commercial business at global scale is starting to make itself felt, because the company has made the first move towards a more commercial model by offering its drivers car leases so they can take more journeys. [16]

It remains to be seen what other steps BlaBlaCar will take as pressure for returns from its investors increases.

UBER

Lyft may have started out with a message of community and sharing, but its bigger and more successful competitor Uber had no such pretensions. As the name suggests, Uber was about status right from the start. Its slogan was "Everyone's private driver"; founder and CEO Travis Kalanick said in a 2013 interview, "We just wanted to push a button and get a ride. And we wanted to get a classy ride . . . That's all it was about."[17] Uber was never a partner of Peers, and although Uber was founded in 2009 it did not refer to itself as part of the Sharing Economy until 2013. Some Sharing Economy proponents don't accept Uber as part of their movement,[18] but for many people Uber now *is* the Sharing Economy.

Uber started as a black car service.[19] Customers called a car on the smartphone app, and drivers of established limo services would respond. Payment was handled by credit card, and customers loved the service enough to pay the premium that Uber charged over other black car services. Between 2009 and 2013 it grew quickly from city to city, but Lyft and other ridesharing services were offering lower prices. Belatedly, Uber recognized the cost advantage that ridesharing companies had, and decided that if it couldn't beat them, it would join them:

> In most cities across the country, regulators have chosen not to enforce against non-licensed transportation providers using ridesharing apps. This course of non-action resulted in massive regulatory ambiguity leading to one-sided competition which Uber has not engaged in to its own disadvantage.[20]

So Uber launched UberX which, like Lyft, relied on unlicensed drivers with their own cars, many without commercial insurance. UberX has expanded with lightning speed: The number of drivers rose from under 10,000 in January 2013 to over 150,000 just two years later;[21] in March 2015 Uber claimed to be available in about 300 cities across 55 countries (unlike Lyft, which operates only in the US); by August it was more like 450 cities in 60 countries.

Uber's expansion has been driven by an unprecedented succession of venture capital funding rounds: as of August 2015, the company has raised $7 billion, which is more than all other Sharing Economy companies in North America put together. By April 2017 that number had reached $11 billion including debt financing. The funding comes from a who's who of Silicon Valley venture capital firms, as well as Google Ventures, Goldman Sachs, the Qatar Investment Authority, Saudi Arabia's Public Investment Fund, select high-wealth investors through Morgan Stanley, Chinese Internet company Baidu, and Amazon CEO Jeff Bezos. Uber is still privately owned at the time of writing, but the investments correspond to a market capitalization of about $70 billion: more valuable than the three leading car rental companies (Hertz, Avis, and Enterprise) combined, and more valuable than the Ford Motor Company or General Motors.

Uber is ambitious: it has explored many variants on its driving services from carpooling to high-end luxury services, as well as delivery and logistics, but for now UberX makes up the bulk of its business. It makes sense to talk of Uber and Lyft in the same breath, despite their different images, because they have ended up offering essentially the same service. When, after a campaign by Peers and others, California became the first state to create a separate set of rules for what it called Transportation Network Companies (TNCs), Uber and Lyft were the main beneficiaries.[22] The TNC framework of lighter regulation requires TNCs to obtain a permit to operate, carry out background checks on its drivers, provide insurance coverage, and provide some anonymized data to the regulator. Unlike taxi drivers, TNC drivers do not have to register with the city, do not have to undergo the same level of vehicle inspection, and do not have to follow other rules such as (in some jurisdictions) operating secure cameras in the car. Similar frameworks were then adopted by Colorado, as well as Seattle, Minneapolis, Austin, Houston, and Washington, and now have been copied with variations throughout the world. While there are differences,[23] the basic principles are the same: the companies "provide prearranged transportation services for compensation using an online-enabled application or platform (such as smart phone apps) to connect drivers using their personal vehicles with passengers."[24] The companies compete against each other for drivers, and some drivers drive for both platforms, keeping both companies' apps in their car.

■

In city after city, debates surrounding ridesharing services are playing out, with Uber front and center. The debates are about many things: they are about us as consumers, but also us as citizens, and us as employees; they are about the role of government and the responsibilities of business. Given the company's success at building an enthusiastic customer base, many media stories present Uber as an inevitable future to which nervous city governments must adjust. Here is an example from journalist Todd Hirsch:

> It's an economic tale told time and again. Camera film makers. Video stores. The music recording industry.

Perhaps most famously, the Luddites—those textile labourers in 19th century England who protested against the introduction of mechanized looms by smashing them. Many of them failed to adapt to new, disruptive technologies and went extinct.

Next on the list may be the taxi industry . . .[25]

Conflating Uber with the broad advance of technology is exactly what the company wants. Who, after all, can argue against the future? But there is a choice, and Uber is not the inevitable future of transit—certainly not Uber on Uber's terms. Thousands of new technology businesses start every year, and many high fliers fail: Groupon turned out not to be the future of shopping; MySpace was not the future of social networking. In 2012, massively open online courses (MOOCs) were going to bring about the end of the university as we know it, but three years later their role has shrunk, rather than expanded.[26] In November 2014, Toronto mayor John Tory wanted to "sit down with the Ubers and the Hailos and others of the world,"[27] but Hailo has already folded its North American operations. Paris has outlawed UberPop (the European equivalent of UberX), but it has Autolib', which, with 2,500 cars, 155,000 members and a total of over 30 million miles driven may be the world's most successful electric-car sharing program.[28] There are many roads to the future—many *innovative* roads to the future—and the best of them don't involve Uber in its current form.

Uber enthusiasts attribute the company's success to its technology, and the efficiency with which it matches drivers and riders, but this misses much of the story. Uber's success also owes a lot to avoiding the costs of insurance, sales tax, mechanical vehicle inspections, and providing a universally-accessible service. Its ability to provide a cheap and effective service for consumers comes from its ability to run at a loss while pursuing its lavishly-funded quest for growth.[29] Uber's success comes from being parasitic on the cities in which it operates.

■

Before looking more closely at Uber, let's step back for a second and think about taxis. Uber CEO Travis Kalanick says that his company is engaged in something like an election race in which "Uber is the candidate and [its opponent] is an asshole called Taxi. I'm not totally comfortable with it but we have to bring out the truth of how evil Taxi is."[30] Kalanick also referred to "Our opponent—the Big Taxi cartel" when he hired former Obama strategist David Plouffe to run Uber's political lobbying efforts.[31] But there is no such thing as "Big Taxi." Taxi firms are generally city-wide, at least until Uber itself came along.

Uber is not only campaigning against taxi firms, it is also campaigning against existing taxi regulations. Law professor Paul Stephen Dempsey spelled out reasons for those regulations in a 1996 paper and focuses on two main motivations: level of service (limiting the number of taxis and regulating fares) and standards of service (universal access, safety standards, and insurance requirements).[32] He also looked at what happened when cities tried deregulation.

In a few cities, being a taxi driver is a skilled occupation, the most famous being London with its examination "The Knowledge." Applicants must memorize all 25,000 streets in the city, along with any businesses or landmarks on them, before they can become a driver, a task that takes several years and which is often compared to qualifying to practice law or medicine.[33] But in most cities taxi driving is not a skilled job, and open entry led to large numbers of empty cabs in the streets, long lines at taxi ranks, and aggressive competition for passengers. Also, oddly enough, it led to higher prices. For example, Seattle deregulated in 1979 but found that "service quality declined and rates were often higher,"[34] and a 2004 report noted that

> . . . several studies, including a 1993 Price Waterhouse study, found that overall, in many cities that deregulated, the supply of taxicabs increased, fares increased, service quality declined and there were more trip refusals, lower vehicle quality, and aggressive solicitation of customers resulting from a higher supply of taxicabs.[35]

The combination of increased supply and increased fares is counterintuitive; in a competitive economic market increased supply should lower the price. But of course passengers don't get to shop around among taxis before they commit to taking a ride and so are vulnerable to being overcharged, particularly in taxi rank locations such as airports and railway stations. Economic generalities are one thing, but the devil is often in the details.

The higher prices did not lead to better taxi driver incomes, as drivers spent more time waiting in the cab stand queue or driving the streets empty, looking for the next ride. In some cities the sheer number of taxis has the potential to cause traffic congestion, and the supply is linked to other traffic management challenges that cities face. Limiting entry to the taxi market and setting out standard fare rates were the response to these problems, balancing the need to provide a predictable service to customers with reasonable conditions for drivers and, in some cases, keeping traffic moving.

Regulating the supply of taxis has been far from a universal success. In many major North American cities, the chosen form of action has been the requirement that taxis acquire one of a limited number of licenses, often embodied in the form of a taxi medallion. Medallions have become valuable investments in recent years, and some say that medallion owners have become like landowners, contributing nothing to the service while extracting extortionate rent from the actual taxi drivers, although the picture is a bit more complex: in cities with a lot of owner-operated taxis the taxi medallion can instead be seen as a retirement investment, a supplement to the low wages of driving rather than a rent-extraction technique that cuts into already low pay. Still, taxi drivers themselves are often middle-aged immigrant men who work very long hours for very low pay at one of the most dangerous jobs around: in Canada and the US, taxi driving appears at the very top of the list of occupations with an on-the-job risk of murder, twice as high a rate as the next on the list (police officers).[36]

Standards regulation addresses a number of concerns around individual vehicles and around the overall level of service in a city. Consumers cannot reasonably inspect the condition of a vehicle's brakes when they get in a car, or know who will be responsible in case of an accident, so regulations require taxis to pass vehicle inspections and carry commercial insurance.

Universal access is one of the tenets of most taxi systems. Cities mandate that taxi services provide a quota of child-friendly vehicles, vehicles suitable for disabled passengers, accommodate service dogs, and meet other universal access requirements. Municipal government means that cities such as Toronto can demand that the entire taxi fleet must be wheelchair accessible over the next decade.[37] As new concerns appear, cities can address them, such as London's introduction of zero-emission vehicles to address environmental concerns.

In many cities the taxi industry is slow to change, but the fact that taxis are managed at a city level does mean that the service can be tuned for the demands and traditions of each city, so that taxis have become iconic in cities such as New York and London. The taxi service is just one part of a larger traffic management problem that cities continually struggle with, and municipal governance allows it to be balanced with other parts of the urban transit landscape such as bus services and subway services, and to fit in with other management techniques such as congestion charging. The sheer number of cities around the world also means that transit innovations can be and are imitated from city to city, such as the municipal car-sharing and bike-sharing programs that have blossomed in cities around the world over the last decade.

From balancing consumer and driver interests, to providing predictable pricing, to ensuring individual cars are safe and that the system as a whole fits into the puzzle that is urban traffic, there is more to transit than a simple market exchange.

Enter Uber. The investors in Uber clearly believe that it is not destined to be one player among many in the taxi space, they believe that the economics of digital technologies will make Uber the clear winner not only in taxi services but in deliveries and other related work.

Not everyone believes that the winner-take-all nature of digital technologies will extend to Uber, which after all is only partly a technology company.[38] There is certainly competition at the global level; in particular Asian competitors to Uber have grown very quickly. Ola in India and GrabTaxi in Singapore and Indonesia have raised over $500 million, and Uber entered a protracted and expensive battle for the Chinese market with Didi Kuaidi, before agreeing to a battered compromise in which it withdrew from China in return for a part ownership stake in Didi Kuaidi. Still, the evidence to date, and the basis of many of the investment bets, is that the market favors the big, especially within a city. That's one reason why Uber CEO Travis Kalanick admitted to undermining the fund-raising efforts of his main competitor, Lyft.[39] The ridesharing model is a "two-sided marketplace" in which Uber manages the supply of both riders and drivers. The more riders on the platform, the better it is for drivers; the more drivers available, the better it is for riders. Getting this spiral kick-started is one of the challenges to any new entrant seeking to gain entrance. The technology component of the business is amortized over all the cities in which Uber operates, so its success in New York helps its business in San Diego.

If the ridesharing market is indeed winner-take-all, then restructuring the transit system to accommodate Uber (allowing them to operate without the expenses and regulations to which taxi companies are subjected) amounts to handing over the taxi market to the company. So what kind of a city would we live in with Uber at the wheel?

■

During 2014 and 2015, Uber made a series of claims about the money earned by its drivers. The tale of these claims is, not unlike those told by Airbnb, not one of direct lies, but it is one of continual exaggeration, selection, and distortion, which have steadily lost credibility over the last year.

The story really starts in May 2014, when the company posted a claim on the Uber web site that the median annual income for an UberX driver is $90,766 in New York City and $74,191 in San Francisco.[40] The claim was greeted with an unskeptical enthusiasm by many commentators. Most prominently, Matt McFarland of the *Washington Post* led with the headline "Uber's remarkable growth could end the era of poorly paid cab drivers."[41] McFarland noted that the typical cab driver's salary is about $30,000, so the difference seems, as he put it, "astounding."

As the story spread, many others jumped on this good-news headline. CNBC led with "Uber's $90K salary could disrupt the taxi business."[42] Entrepreneur.com claimed "The Median Income of an Uber Driver in NYC Is Nearly $100,000."[43] From the technology industry, CEO Mike Jones laid it out at Code Conference: "You're qualified to drive a car, but not professionally doing it. Congratulations, boom, you're making [a] $90,000-a-year average Uber salary."[44]

For many economists the story was simple and the villain was clear: "regulatory capture" by those taxi medallion owners who suck all the money out of the taxi system without delivering value.[45] Take them out of the picture, improve efficiency by better matching drivers with customers to cut down on the dead time between rides, and we have a new age for urban transit.

Over time, however, what Uber left out of its numbers was to prove as illuminating as what it included.

The *Washington Post* did mention in the body of its text that the figure is the median of "drivers working over 40 hours per week," and if that's the sample then, as financial journalist Felix Salmon pointed out,[46] "the median number of hours worked, for drivers in this sample, is going to be well over 40." His continued attempts to get clarification from Uber fell on deaf ears.

And then there is the matter that, as McFarland wrote, "Uber's numbers don't account for the costs a driver incurs to own and operate a vehicle." Like many people, McFarland thought those costs could not be big enough to make a serious difference to the picture.

Taxi earnings and employment models vary greatly from city to city, but comparing Uber's estimates to taxi reports from Los Angeles, San Diego, and Toronto shows that Uber's 20% cut of the fare, plus its $1 "safety fee" was about the same as that taken by medallion owners; there was no magic there after all.[47] Payments for gas, maintenance, car depreciation, and insurance together with additional expenses (tolls, parking) accounted for about half of each dollar of taxi fare, which would take the earnings down to more like $45,000 in New York and $37,000 in San Francisco.

Uber did not choose New York City and San Francisco at random for their report: the company selected these two cities because that's where Uber drivers earn the most. A later report[48] showed that New York City earnings were 50% more than those in any other city except for San Francisco, which was comfortably in second place, so in many cities the earnings would come to about $30,000, which is the average for a taxi driver. Once additional expenses are accounted for, the "astounding" gap between Uber earnings and taxi earnings vanished.

Since Uber made its $90,000 claim, it has become less and less plausible. Journalists looking for drivers making $90,000 called their efforts a search for Uber's unicorn, and came up empty-handed.[49] The company never backed up its claims with more complete data, or addressed the question of expenses. The year 2014 saw Uber drivers protesting over low income in Seattle in April and August, San Francisco in May and October, Los Angeles in September, New York in September and October, and London in October: an unlikely development if they were earning as much as the company suggested. Low income became a consistent complaint on active Uber driver forums at UberPeople.net and at Reddit. Reports from individual Uber drivers failed to come anywhere near to the income figures that Uber claimed.

When Uber expands to a new city it provides subsidies and special offers to drivers and customers to get the service kick-started. As it becomes established, Uber takes a bigger slice of each dollar and often cuts fares.

Over time, Uber has taken a larger and larger slice of every fare. In April 2014, Uber introduced a $1 per trip safety fee, increasing the company's slice to around 30% for short trips. In July it started charging drivers $10 per week for use of a smartphone.[50] In September Uber increased their commission for new drivers in San Francisco to 25% of the fare,[51] and in May 2015 they started experimenting with taking 30% of the fare: more than most medallion owners.

Before this most recent trial, Uber CFO Brent Callinicos mentioned in a meeting with potential investors that Uber could easily raise rates to between 25% and 30%. Venture capitalist Mike Novogratz asked him a question: "You've got happy employees, you've got happy customers, you've got happy shareholders. The holy triumvirate are all really excited about your company. Why are you going to risk that and push the employees' salary down 5%?" Callinicos responded "because we can."[52]

When it cuts prices, Uber insists that it's good for drivers: that a greater number of rides per driver makes up for the price cuts. In October 2014 it put some numbers behind these claims.[53] In a company blog post, Uber showed that as it cut fares in New York City the average gross hourly earnings of drivers increased from $25 in 2012 to $27 in 2013 to $36 in 2014 before Uber's take or other deductions. (The 2014 rate after Uber's take and after taxes, but before any driver expenses, was around $25 per hour.[54] As an aside: at that rate a driver would have to work 70 hours a week every week of the year to bring in that $90,000.) Drivers were busy more of the time, and so although each fare was less, their total income increased.

Again, however, a key piece of data needed to provide a realistic estimate of actual income is missing, in this case the number of miles that a driver puts on the clock. More rides obviously means more gas and more wear and tear on each driver's car. Data about driver expenses was also missing from a report commissioned by the company and written by eminent economist Alan Krueger and Uber Head of Policy Research Jonathan Hall.[55] Their main conclusions were that Uber is growing really quickly—impressive, but no surprise—and that Uber drivers are paid better than taxi drivers. They report earnings of $30 per hour for New York (though more modest for other cities: $19 per hour for Boston, $17 for Los Angeles), and compare them to government figures showing that taxi drivers take in about 30% less. As with previous Uber reports, Krueger and Hall shrug their shoulders at these expenses:

A detailed quantification of driver-partner costs and net after-tax earnings is a topic of future research. Nonetheless, the figures suggest that unless their after-tax costs average more than $6 per hour, the net hourly earnings of Uber's driver-partners exceed the hourly wage of employed taxi drivers and chauffeurs, on average.

Several commentators picked up on the gap.[56] A reasonable estimate is not that difficult to make if you know the distance driven, which Uber obviously does, as it tracks all the cars on its system. *Washington Post* journalist Andrea Peterson writes:

The Internal Revenue Service . . . sets standard mileage rates for tax purposes. For 2015, taxpayers can deduct 57.5 cents a mile for operating a car for business purposes. That rate is based on an annual study of the costs of vehicle operation—those things like repairs, insurance, maintenance, gas and depreciation that were not factored into Uber's study.[57]

Based on this figure Dean Baker of the Center for Economic and Policy Research estimated that the average length of a drive would have to be "considerably less than 8 miles" for Uber drivers to come out ahead of traditional cab drivers.[58] Baker also notes that if Uber drivers do not pay for commercial insurance, or do not invest in the upkeep of their cars to the extent that commercial drivers are expected to, they would have fewer expenses and more take home pay: "If that's the case, this would be a typical story of getting rich in the new economy. Find a way to get around the rules and then claim it as a great innovation."

We do have one other source of information about driver pay, which is the drivers themselves. One of the most multifaceted and careful is an account by Philadelphia journalist Emily Guendelsberger of her time as an Uber driver.[59] After meticulously tracking her own expenses and those of other drivers who shared them with her, she made about $17 per hour gross, and after Uber's 28% cut and the 19% that went to expenses she ended up with just $9.34 an hour. Uber is not going to end the era of poorly paid cab drivers any time soon.

If the pay is really so poor, why do so many people drive for Uber? For those who have a car, driving for Uber is a way of converting that capital into cash; some underestimate the costs involved with full-time driving; for some the flexibility is a boon; for many, driving for Uber offers what taxi driving has offered for years—a job that requires little skill and has a low cost of entry is better than nothing. And as Uber has cut into the demand for taxis in many cities, individual taxi driver income has fallen, leaving Uber as the best alternative. And still, Hall and Krueger reported that about half of Uber drivers leave the platform within a year.

This discussion of Uber driver income only touches the surface of what is a complex and ever-changing topic. But what comes out of this is that the real story is a long way from $90,000, even though that number is still out there (Guendelsberger refers to "that $90,000 a year figure that so many passengers asked about"). Uber drivers appear to take home about the same as a taxi driver once expenses are figured in, while Uber itself has stepped in and takes as much of the fare as do medallion holders.

■

One of the complaints that taxi companies have against Uber and Lyft is that they are subject to different standards, and that the taxi standards are more onerous than those that the ridesharing companies have to follow.

Uber maintains that its drivers are subject to a thorough screening process, but a series of assaults on the service has put this largely automated process under scrutiny. It has not held up well. Most dramatically, *The Guardian* worked with a whistleblower who applied for work as a driver with Uber UK. Part of the process is to upload car insurance documents; the whistleblower uploaded a fake insurance policy using a made-up insurance company, "Freecover," but Uber still approved him to drive. Another driver said that some drivers Photoshop documents,[60] and in the US drivers have claimed that it is easy to get around the screening by driving on somebody else's account.[61] District Attorneys in California have filed a complaint claiming "systematic failures in Uber's background check process", so that "registered sex offenders, identity thieves, burglars, a kidnapper and a convicted murderer had passed the firm's screening process and were driving for the company."[62] More recently, the state of Massachusetts removed over 8,000 of the 71,000 Uber and Lyft drivers in the state, even after they passed company reviews.[63]

There have been numerous cases of assault on both Uber drivers and passengers, but taxi driving is dangerous too and there are also cases of assault by taxi drivers. The difference between the two is that there is a mechanism for people or communities to demand better of taxi companies, and to hold them accountable. Uber maintains that while safety is, they never forget to say, always its highest priority, the drivers are not Uber employees and Uber is not responsible for what happens on the ride.

The same story can be told of car safety standards. Uber has adjusted its policies in different cities when it has come under pressure: in Toronto, for example, it introduced an inspection by a certified mechanic as the debate about the service grew in profile (the city inspects taxis every six months), but again the company can unilaterally change its standards when it wants; for example, in February 2015 it increased the maximum age of UberX cars to fifteen years in many major markets.

∎

One of the reasons for regulation in many cities is to ensure universal access to a city's transport system. Two common requirements of taxi services are that they have to cover all areas of a city, and that they have to be ready to transport anybody without discrimination, including people with disabilities. The reactions to Uber from different segments of the population tell a complex story about the how taxis and Uber fit into the urban environment.

In California, when the company was certified as a Transportation Network Company, the regulators "required the TNCs, which provide paid rides mostly by freelance drivers using their own cars, to submit reports on how they will accommodate disabled users." Disability rights advocate Larry Paradis commented that "The plans are all quite tentative and don't address the fundamental challenge, which is ensuring enough accessible vehicles to make this transportation system at least minimally accessible for people with mobility disabilities."[64] Since then, Uber and other TNCs have made little progress in addressing the issue of universal access, and disabled groups and individuals have been vocal in their opinion that these services are not living up to the standard of universal access.

In September 2014 the National Federation of the Blind sued Uber, claiming that "Uber is violating basic equal-access requirements under both the ADA (Americans with Disabilities Act) and state law," and there are also ADA-related cases being pursued in California, Texas, and Arizona. Individual events include drivers refusing to pick up blind customers accompanied by dogs and driving away from riders with wheelchairs without trying to find an alternative.[65] The ADA requires vehicles for hire to offer "reasonable accommodations" for wheelchair users, but as urban planning professor Sandra Rosenbloom said when interviewed by Ted Trautman of non-profit publication Next City, "generally that phrase has meant nothing." Trautman also interviewed a Lyft spokesperson, who acknowledged that it's a challenge for Lyft and UberX to supply wheelchair-accessible vehicles "because these are people's own cars that they use in everyday life to drive around." One effect of the transportation network companies' rapid rise is that, in some cities, it could remove transit options for wheelchair users.[66]

If Lyft and Uber claim to provide urban transit then universal access is a challenge they must address, but there is little indication that they are doing so. In some cities Uber has introduced programs called UberAccess and UberAssist to enable customers to call an accessible vehicle but there is little evidence that these programs are effective, and the company has not made any data available about them. And Uber is pursuing a second track, which is to argue that the ADA does not apply to them. In one of the many cases of Sharing Economy companies wanting to eat their cake and have it too, Uber gives a big shrug of its shoulders: the law does not apply to them because they are not a public service, they are merely a technology company that matches drivers with riders, and they have no "legal or con tractual duty to control compliance with the law."[67]

Elsewhere, in Washington DC, council member Mary Cheh proposed legislation that would require taxicab companies to have 12% of their fleet accessible by the end of 2016, and report the number of people who request disability-accessible vehicles. Uber has opposed this legislation too, saying that it could "place excessive regulatory burdens on private vehicle-for-hire companies."

Airbnb also asserts that requirements for non-discrimination and disabled access do not apply to most properties advertised on its site, and disability advocates have argued that the Airbnb web site fails to help disabled people find appropriate accommodations (there is no way to search for listings that provide disabled access, and few listings say whether they are accessible).[68]

Airbnb, Uber, and Lyft each take steps to nudge or encourage their service providers to provide disabled access, using language that emphasizes their commitment to helping disabled people. But that commitment stops short of taking responsibility for the services that provide them with their revenue.

In many cases, Sharing Economy companies have been arguing that municipal regulations are obsolete in the face of their new technologies and new business models. Disabled access rules are clearly not obsolete, so instead the companies argue that it's not their problem. It is difficult to take companies seriously when they so clearly align their stated principles with their financial interests.

■

The situation regarding ridesharing and race is complex.

In many major American cities, and particularly in New York, people of color have long maintained that they are routinely ignored by taxi drivers and that, despite the rules surrounding universal access, cab companies do not service their neighborhoods. For example, in 2012 Latoya Peterson wrote at the Racialicious blog about her repeated experiences of taxis "not even bothering to pull to the side for the lone black girl on the corner but happily picking up the white couple a few feet away" and contrasted that to Uber's premium service: "The price made me gag, but the rest of the experience was flawless: I knew exactly when my car would arrive, I received a text when they reached my location, I gave them a location without quibbling, and rode there in peace."

But as Peterson notes in a more recent post, it's worth unpacking what it is about Uber that led to her experience.[69] Taxi drivers may not get much control over their jobs, but one thing they do get to control is who they pick up and who they leave at the side of the road. So any discriminatory tendencies (implicit or explicit) among the taxi driver population has an easy way to make itself known: they will tend to leave people of color standing at the curb. For Uber drivers, the summons that they get on their app does not show a picture of the customer, just a name, and so drivers must accept or reject fares without all the cues that taxi drivers have. Second, Uber requires drivers to accept 90% of all rides that are sent their way, on pain of being removed from the service, so rejecting a potential ride comes at a cost.

A more recent study suggests that Uber passengers may be experiencing the same kind of discrimination that Peterson complained of from taxis, based on their names. A study from the National Bureau for Economic Research sent passengers to Seattle and Boston to hail nearly 1500 rides on Uber and Lyft, some with clearly African-American sounding names such as Aisha, Darnell, Kareem, or Ebony and some with "white sounding names" (Allison, Brendan, Greg, or Anne). Here are their highlight findings:

> Results indicated a pattern of discrimination, which we observed in Seattle through longer waiting times for African American passengers—as much as a 35 percent increase. In Boston, we observed discrimination by Uber drivers via more frequent cancellations against passengers when they used African American-sounding names. Across all trips, the cancellation rate for African American sounding names was more than twice as frequent compared to white sounding names. Male passengers requesting a ride in low-density areas were more than three times as likely to have their trip canceled when they used an African American-sounding name than when they used a white-sounding name. [70]

Uber drivers are not told where to drive, so they may avoid what they consider as "sketchy" parts of town, and both Uber and Lyft have been accused of "redlining": not providing services to poor and minority neighborhoods.[71] For example, data journalists Jennifer Stark and Nicholas Diakopoulos studied a month's worth of Uber data from Washington DC and concluded that "The neighborhoods with better service — defined as those places with consistently lower wait times, the pickup ETA as projected by Uber — are more white." [72]

Numerous comments on social media suggest that one of the appeals of Uber and Lyft to young and well-off early adopters was that the drivers matched their age, educational-level, and social background more than did taxi drivers. Instead of being driven by a middle-aged immigrant man who had 60 hours on the clock that week, you could be picked up by "a friend with a car," more likely to be female, more likely to be well educated, and more likely to be white.[73] As the companies have expanded, however, the driver population more closely matches taxi drivers and this opportunity to discriminate has faded.

Discriminatory behavior does affect minority hosts on Airbnb. The listings include pictures of hosts and guests, so allowing any discriminatory tendencies among the user base to be expressed. Researchers Benjamin Edelman and Michael Luca examined a set of listings and concluded that "non-black hosts charge approximately 12% more than black hosts for the equivalent rental. These effects are robust when controlling for all information visible in the Airbnb marketplace." [74] Uber does not record race information about its drivers, and does not publish data about rating distributions. There is so far no published research about ratings bias on Uber, but in addition to Airbnb there has been research showing bias on TaskRabbit [75] and other platforms,[76] so it would be remarkable these attitudes did not also manifest themselves on ridesharing platforms. Meanwhile hotels in the USA are required to follow the Civil Rights Act of 1964, which guarantees full and equal access to any place of public accommodation.[77]

Discriminatory tendencies will show themselves if there is the opportunity to do so. The taxi, Uber, and Airbnb systems each let those tendencies express themselves in different ways.

A similar effect happens when comparing methods of traffic policing. Individual traffic police officers can and do have a pattern of disproportionately stopping black drivers,[78] while traffic cameras with automatic license plate recording act irrespective of the race of the driver. So in this way, a change of technology can cut down on specific incidents of racist behavior. Yet we should be careful about drawing general conclusions about the overall effect of any new technology: as criminologist Clive Norris has shown, license plate recognition has now become a way of tracking known individuals as they move around, and it is no surprise who is tracked more and who is tracked less.[79] The underlying problem remains: there is still racism in the system, but it is now manifested in different ways. Data acquisition shifts the place where racism happens from the street to the database query.

It seemed for a while that the opacity of the ridesharing apps may provide a solution to the problem of taxi discrimination, but the newer investigations described above suggest that, if discrimination is present in a society, it will show itself when given the opportunity. A particular concern is the rating systems that Uber uses to manage ride quality. These systems can be used to deprive a driver of a livelihood, and this opens the question of whether Uber's employment practices may themselves have a discriminatory side.[80]

■

Money is one of the main points of contention for many jobs, but Uber is not just another employer. In fact, it's not an employer at all: Uber drivers are "partners," self-employed entrepreneurs who choose to work on the platform. The model of "micro-entrepreneurs" who can choose when to work independently is what makes Uber part of the booming Sharing Economy along with others such as Airbnb. What seems at first like a light-weight and flexible model of work turns out, in Uber's hands, to be another way for the company to have it both ways.

Uber makes it easy for new drivers to sign up: it publicizes what many drivers describe as unrealistic earnings to attract interest, it subsidizes its expansion into new cities, and its vehicle approval process is cursory. As journalist Nitasha Tiku uncovered, the company's partnership with Santander bank encouraged drivers to take out what amount to subprime loans in order to buy a car,[81] and when that partnership expired Uber took to directly leasing cars to drivers.[82] It sometimes seems as if Uber is re-introducing each of the problems of the taxi industry: a long-standing criticism has been that some taxi drivers have to pay to use a cab, and so start each shift in the red; now Uber drivers too put in long hours to pay off a purchase, and being kicked off the platform becomes even more of a threat.

Uber has taken advantage of its drivers' vulnerability by imposing more and more strenuous rules. Drivers must accept 90% of ride requests or they get a notification to "Please improve your acceptance rate if you want to continue to use the Uber platform." Drivers claim to have been deactivated for being critical of the company on Twitter.[83]

Drivers on the premium Uber Black service have been forced to take requests for the lower-pay UberX service and UberX drivers have been forced to take the unpopular UberPool requests. The company tracks driver locations and complains if they are not to the company liking.

Over time, Uber has collected more and more data about every aspect of rides on the platform, and this data gives the company novel opportunities to control driver behavior and shape customer experiences. Uber knows that customers will pay higher prices when their phone batteries are low; it knows that we are happier to pay a surge price with a multiplier of 2.2 (compared to the base price) than a multiplier of 2, because the spurious precision of 2.2 looks like the dispassionate output of an algorithm, whereas the round number "2" looks more like a human decision to take more money from customers. [84]

Uber has studied the psychology of persuasion and uses it to optimize its own operation, adopting techniques from video games to keep drivers at the wheel. [85] Many drivers are convinced that Uber's systems deceive them, for example showing ride requests that vanish before they can be accepted, so that the driver fails to achieve the acceptance levels needed for a bonus, or inaccurately recording the time a driver waits for a customer to turn up, so as to deny them the cancellation fee.[86]

Uber's application and algorithms are not directly accessible to anyone outside the company, so it is difficult to know which actions are real and which are perceived. But two revelations in early 2017 showed that Uber is capable of active deception. Uber's "Greyball" program identified city government officials who used the application to enforce local taxi regulations, and "served up a fake version of the app, populated with ghost cars, to evade capture".[87] A second program, called "Hell" to contrast with the "Heaven" program that provided executives with a "God view" of Uber operations in a city (see below), used fake Lyft accounts to collect the number and location of drivers for the rival service, and so could identify drivers who drove for both services. Uber used the data to tweak its pricing and to offer the drivers incentives to use only Uber.

But at the heart of the control is the rating system that permits riders to rate drivers. Chapter 6 explores rating systems in more detail, but a few words about Uber's belong here. Most riders give their drivers five stars out of five as a courtesy ("five for five"), but if a driver's rating slips even slightly—below 4.7 in many cities— they can be "deactivated" or kicked off the platform. The system makes drivers vulnerable to the most demanding of riders, as a small number of complaints can lead to the driver losing their livelihood. And of course there is no appeal, as the driver isn't an employee and the contract is not a work contract. The reports of happy and friendly Uber drivers take on a different meaning once you know the precariousness of the drivers' situation. As *Forbes'* Jeff Bercovici reported, "Uber likes this system because it enjoys being able to say all of its drivers have near-perfect ratings. But it's a harsh one for drivers, and also for customers, who find themselves repeatedly forced to choose between guilt, spite and ignorance."

While Uber dictates the behavior of its drivers in more and more specific ways, it still takes none of the responsibility when things go wrong. Section 230 of the "Communications Decency Act" may seem like an odd law to protect the company, but here's how it works. The law was initially introduced to say that blogs and other user-content sites such as YouTube were not responsible for content posted by its users. Fair enough. But now Uber says it's not a taxi company, it just runs a web site and an app, and puts drivers in touch with riders. Anything that goes wrong is not Uber's responsibility, it's the driver's. The law is an American one, but challenging Uber is going to be expensive in other countries too, and maybe prohibitively so, given the company's formidable bank account.

Uber's rules seem to step over the line regarding whether a driver is, or is not, an employee according to Canada Revenue Agency rules. Sharing Economy workers are facing this issue with other companies too (see Chapter 9). It's an issue that other industries face, such as construction, and the root cause is always the same: classification as an independent contractor relieves the hiring company (Uber in this case) from having to pay employment insurance premiums, sick leave, and from having to abide by employment standards. The risk is pushed entirely onto the subcontractor.

■

If cities decide to put taxi regulations to one side for ridesharing companies, many important decisions are handed over to the company. As shown in Chapter 7, technology industries are often a winner-take-all market, where the winner has significant market power, so it matters what kind of company Uber is.

It's a company that has experienced a lot of controversy. Among the most high profile events was a dinner in which Uber executive Emil Michael told journalist Ben Smith that he had considered investigating the private life of Sarah Lacy, a journalist who had criticized Uber. (Unlike a driver with a bad rating, Michael was forgiven by the company).[88] Uber is a company that spies on its customers using what it calls its "God View" of company data, which it has shown at company events for entertainment[89] and posted about on its web site.[90] It's a company whose New York general manager

Josh Mohrer is being investigated internally for tracking a female journalist without her consent.[91] It's a company whose employees have warned
another female journalist that "company higher-ups might access [the journalist's] rider logs."[92]

I emphasize "female journalist" here because the culture of the company is a big part of the problem. Do we want to hand over city streets to
a company whose CEO wisecracks about women on demand ("Yeah, we
call that Boob-er")?[93] Which "can and does track one-night stands" and
posts a blog entry about the data called "Rides of Glory" (now removed)?[94]
Which, more damagingly, ran a campaign in France (now also removed)
called "Avions de Chasse" to pair Uber riders with "hot chick" drivers?[95] As
the company posted on the English version of its web site:

> "Avions de chasse" is the French term for "fighter jets,"
> but also the colloquial term to designate an incredibly hot
> chick. Lucky you! The world's most beautiful "Avions" are
> waiting for you on this app. Sit back, relax and let them
> take you on cloud 9![96]

The promotional material focused, unsurprisingly, on the drivers'
breasts.

This is a company that responded to a complaint by a female customer
that she was driven twenty miles out of her way to an abandoned lot by
saying it was an "inefficient route."[97]

It's also a company that coaches Miami drivers how to circumvent
laws.[98] It's a company that ordered and cancelled over 5,000 rides with its
main competitor to interfere with their service.[99] It's a company that sets
out to dupe newspapers with fake PR,[100] and which now talks of "weap-
onizing facts" in its PR campaigns (this company really likes its military
analogies).[101] In short, it's a company that reflects the worst of the macho
culture of some parts of the technology industry.

Uber's commitment to the places where it runs is minimal. It is
remarkable that, among all the privacy problems, Canadian cities are generally allowing Uber to operate. Although the company has a privacy policy
for the US, it has no Canadian privacy policy.[102] That's how much Uber is
thinking, for all its massive funding base, about privacy issues and about
the different requirements of operating in different cities.

From a tax point of view, Uber is parasitic on local economies. When you pay a taxi driver, part of the money goes to the taxi company he or she drives for, that taxi company pays taxes in the city, and so the money feeds back into the local economy. When you pay an Uber driver, the situation is different. After a Toronto Councilor obtained an email stating that there is no tax charged on Uber rides, the company claimed that its drivers are expected to collect sales tax, even though the cashless transaction is part of the service's appeal.[103]

Whatever happens to the driver's portion of the fare, the company's cut is tax free. Like many digital companies, Uber has set up subsidiaries around the world. Uber Canada, for example, pays no tax because it makes no income. If you take an Uber in Canada your credit card payment goes to Uber BV, incorporated in the Netherlands. Uber BV takes in a lot of revenue, but does not make a profit (and so pays no tax) because it pays a large license fee for the intellectual property it uses to another Uber subsidiary, Uber International CV. Intellectual property licensing fees are not taxable in the Netherlands, so Uber International also operates tax free, and can transfer its money to its headquarters in Bermuda. For now, like other global technology programs, Uber's pile of money in Bermuda is not being moved back to the USA because Uber does not want to pay the corporate tax such a move would trigger. The arrangement, called "Double Dutch" because of the two Dutch subsidiaries, shows the lengths to which Uber will go to avoid contributing to the cities where it operates.[104]

In the early months of 2017, Uber suffered a series of revelations that showed the leopard has not changed its spots. A blog post by Susan Fowler, a software engineer who had left Uber after a year with the company, highlighted the continuing sexism in the internal culture of the company. Fowler's post came from a demonstrated expert in her field (she had published a book with respected technical publisher O'Reilly), dispassionately and meticulously documented the harassment she experienced from her manager, and made it clear that Uber's human resources department had been no help. [105] It was convincing enough that Uber had little choice but to carry out an internal investigation. Fowler's revelations were followed in quick succession by the revelation of the Uber "Greyball" program to deceive government officials and the Uber "Hell" program to obtain underhand information about its competitors and drivers (see above), by a videotaped exchange in which CEO Travis Kalanick insulted one of his drivers, by the departure of several senior executives, and by accusations from Google that Uber's self-driving car initiative was built on a foundation of stolen intellectual property.

At the same time, Uber's financial situation was coming under increased scrutiny. For years, the rapid growth of Uber was compelling evidence that the company had unlocked a new model of transit, and Uber was in a position to challenge city governments to get on board with the inevitable future or be left behind. The company's ambition was clear: Uber is not just a big taxi company, it would reshape transit and disrupt logistics. It lived in "the place where bits and atoms come together".[106]

But Uber has continued to postpone what was expected to be a spectacular initial public offering of shares. As a private company it does not have to make its books public—even high wealth investors who bought part of the company through Morgan Stanley did so without a look at the accounts. Through a sequence of leaks it became clear that Uber was losing money in an unprecedented fashion, and in late 2016 a series of blog posts by transport analyst Hubert Horan suggested that during 2016 Uber had taken in $3 billion of revenue, but had spent $6 billion.[107] What's more, Horan argued, Uber's case was fundamentally different to the company with which it has been most frequently compared. Amazon postponed making a profit for years in order to reinvest in growth, but Horan argued that there was nothing about Uber's model that promised profitability in the long run. Horan argued that Uber's ability to match riders and drivers, and the efficiencies of its surge pricing models, were not the primary factors responsible for Uber's growth. These were clever, but the difference they made to the business had been overstated. Instead, Uber's growth was driven by an unsustainable level of subsidies for both riders and drivers. On average, riders are paying under 80% of the cost of a ride.

Under pressure, Uber finally released financial information in April 2017, and it showed that "Net revenue was $6.5 billion, while adjusted net losses were $2.8 billion, excluding the China business, which it sold last summer."[108] Losses according to generally accepted accounting principles would, it was accepted, be even bigger. It looks increasingly as if Uber's self-promotion has been a repeated game of misdirection. Its original Uber Black service was not profitable, but maybe the mass-marked UberX would be. UberX, it now seems, is not a profitable business but maybe the still uncertain UberPool service will be. Maybe the services will become profitable once we have all given up our own cars and adopted Uber as our main mode of transport. If UberPool is not profitable, maybe the bigger game of logistics will deliver (even though Uber's efforts in that area have so far not delivered significant revenue). If logistics is not the future, maybe it's self-driving cars (a topic beyond the scope of this book, but which—despite impressive advances—is still wrapped in uncertainty). Uber has even released two whitepapers about flying cars, the most recent suggesting prototypes by 2020 and claiming that these "air taxis" may be cheaper than owning a car. Maybe. Maybe.

By the time this book gets to press, this chapter will be outdated in that new events will have superseded old ones. But what won't change is the question of how to build an accessible, affordable, and sustainable transit system for cities around the world. And what won't change is that, for Uber to be a constructive part of such a system, it cannot be allowed to set its own rules and own agenda in the way that it has done. If Uber is intent on delivering, there are some chickens that need to come home to roost.

5. Neighbors Helping Neighbors

Personal and home services like housecleaning, handyman tasks, and deliveries is a disparate, crowded and rapidly changing field, with many competing companies and, as yet, no clear winner. In this way it is different from the world of Airbnb and Uber; the evolution of the sector tells us what happens when competition forces an evolution of business models.

TASKRABBIT

The first company in the space was TaskRabbit, which started at the same time as Airbnb, Lyft, and others. The listing for TaskRabbit on the business information web site CrunchBase describes the moment when the company founder had her idea:

> It was a cold night in Boston in February of 2008 when Leah Busque realized she was out of dog food for her 100-lb yellow lab, Kobe. Leah thought to herself, "Wouldn't it be nice if there was a place online I could go to connect with my neighbors—maybe one who was already at the store at that very moment—who could help me out?"
>
> From this experience, TaskRabbit (formerly RUNmyERRAND), an online and mobile marketplace that connects neighbors to get things done, was born . . . Neighbors helping neighbors—it's an old school concept reimagined for today.[1]

TaskRabbit was set up as an "eBay for errands," and offers a range of services. The two that gained most attention could be done by any young, healthy person: standing in line for concert tickets and for new iPhones, and assembling Ikea furniture (well, *almost* anyone). The going rate for a task was settled by an auction, with TaskRabbits bidding for a job. The practice reflected the way homeowners might negotiate with someone who offers to clear their driveway of snow, or the way babysitting rates are settled informally, or the way that eBay used auctions in its early years. Leah Busque used the familiar language of empowerment:

> providing people with the tools and resources to set their own schedules, be their own bosses and say how much they want to get paid is incredibly empowering. It has huge implications for the global labour force.[2]

The earliest investors in TaskRabbit came in 2009 when the company received $25,000 from fbFund, a joint venture of Founders Fund and Accel Partners. Founders Fund was co-founded and is managed by Peter Thiel, a person whose politics are far more about rejecting government than about the neighbor-to-neighbor connection that Busque envisaged.

And quickly, as with the other examples of the Sharing Economy, the idea that the TaskRabbits, as they were called for a few years, would be neighbors helping neighbors vanished, and the harsh world of the free market took its place. Just as Airbnb traded on the idea of a welcoming host and Lyft traded on the image of "your friend with a car," so the values of neighborliness were invoked to justify a new form of precarious employment.

In an extended report written in 2013,[3] journalist Kevin Carhart unpacked many of the problems with TaskRabbit. Carhart quotes a TaskRabbit blog post (now removed) "rhapsodizing over networked mobile devices as an exciting kind of metaphor for spontaneous order," which goes back to Adam Smith's idea of the "invisible hand" of the free market. Here is TaskRabbit:

> [Adam] Smith is saying that governments should simply provide an unrestricted market system for people to easily exchange goods and services, and then get the heck out of the way! Market forces will take care of the rest. Yep, we totally agree! . . .

The interconnectedness and transparency offered by the Internet and social networks make it possible for Smith's vision to be realized for individuals in a community . . . We are hopeful that Service Networking is continuing to foster Smith's philosophy—making it increasingly possible for markets to be truly free for the betterment of the community.

The company's now-familiar narrative was that they provided a way to earn some extra money by acting as a "micro-entrepreneur." Carhart's interviews with TaskRabbit workers showed another side of the coin. One middle-aged TaskRabbit told him that the company is "filling in the gaps. They're opportunists. If they can go around labor law, they're going to do it, and if they can get young people, inspire people with their doublespeak rhetoric, they've got recruits." She went on to say that TaskRabbit workers "would like to have a job and they can't get one. I think they're worth more. I think they're great people or they wouldn't be asked back. I've seen what they do to get this money and you would think they would be properly compensated for what they do . . . I feel really bad for them . . . People are making less than minimum wage for everything."

Reporter Alyson Shontell interviewed another TaskRabbit who supported the claim of less than minimum wage:

No one is obligated to pay minimum wage, and that happens again and again and again. I have worked 12 and 15 hour days doing really strenuous physical labor and had $80 to show for it . . .

You're always aware of the fact that a task could be more difficult and more cumbersome than what you're imagining. And you're always aware of the fact that a task poster may indeed downplay what's involved to get a cheaper price.

I had a client a couple of months ago who wanted me to do his laundry.

He always posts that it's four loads of laundry and every time I did his laundry it filled 10 or 15 double loading washers. It was a mountain of laundry and it was all covered in cat diarrhea.[4]

Leah Busque responded to Shontell, and emphasized that "TaskRabbits take on only the jobs they want to complete. TaskRabbit is an open marketplace. As such, TaskRabbits are free to bid on the jobs they find attractive—taking into consideration the amount of time involved, the nature of the work, etc. No TaskRabbit is ever forced into any job or task. One thing to note is one person's imperfect task is another person's ideal task. It is not up to us but rather the TaskRabbits themselves to decide which tasks to bid on."

Carhart took up the claim "that violations of employment standards are 'not our problem' and 'not up to us,' with labor lawyer Catherine Ruckelshaus, who responded:

> That's the narrative that employers who misclassify their workers as independent contractors use. They say even to a day laborer, a strawberry picker, "it's up to you, you can come or go." And they don't set the price and they don't set the hours. They try to cloak it as an independent, free exchange, which it's not.

TaskRabbit has gone through a range of business models and seems to be struggling. For some time they promoted a "TaskRabbit for Business" program, which was essentially an all-purpose temp agency. Then in June 2014 they changed their model: no more auctions, work would now be done at a fixed price; a computer algorithm would match clients with "taskers" as they are now called; taskers were asked to wear a company-green tee shirt.[5] The changes reflect the way that other online platforms have moved from a model that mimics personal interactions to one that models the consumer experience: eBay moved away from auctions toward fixed prices, Lyft gave up on "donations" for fares.

The changes are unilateral. The idea (promoted by the company) that they empower taskers turned out to be empty. As Juliet Schor commented:

> One thing we found in interviews with taskers was that the ability to have control over when they work, who they work for and how much they work was central to the appeal of this platform for many people. These changes have reduced that. The platform is exercising more power and control.[6]

TaskRabbit's most recent change is to ally with Amazon with its new "Amazon Home Services" offering.[7] The additional control that the company now exerts over its "micro-entrepreneurs" raises the question of whether they are really independent agents at all. It's a question that continues to haunt some of the more recent startups that have followed in TaskRabbit's path.

HOMEJOY

House cleaning is not an obvious industry for Google to expand into, but in 2013 the company's venture capital wing, Google Ventures, joined other investors in putting $38 million into a small company called Homejoy, run by sister and brother Adora and Aaron Cheung. Joining Google Ventures in the early investment round was Max Levchin, co-founder (along with Peter Thiel) of PayPal, and Andreessen Horowitz.

Homejoy's web site says "Get your place cleaned," but the terms of service (over 4,000 words) emphasize that "THE COMPANY DOES NOT PROVIDE CLEANING SERVICES, AND THE COMPANY IS NOT A CLEANING SERVICE PROVIDER" and "The Service is a communications platform for enabling the connection between individuals seeking to obtain cleaning services and/or individuals seeking to provide cleaning services."

Homejoy provides a web site on which you pick what time you want your house cleaned. As *Wired* magazine says, "A key selling point is that the housecleaners themselves are insured and vetted by Homejoy. Like Uber's drivers, however, they're not technically employed by the company. Instead, they work as freelancers who set their own hours and receive assignments based on availability."[8] The arrangement has come to be known as the "1099 model," after the 1099-MISC "independent contractor" form that the workers in the US have to fill out at tax time. Venture capitalist Jeff Jordan of Andreessen Horowitz is enthusiastic about companies like Homejoy.

> The proliferation of mobile devices is enabling what I call "People Marketplaces": two-sided marketplaces that connect consumers with people providing specific services. From finding a ride with Lyft, to getting your house cleaned with Homejoy, home-delivered restaurant meals from DoorDash and Caviar, and instant pet-sitting from

DogVacay, the variety and usage of People Marketplaces are exploding. It's really becoming a thing![9]

(Jordan was writing as Andreessen Horowitz announced its funding for yet another sharing-economy startup, Instacart, discussed below. Jordan now has a seat on Instacart's board.)

Homejoy's pitch makes three claims: they are cheap compared to other cleaning services, offer good pay to the cleaners, and carry out "extensive screening" to ensure high standards. Lydia DePillis of the *Washington Post* talked to a Homejoy cleaner, and her report makes it clear how Homejoy kept its prices low.[10] Anthony Walker gets to his first appointment, on the other side of Washington, on the bus, carrying his cleaning supplies in a rolling suitcase. Homejoy says its cleaners earn about $20 an hour, and sure enough the job will earn him $51 for the two-and-a-half hours he spends cleaning, but like Uber's claims about their drivers' income, Homejoy neglects half of the picture: Walker's two-and-a-half hours travel time is not included, he pays the bus fare, and the cleaning supplies are his own. His afternoon appointment cancels, but that's no loss to Homejoy; it doesn't have to pay Anthony Walker for the lost afternoon. Walker gets no unemployment insurance, no workers' compensation, and no retirement benefits. And if he is sick that's his problem.

Early funder Peter Thiel may see government as broken, but Homejoy's services are state-subsidized. DePillis writes that Anthony Walker "gets transit refunded through D.C.'s welfare programs, although it took some doing to prove his employment status, as Homejoy doesn't give traditional pay stubs."

In Chicago, Homejoy works with the mayor's office to find cleaners. "For many people in the program, they have to show proof of employment to receive government assistance, so the Homejoy program is important to them." Once more there is the suggestion that this is not really a job in the normal sense. Homejoy's Marlo Struve says: "A lot of people use it as a flexible option to bring in extra earnings to a family and sometimes supplement another part-time opportunity. A lot of times it's part of a bigger picture for them and their families."[11]

They may not be employees, but Homejoy cleaners are continually ranked by the company. "On its internal system, cleaners can see how they rank by customer rating. Walker sits at 13 out of D.C.'s 42 cleaners with a 4.6;

almost all 5s, except for a woman who complained that he hadn't gotten the mildew entirely out of her shower grout."

Interviewed by the *Washington Post*, a Homejoy spokesperson gave the standard Sharing Economy line, emphasizing the quality of the service by claiming that "only 30 percent of applicants make it through to become cleaners," but was somehow unable to find answers to more pressing questions. He "declined to disclose any of the company's other metrics, such as the average wage earned by its cleaners in a week or the distance they travel to jobs."

Sharing Economy entrepreneurs like to talk about "earning a little extra money" and making life a little more affordable, but Anthony Walker shows that the business model is a race to the bottom for the service providers. The most that can be said for the practice of replacing actual jobs with the kind of precarious, state-subsidized work that Walker gets from Homejoy is that it is better than nothing, but it is undermining other workers as it does so, and while Walker gets some money he has no chance of moving on to actual employment.

Kevin Roose of *New York* magazine was living in the San Francisco Bay area and asked for a house cleaning through Homejoy. A young man turned up and Roose made small talk, asking where he lived.

> "Well, right now I'm staying in a shelter in Oakland," he said. I paused, unsure if I'd heard him right. A shelter? Was my house cleaner—the one I'd hired through a company that has raised $40 million in venture-capital funding from well-respected firms like Google Ventures, the one who was about to perform arduous manual labor in my house using potentially hazardous cleaning chemicals—homeless?
>
> He was, as it turned out. And as I told this story to friends in the Bay Area, I heard something even more surprising: Several of their Homejoy cleaners had been homeless, too.[12]

By August 2015 the Homejoy story had come to an end. The company was able to offer cheap prices and claim reasonable pay for reasons that had nothing to do with the efficiency-improving wonders of digital technology; the company was simply burning through venture capital money, trying to raise enough business to gain momentum in the winner-take-all world of the Sharing Economy. Once the money ran out, Homejoy had to look for a buyer. A German company called Helpling looked at the company's books and walked away; then it seemed that Homejoy's competitor, Handy, might buy them up, but in the end the company just folded. Many of the technology team were hired by Google, so maybe the era of Internet-driven cleaning services is not over yet.

HANDY

Handy, originally called Handybook, is similar to Homejoy in many ways. It goes beyond cleaners to add plumbers and other home services into its offering, but about 85% of its revenue comes from cleaning.[13] And of course it has an "origin story" on its web site. Here it is:

> Oisin Hanrahan was a 19-year old college student in Ireland when he decided to become a real estate developer in Eastern Europe. After scouring various cities on weekend breaks from Trinity College in Dublin, Hanrahan started buying and renovating apartments in Budapest. While renovating a series of apartments around the city, Oisin found it difficult to find quality handymen he could trust to get the job done. There was no easy way. A few years later, while attending Harvard Business School, Oisin and classmate, Umang Dua, realized the same was true in the U.S. They developed Handy to fill that void, with the goal of building the easiest, most convenient way for busy people everywhere to book household services.[14]

Handy has (as of April 2015) raised $60.7 million in venture capital funding, and its funders include Revolution LLC, led by ex-AOL president Steve Case, a prominent Sharing Economy booster.

The benefits of Handy will be familiar. Hanrahan says "We are building a brand that's based on trust. We need our customers to trust us to let us into their homes."[15] The benefits for consumers are touted: co-founder Umang Dua said "We're focused on creating the best end to end consumer experience at Handybook. From ease of booking to working with trusted professionals to provide best in class service, our goal is to build an ongoing relationship with our customers who continue to turn to us for all their service needs within the home."[16] And the status of "service pros" as independent contractors: "the flexibility in terms of scheduling and earnings—is a very meaningful part of the value they see in the platform."[17]

The terms of service paint a different picture. According to the 8,500-word document, "The Handy Platform is Solely a Venue for Communications; Background Checks." It continues:

> Handy does not itself provide Services . . . HANDY, THROUGH THE HANDY PLATFORM, OFFERS INFORMATION AND A METHOD TO OBTAIN SUCH SERVICES, BUT DOES NOT AND DOES NOT INTEND TO PROVIDE SUCH SERVICES ITSELF OR ACT IN ANY WAY AS A CLEANING, HANDYMAN, OR OTHER HOME-RELATED OR MOVING-RELATED SERVICE PROVIDER, AND HAS NO RESPONSIBILITY OR LIABILITY FOR ANY SERVICES PROVIDED TO YOU.

The picture we get of the typical "service pro" is shaped by the well-lit, smiling faces on the Handy web site, and by many of the portrayals in the media that cover the area. Unfortunately (with notable exceptions, many of whom have been quoted here), too much of the technology press and business press seem to take an uncritical attitude to the employment conditions. And why not? Handy offers "great pay," claiming that its workers "make up to $22/hour as a cleaner or $45/hour as a handyman. Our top professionals make more than $1,000 a week."[18] When *The Economist* ran a story on freelance workers for Handy and other platforms, they bought into the extra work story, talking to a law graduate for whom "the on-demand model allows her to combine a career as a lawyer with her taste for travel," and to the founder of a group that represents "elite workers who want to wind down after decades of selling their soul to their company."[19]

Although Homejoy and Handy have adopted many of the tropes of the Sharing Economy, something is missing, and that's the neighborhood and community aspect that other digital platforms emphasize. There is no pretense of anything other than a straightforward commercial transaction.

While Sharing Economy advocates point to web platforms as enablers of peer-to-peer exchanges, removing corporations from the picture, the home services wing of the movement is resolutely marching in the other direction: one of the major benefits that the new technology-based services offer, compared to more traditional cleaning services, turns out to be that it enables customers to hire cleaners without having to actually speak to anybody.

Ellen Huet is a journalist who has covered the ins and outs of the Sharing Economy for several years. She quotes Handy's Hanrahan:

> If you want someone to go through the process of scrubbing the mold off the top left corner of the shower because you're too busy or lazy to do it yourself, it's really hard to ask that person, particularly if you're 22, you've never had the responsibility of employing someone your whole life, you've interned two places and now you're asking someone to do this for you.[20]

Huet's interviews with Hanrahan and with Homejoy's Adora Cheung have a clear lesson for online services: separate the service provider from the customer. Phone is better than face-to-face: as Hanrahan says, "That's the worst—asking the cleaner in person, 'Hey, while you're here, can you clean the bathroom?'" Text is better than voice. Indirect is better than direct: "People prefer to hit the chat box in the lower left hand corner of the site and ask someone who is in the position to influence a booking to put in a special request, rather than ask the person who will be doing the cleaning." Check boxes are better than text: Huet quotes design specialist Steph Habif that "Handybook and Homejoy both prompt users with cleaning add-ons like interior windows, ovens, fridges, cabinets and laundry. Such choices let people feel in control, even if they aren't creative enough to come up with their own instructions."

The problem of trust is solved, according to Huet's interviews, mainly by introducing a feeling of familiarity, normality, and routine to the process of ordering online services. "We wanted to make it like shopping on Amazon," said another of Huet's interviewees. Adora Cheung adds that "In the past decade, purchasing products online has become trusted—we trust the product will show up at your address at some point," Cheung said.

"Now, people are beginning to trust purchasing offline services, whereas a decade ago they maybe wouldn't have."

The lack of direct contact and the now-routine familiarity of a click-to-purchase or app-based model helps in another way: it makes users avoid a feeling of guilt about paying to avoid chores. Huet quotes design specialist Habif again: "The more time a person has to practice a behavior, the less guilty they're going to feel about it, especially if they have a rewarding and successful experience. My guess is their customers feel less guilty over time."

DELIVERIES

Delivery was one of TaskRabbit's common tasks, but now more specialized firms have moved in (as well as Uber, making a so far largely unsuccessful attempt to expand its business). Of these, two are particularly interesting.

Instacart's web page offers, in big letters, "Groceries Delivered in an Hour," but according to its terms of service Instacart is not a delivery service:

> Instacart is a communications platform for facilitating the connection between individuals seeking to order food and beverage products and other grocery items ("Groceries") from selected retail premises ("Customer(s)"), and individuals seeking to assist Customers by retrieving and delivering the Groceries to and on behalf of Customers who have authorized the purchase of such Groceries.

Instacart was founded in 2012. The required founding myth is a little less than inspirational. Twenty-seven-year-old Apoorva Mehta had spent two years working as an engineer at Amazon: "I had this problem of never having groceries in my fridge and never having the motivation and energy to go to the store," and most grocery services made him submit his order hours in advance.[21]

Instacart has already raised over a quarter of a billion dollars from big-name firms like Andreessen Horowitz and Sequoia Capital. Initially Instacart ran a typical Sharing Economy model, charging customers delivery fees and a price markup, paying your personal shopper, and pocketing a portion of the exchange. But in 2014 it jettisoned even the pretense of peer-to-peer exchange, partnering with grocery stores who pay Instacart a fee to service their locations.[22] Just as eBay became a storefront for major retailers, so Instacart is becoming a new supplier of customers to major fast food chains and retailers; it even gives customers the option of sharing their personal data and shopping history with retailers.[23]

Like Homejoy's Anthony Walker, Instacart shoppers are promised "up to $25 an hour," but the important words are "up to." Reporter Joseph Erbentraut interviewed several Instacart shoppers, who "said their minimum hourly base pay was $10, and that their typical hourly pay usually hovered around that figure."

> "It's a really strange job, and there are many weeks where you're just sitting in the car waiting for orders and hoping something comes in, not being paid to be there," one of Instacart's personal shoppers, a 24-year-old college dropout based in Chicago, told the *Huffington Post* in an interview. "But it's keeping gas in my car. I'm working a job that requires gas that is essentially just paying for my car. It feels like selling my hair to buy a hairbrush."[24]

Maybe the shopper should take heart from economist Tyler Cowen, who cheerily opined (based on no quoted evidence at all) that "I wouldn't want to suggest people will become grocery-delivery millionaires, but if you don't have a college education but you're smart and responsible, could you make a living doing this and maybe piecing it together with some of these other kinds of jobs? Absolutely."[25]

Postmates is a competitor to Instacart, although more of its deliveries are prepared meals rather than groceries. Also founded in 2012, it took 116 weeks to make its first half-million deliveries, twenty weeks for its next half-million, and ten weeks for its third half-million.[26] Like Instacart, Postmates started with the Sharing Economy model by charging customers, paying delivery workers, and taking a 20% cut. Also like Instacart, it has added a Preferred Merchant program in which companies pay Instacart to provide a delivery service, and Postmates has now partnered with Whole Foods, Starbucks, Apple, McDonald's, and Chipotle. Asked about worker security, salary, and benefits, the Postmates CEO said "We're talking about a different sector of the labor market. We like to think of Postmates as America's best part time job. It's complementary income."[27] He did not say whether Postmates delivery workers like to think of their work that way.

The on-demand delivery segment of the Sharing Economy has morphed into a concierge economy "where serfs deliver stuff to rich folk."[28] The range of on-demand services available in San Francisco and New York has become self-parodic. Magic asks you to "Text this phone number to get whatever you want on demand with no hassle." Alfred offers an on-demand butler. Dufl is "a personal valet that simplifies business travel by shipping, cleaning and storing your business attire." And there are many more, in a phenomenon that Umair Haque calls the "Servitude Bubble."[29]

Any promise of community and connection has been left behind together with ideas of sustainability and anti-materialism as venture capital races to create an emerging demographic of ever-more entitled consumers, providing them with a frictionless, hermetically sealed experience in the name of Sharing.

6. Strangers Trusting Strangers

Sharing Economy companies love to talk about trust: they claim that we can trust stranger-to-stranger exchanges on their platforms because of what Brian Chesky calls "these magical things called reputation systems."[1]

Some go so far as to call reputation systems the central innovation of the Sharing Economy. *New York Times* columnist Thomas Friedman lauds "Airbnb's real innovation—a platform of 'trust'—where everyone could not only see everyone else's identity but also rate them as good, bad or indifferent hosts or guests. This meant everyone using the system would pretty quickly develop a relevant 'reputation' visible to everyone else in the system."[2] Friedman was writing just a couple of weeks after his *New York Times* stablemate David Brooks described "How Airbnb and Lyft Finally Got Americans to Trust Each Other": "Companies like Airbnb establish trust through ratings mechanisms . . . People in the Airbnb economy don't have the option of trusting each other on the basis of institutional affiliations, so they do it on the basis of online signaling and peer evaluations."[3]

Sharing Economy companies are not the first to use ratings and algorithms to guide behavior. Their trust systems build on the rating and recommendation systems used by Amazon, Netflix, eBay, Yelp, TripAdvisor, iTunes, the App Store and many others. Each takes individual ratings as their input and transforms them into some form of recommendation. As rating systems have become ubiquitous their usefulness has become a matter of faith in the world of software development.

The Sharing Economy is at the cutting edge of a push for "algorithmic regulation" in which rules protecting consumers are replaced by ratings and software algorithms. Law professor Lior Strahilevitz enthuses: "Imagine if every plumber, manufactured product, cell phone provider, home builder, professor, hair stylist, accountant, attorney, golf pro, and taxi driver were rated . . . In such a world, there would be diminished need for regulatory oversight and legal remedies because consumers would police misconduct themselves."[4] Your online history becomes more important than your credit history.[5]

As in so many other aspects of the Sharing Economy, Airbnb and Uber are leading the way. Airbnb CEO Brian Chesky expresses his company's confidence when he says of city-level rules, "they're primarily set up for screening. To protect consumers. Well it turns out that cities can't screen as well as technologies can screen. Companies have these magical things called reputation systems . . . We think government should exist as the place of last recourse."[6] Uber CEO Travis Kalanick is even blunter about his disdain for old-style regulations, which he sees as just a way to keep entrenched interests happy: "Every city we go to, eventually the regulators will make something up to keep us from rolling out or continuing our business."[7]

The promise of reputation systems is a mirage.

The broad-brush talk of trust misses the point that most regulations exist to screen those things that customers cannot see for themselves. Most tourists cannot assess whether their accommodations are properly protected in case of fire, restaurant customers will not know whether the kitchen handles food properly, taxi passengers will not know whether the brakes of their car are in good condition, and most will never find out. Ratings will never solve these problems, and for this reason alone algorithmic regulation is a non-starter.

Reputation systems are also the wrong tool to deal with extreme failures of trust. A one-star rating is no way to deal with assault, fraud, or theft, for which reparations and perhaps even prosecution are required. Sharing Economy companies have proved ill-equipped to deal with these failures when they do occur. In a dramatic recent case, a nineteen-year-old Airbnb guest in Spain was sexually assaulted by his host. He texted his mother in the USA that his host had locked him in the apartment where he was a "guest", and when she called Airbnb they told her to get in touch with the police instead.[8] When push comes to shove, Airbnb maintains that is not responsible for what happens during visits that it arranges, and rating systems do nothing to address these rare but extreme breaches of trust.

We are left with a relatively narrow range of trust problems that reputation systems can even claim to address: cleanliness, punctuality, friendliness, and so on. Even there, reputation systems are failing in their basic task of discriminating between the good and the bad. The failure has been covered up by continually re-inventing rationales for the systems, by using reputation systems as a front for centralized and unaccountable disciplinary styles of management, and by a star-struck public discourse that focuses on the "magical" aspect of all these effortless clicks and algorithms. Technologists routinely misunderstand what we are doing when we rate each other, and as a result reputation systems are eroding the very person-to-person relationships that the Sharing Economy supposedly values.

SIGNALING TRUST[9]

Trust is a word with many rich connotations, so let's start by making it clear what kind of trust we are dealing with in the Sharing Economy.

Imagine that Jill must decide whether to make a loan to a stranger named Jack; if Jill makes the loan, then Jack must decide whether to repay it. We say Jill *trusts* Jack if she expects him to repay, and we say that Jack is *trustworthy* if he would repay the loan.

Trustworthiness is not a quality like eye color or height that can be observed directly; Jill must look instead for signals of trustworthiness (a firm handshake? evidence of past good behavior? membership of a similar social group?) If she sees these signals she must decide whether they are genuine, or whether Jack is mimicking signals of trustworthiness in order to deceive her. Jack has a problem too: even if he has every intention of repaying the loan he must convince Jill of this fact; he must convince Jill that he is not a con man mimicking the signals of trustworthiness.

An effective signal—one that Jill could believe in—must separate trustworthy from untrustworthy people. Thinking economically, it must be a signal that is easy for a trustworthy person to display but too costly for an untrustworthy person to display.[10] If no such signal is available, then Jill has no way to know whether Jack is trustworthy or is just mimicking trustworthiness—an outcome that is called *pooling*. In the pooling case Jill will not loan Jack the money, even if he is perfectly trustworthy, because Jill cannot trust the signals that Jack sends. In real life we deal with probabilities rather than certainties, but there is a spectrum from separating to pooling outcomes in problems of trust.

In the commercial world there are many signaling mechanisms for solving the problem of trust, some of which work better than others. Group membership has always been an important signal: Quakers became wealthy in the early days of transatlantic commerce because their reputation for honesty encouraged people to trade with them. There are regulations (you can trust this restaurant because it has passed a food safety inspection), professional qualifications (you can trust this person to fix your leg because she is a doctor, you can hire this graduate because they got a good degree from a good university), voluntary industry certifications (you can trust this coffee to be fair trade because there is a fair trade label on the package, or this French wine because of its Appellation Contrôlée designation), independent rating agencies (you can trust this business because they rate highly in Consumer Reports, J.D. Power reports, or on the Better Business Bureau), individual firm commitments (you can trust this retailer because they have invested heavily in their brand, and so must act accordingly), and many others.

Reputation deals in a more informal, social, and personal kind of signal: reputation is the social distillation of other people's opinion. When my neighbor says "Don't hire John the Plumber: he came to fix my sink but it's still blocked," she is providing information that lets me decide whether to trust John to fix my drains. In a community with strong word of mouth, it is easy for a good plumber to establish a reputation as reliable, punctual, and skilled simply by being reliable, punctual, and skilled; it is difficult for an incompetent or lazy plumber to do the same.

In the sense used here, reputation is peer-to-peer, informal, decentralized, and community-driven, and it is those qualities that Sharing Economy advocates claim can be scaled up by using internet reputation systems. Airbnb and BlaBlaCar both describe themselves as "a trusted community marketplace;" Lyft's one million rides show "the power of community." Instead of passing on comments by word of mouth, we now click to rate John the Plumber with a one-star rating.

Reputation is far from a perfect signal. In the offline world, testimonies are often private ("he fixed my sink and came on time, but there was something about him . . . I just didn't like having him in my house") and there are good and bad sides to this. Word-of-mouth reputation can pass along legitimate but unprovable concerns when the speaker does not have to be publicly accountable for their statements. But reputation also makes it difficult for John to gain a good reputation—no matter how trustworthy he is—if he is a black man trying to find work in a white community with a history of racism, or difficult for Jane the Plumber's skills to be taken seriously if the community has traditional norms about women's roles. "Old boys' clubs" and other insider groups provide members with an inbuilt advantage when it comes to establishing a reputation.

Reputation is effective only if the testimonies are impartial and free from the taint of collusion or retaliation. Testimony from John's brother does not carry the same weight as that of someone who has no stake in John's success or failure. John may not want my neighbor to tell me about his failure to fix their sink, but there's not a lot he can do about private conversations over a garden fence.

In her TED talk, influential author Rachel Botsman says that in the new economy "reputation will be your most valuable asset," but thinking of reputation as an asset is a dangerous path to take. Markets grow around assets, and these markets undermine the impartiality on which reputation relies. Intermediaries such as reputation.com will help you boost your reputation, for a fee, but why would you trust a reputation that has been paid for? As soon as we invest in actions explicitly to promote our reputation, then reputation fails to work from a social point of view. If you can buy and sell testimonies, those testimonies lose their ability to discriminate between trustworthiness and opportunism.

In many cultures self-promotional activity is not generally acceptable in the social world, seeming crass and selfish, but it is widely accepted in the commercial world in the form of branding and marketing activities. As Alice Marwick writes, ideas of personal branding and investment in self-promotion have taken off in a big way in Silicon Valley; part of the region's belief in the value of entrepreneurship,[11] so now Sharing Economy companies have coined a word for "people as companies." Airbnb hosts, Lyft drivers, and TaskRabbit errand-runners are "micro-entrepreneurs": the self as corporation, and one's reputation as personal brand. If investment in "reputation as an asset" gains ground, then reputation may become a measure of how well we conform to the prejudices and expectations of Silicon Valley culture.

RATINGS DO NOT DISCRIMINATE

Start by looking at ratings on Netflix: the ratings of movies and TV shows by Netflix customers. There is every reason to believe that most Netflix ratings are independent and honest. When you rate a movie you can offer your opinion freely, having no reason to expect reward or punishment for any particular rating. You also have an incentive to give a rating that matches your actual opinion, as it enables Netflix to recommend movies that better match your tastes. Figure 3 shows the distribution of ratings for a set of 100 million ratings that Netflix released for its Netflix Prize competition.

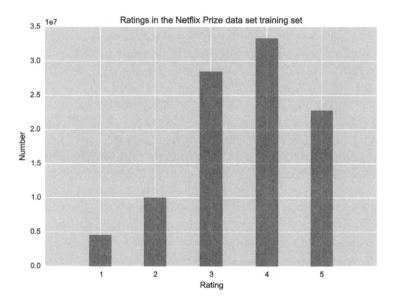

Figure 3. Ratings in the Netflix contest data set.

The ratings are distributed among the available scores with a peak at about 3.5, so a rating of 4 or 5 is a pretty good rating and Netflix ratings help us to discriminate between one-star stinkers and five-star favorites.

Yelp is a rating site for restaurants and other small businesses. Each rating is made by an individual customer (who may remain anonymous).

Businesses do not choose to participate on Yelp; they are listed whether they want to be or not. The incentive for individual customers to rate their experience is less obvious on Yelp than on Netflix, as Yelp does not yet provide personalized recommendations to the users of its site. Instead, Yelp builds on the idea of community to nudge its users to provide reviews: if you use the Yelp application to get ratings, you may want to provide your own reviews as a contribution to improving the experience.

Yelp recently made a data set of its own ratings available for use. Figure 4 shows the distribution of ratings for restaurants, which is the most widely reviewed classification on the site. The distribution is similar to that of Netflix, suggesting that Yelp reviewers rate restaurants in a similar manner to the way that Netflix reviewers rate movies.

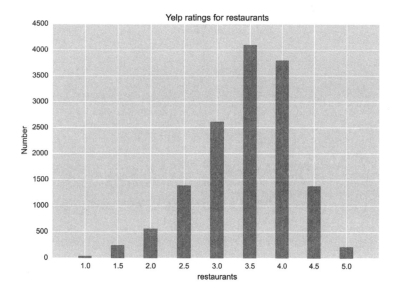

Figure 4. Yelp ratings for restaurants.

So what about Sharing Economy ratings? The distribution of ratings on Airbnb for a number of representative cities is shown in Figure 5. The distributions are quite different: each is a "J-curve," where the bulk of the ratings are at very high values. Rating system designers typically see curves like this as a problem: are there really so many more excellent Airbnb experiences than there are excellent restaurants? Commonly suggested causes are filtering (only customers with a good experience are rating the site), or bias (customers are being guided in their ratings by something other than the quality of the experience itself).[12]

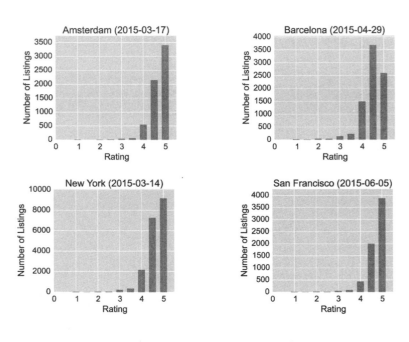

Figure 5. Airbnb ratings in a selection of cities.

Even more dramatically, Figure 6 shows the ratings distribution for a set of over half a million ratings that I collected from the ridesharing web site BlaBlaCar, on which over 98% of ratings are five stars. Ratings are not publicly available for Uber and Lyft drivers and riders, but both sites are known to "de-activate" drivers from the site if their rating drops below a cutoff in the range of 4.5 to 4.7 (out of five stars) so most ratings must be five stars out of five in these cases too. Similarly, newspaper articles suggest that average ratings on Handy and Homejoy are between 4 and 5.

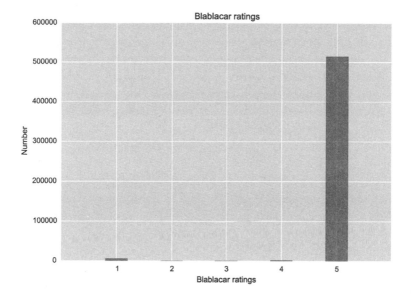

Figure 6. BlaBlaCar ratings.

∎

Even though Sharing Economy ratings are typically crammed into a small range, could a 4.9 rating still indicate a better experience than a 4.7? All the evidence to date says no, it cannot.

Even in rating systems with widely-distributed ratings like Netflix, the relationship between an individual rating and the quality of user experience is murky. One of the results of the Netflix Prize competition was that individual ratings turn out to depend on factors that have nothing to do with the movie itself: people tend to grade relative to the existing rating, so highly rated films tend to stay highly rated. The best competitors managed to compensate for these effects, but only in an environment where individual movies were getting millions of ratings, quite different from the Sharing Economy case. Despite the fact that more expertise was poured into improving the Netflix rating system than any other, Netflix has moved away from using sophisticated rating algorithms when making its recommendations.

The fragile relationship between quality and ratings was confirmed in an experiment by three sociologists.[13] Matthew Salganick, Peter Dodds, and Duncan Watts created an artificial music market in which over 14,000 participants listened to a set of songs they had not heard before, rated them, and were given the chance to download the song. The participants were split into nine groups, and eight of those groups were shown a single piece of rating information: how many times songs had been downloaded by others in the group. The ninth was not shown any download information. The experiment's conclusion was that even this form of rating influenced people's behavior: they were more likely to download songs that others had downloaded. Ratings led to a greater inequality (those which had been downloaded got downloaded more), but the set of popular songs was different in each of the groups, showing that download ratings did not provide a reliable guide to quality. "The best songs rarely did poorly, and the worst rarely did well, but any other result was possible." In a Sharing Economy context, this means that early ratings influence how later raters behave: a bad early rating may influence reputation far more than later ratings.

As ratings are compressed into a smaller range, the already tenuous relationship between score and quality suffers further. A recent working paper studying accommodations listed on both Airbnb and on TripAdvisor concluded that "Overall, Airbnb and TripAdvisor reviewers exhibit little agreement. TripAdvisor and Airbnb ratings are only weakly correlated, with the relative rankings of properties varying to a significant degree across the two sites."[14] The paper is a detailed and careful analysis that comes to the same conclusion about Sharing Economy ratings as did *Wired* magazine's Kat Kane, a regular Uber and Lyft customer. She admits to giving five-star ratings after white-knuckle rides, and her experience tells her that ratings are no indication of quality: "I've ridden with 4.7 star drivers who wear gloves and open passenger doors and 4.7 star drivers who couldn't pass a road test."[15]

Together, these studies confirm that reputation systems fail in their basic task of distinguishing high quality or trustworthy offerings from lower-quality or untrustworthy offerings. There is no evidence that an Uber driver or a Handy cleaner with a rating of 4.9 is better in any way than someone with a rating of 4.6. Sharing Economy reputation systems are broken. The influential idea that these systems can be relied on in situations where bad behavior can have serious consequences is simply magical thinking: the system designers are so wrapped up in the elegance of the software that they are convinced it will work, and too many journalists are bowled over by the promise of something novel.

Reputation systems are no substitute for regulation. Instead, they are a substitute for a company management structure, and a bad one at that. A reputation system is the boss from hell: an erratic, bad-tempered and unaccountable manager that may fire you at any time, on a whim, with no appeal.

■

J-curve rating distributions, like those of the Sharing Economy reputation systems, show up whenever people rate each other. By far the most widely-studied reputation system in which customers and service providers rate each other is the eBay system. In its early years, buyers and sellers rated each other on a simple scale of positive, neutral, or negative, and each could see how the other rated them. In some studies, as much as 99% of all ratings on eBay are found to be positive, and researchers suggest that this extreme J-curve is evidence of bias. For example:

> The fact that from 742,829 eBay users . . . who received at least one feedback, 67% have a percentage positive of 100%, and 80.5% have a percentage positive of greater than 99%, provides suggestive support for the bias.

An early explanation for bias on the eBay system was fear of retaliation: if you give a bad review and the target retaliates by giving you one in response, then your own reputation takes a hit. Why take the risk? EBay has made a number of attempts at removing the threat of retaliation (not allowing sellers to rate buyers, for example) to improve the experience for the marketplace as a whole, but the very high proportion of positive reviews remains. There is more to high ratings than fear.

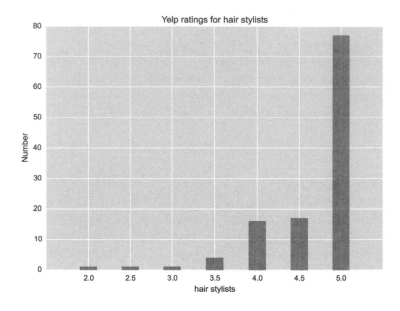

Figure 7. Distribution of hair stylist ratings in the Yelp data set.

While Yelp is primarily a rating site for restaurants, it also covers other kinds of small businesses, and the rating distribution for hair stylists is shown in Figure 7. Even though there is no fear of retaliation here, the ratings form a clear J-curve. Some have suggested that this is because when we deal with other people, especially when we have a relationship over time, norms of everyday courtesy make us reluctant to criticize in public: we will more often behave like *Forbes* writer Jeff Bercovici when he rated his Uber driver:

> I took a ride in a car as grimy and musty-smelling as a typ-
> ical yellow cab. The driver was friendly and knew his way
> around, but he was clearly falling short of Uber's standard
> that the sedans in its UberX fleet be in "excellent condi-
> tion." Since customer feedback is "important to insuring a
> high-quality experience," according to the company, when

it came time to rate my trip, I only gave the driver three out of five stars.

Just kidding. I gave him five stars, of course. What do you think I am, a psychopath?[16]

A norm of courtesy applies to market transactions. It is customary to express thanks at the conclusion of many exchanges: even the screen of the vending machine at my workplace shows "Thank you, enjoy your beverage" when I fill a mug of coffee. Guest books at bed & breakfasts and at museums are filled with polite and appreciative comments. The positive rating at the end of an eBay exchange is not so much an assessment (honest or dishonest) but is rather a courtesy.

Stronger norms apply to more personal exchanges. We feel free to talk critically about impersonal market transactions to third parties (nobody thinks it impolite to say "I didn't enjoy that movie"); but when it comes to personal relationships it is impolite to bad-mouth someone in public without at least trying to solve the problem privately first. "Don't kiss and tell" and "if you have nothing good to say, say nothing at all" are two ways this norm is expressed, but there are others. Managers are told to "praise in public, criticize in private": to do otherwise puts people in the position of being shamed, and leads to "fight or flight" reactions. When groups get into trouble, there are norms to not be a splitter, a rat, a snitch, a tattletale.

Reputation systems present a rosy picture of the Sharing Economy as a Lake Wobegon in which everybody is nicer than average, because people under-report bad experiences. A study of the eBay reputation system showed that about one in five of all eBay transactions led to some level of dissatisfaction, but that people tend to follow the maxim of "if you can't say anything nice, say nothing at all." Dissatisfied eBay customers give, not a bad rating, but no rating at all.[17] Keeping a system that has an overwhelming number of visible high ratings creates an atmosphere in which customers are likely to book, and provides a veneer of familiarity for people used to doing business on Amazon and Netflix.

Fortunately for Sharing Economy companies, trusting strangers is not always as perilous as the hype suggests, and we know this in our daily lives. *Wired* may run a story with the title "How Airbnb and Lyft finally got Americans to trust each other," but the truth is that Americans and others have been trusting each other for centuries.

Trust is a problem only if there is a real incentive to behave badly, which is why trusting strangers is commonplace. When we get lost we ask strangers for directions and trust their answers: why would they lie? When I look up the date that Henry IV died on Wikipedia I trust the answer because, again, why would someone lie?

Even when there is an opportunity to take advantage of others, most people are decent most of the time. Shop assistants give us the right change. People buy and sell through Craigslist, Kijiji, and classified ads without any reputation system to help them. For decades, people hitchhiked and almost all of those rides were safe.

The headlines that express surprise about "letting a stranger into your house" are overly dramatic: we let plumbers, furnace repair people, cleaners, and other service providers into our houses and apartments routinely; taxi drivers let strangers into their cars all the time, and we get in the car with taxi drivers who are strangers. And when things don't go perfectly, we sigh and move on. If the shop assistant is grumpy, if the plumber turns up late, if the bus driver stops and starts too suddenly, it's not that important in the big scheme of things.

(Aside: I traveled from the UK to Canada—my first ever plane ride— as a naïve twenty-one-year-old in 1981, planning to fly into New York and take the bus through Buffalo. On the plane I got talking to another young man who invited me to spend the night with him and his mother in Queens before sending me on the next day with a packed lunch. What a wonderful introduction to a new continent!)

I'm a middle-aged white man, and not everything is so rosy for others. Things do go badly, both in Sharing Economy transactions and in our dealings with strangers, and individual examples of extreme trust violations are felt across whole industries. But reputation systems are the wrong tools to cope with occasional extreme violations of trust, as they rely on an accumulation of feedback over time to present their ratings. When things go badly wrong, customers do not want to post a three-star review, they want a direct line to the company itself, and too often this is not always available: Uber has had an F rating from the Better Business Bureau for some time, primarily because of its persistent failure to respond to customer complaints.[18]

Airbnb had to set up a safety division when guests trashed the apartment of San Francisco host EJ in June 2011, and stole her jewelry, hard drive, passport, and credit cards.[19] It continues to have its share of scandals, some of which make the press. The headlines tell the stories: "Hookers turning Airbnb apartments into brothels,"[20] "Airbnb renters who trashed Calgary house used fake credit cards to fuel party,"[21] "Airbnb host left violated after busting fanny pack–clad male prostitutes in her apartment,"[22] "Nightmare Palm Springs AirBnB Renter Refuses to Leave," and even more seriously, "AirBnB Flat Owner Jailed For Raping US Tourists," and more. Such events cannot be flagged ahead of time by a reputation system, although to be fair the very positive reviews for one set of guests, who turned out to be using apartments for prostitution, did contain the enigmatic and yet revealing comment: "It was very difficult to clean up the oil marks." The curious can find an extensive collection of generally less-dramatic (and less substanti-ated) cases at http://www.airbnbhell.com.

Uber has had more high-profile scandals than Airbnb, with cases of assault (both driver on passenger and vice versa), threats, hacked user accounts, and accidents.

The companies' responses to these events is always to emphasize their rarity, but rare events can change a practice for good. Rates of hitch-hiking in the UK, for example, plummeted in the 1990s in the wake of two highly-publicized murders, even though the danger to any individual hitch-hiker remained very low.[23] When an Indian woman sued Uber in India after being raped by her driver, the city of Delhi banned Uber for failing to carry out adequate driver checks.

Terrible things happen to people in hotel rooms and taxis too, but there is a mechanism to hold hotels and taxi companies responsible for these events, and that mechanism provides a lever that can improve safety over time. Sharing Economy platforms retreat behind the language of their terms of service agreements to claim that they have no legal responsibility for the events. Press coverage is too often the only method to force them to take steps.

Missing reviews continue to be a thorn in the side of reputation system designers and companies. In July 2014 Airbnb tried to encourage more crit-ical reviews by holding back the publication of reviews until both parties had submitted a review of the other; neither the company nor researchers with access to the company's data have commented on the success of the change. In another experiment, Airbnb staff are working with external researchers to test whether offering a reward to encourage reviews has any effect on the number of critical reviews that guests provide.[24]

Other efforts are trying to squeeze more critical information from what is already there. Airbnb is using natural language processing to parse critical comments from review texts.[25] Researchers have shown that taking missing reviews into account can give a much more effective measure of seller quality.[26] The problem with such efforts is that, if systems were changed so that missing reviews or passive-aggressive text comments were known to be recorded (and so became, implicitly, a negative review) customer behavior may change to avoid the threat of a negative (non-) review in return.

RATINGS AS SURVEILLANCE

Despite their failings, reputation systems do serve a useful purpose for Sharing Economy transactions. The orthodoxy around reputation systems is that critical reviews provide information to other peers, but we have seen that there is little information about quality to be gained from Sharing Economy reputation scores. Instead, critical reviews act as a complaint to the central authority (the Sharing Economy company).

The reputation system is useful to keep service providers in line. Most people are going to give a good review unless their experience is very bad, but there is a small group of customers who are happy to provide critical reviews, and those reviews can have a big impact. A slip from 4.6 to 4.5 in an Uber driver's rating is not like the slip in the rating of a movie on Netflix. It does not meaningfully affect the perception of the driver by other customers. Instead, a bad rating is a complaint to Uber itself, which has its own unaccountable disciplinary system that can remove drivers from the platform for any reason. The threat of a bad review becomes a trap waiting to open in front of the driver.

Uber drivers' discussion boards show a consistent fear over occasional bad ratings—how did they come about? can they be appealed? (no), how can they be avoided? Drivers must continually worry about that one-in-ten customer who will complain that you didn't offer them bottled water, or that you were overly friendly, or not friendly enough.

That's not how Sharing Economy companies present the situation. Their reputation systems ask people to speak "honestly" when rating service providers, and to make criticisms of services that do not match up to expectations.

Yelp gives an example of how this search for honesty plays out. Yelp filters the reviews that come into its site, including only trusted reviews in its overall rating. It gives priority in its selection of reviews to people who have a strong relationship with Yelp (its "Elite Squad"), but discounts the views of those who have a strong relationship with the service provider (which they see as a source of bias).

Yelp encourages a norm of market transactions, while many restaurateurs promote a norm of personal service. Is a bad review an "honest rating" or is it a "drive-by trashing"? Is the reviewer providing a public good by notifying the broader public of their opinion through the platform, or acting in bad faith by not engaging with the service provider? It is no surprise that many restaurants don't like Yelp's ratings: reviews by their most trusted customers are discarded, while anonymous reviews by a one time visitor are given pride of place. A restaurateur's objection to a bad review on Yelp by a customer who never complained in person is not just sour grapes at an "honest" review, it is a clash of norms. If there are problems, restaurateurs hope customers will give them a chance to set things right, rather than going straight to the public shaming of a low review. If a rating is a mark of courtesy, then asking customers to provide critical feedback is to encourage violation of the norms of courtesy. The more personal the customer–service provider relationship, the more the friction between the reputation system and the norms of exchange.

As Airbnb continues to tune its reputation system, it seems likely to follow the path that Yelp has forged. Airbnb researchers seeking to collect feedback from their customers suggest that "guests may be choosing to omit negative feedback from public reviews even when there is no possibility of retaliation because they do not want to hurt the hosts they have socially interacted with," and conclude:

> Based on our results, marketplaces should design reputation systems to induce a higher share of participants to leave reviews and to solicit feedback in such a way that maximizes the perceived social distance between the reviewer and the reviewed.

Airbnb marketing emphasizes the personal nature of its service, but the reputation system needs a "social distance" between host and guest if it is to collect the right input.

In the cases of both Yelp and Airbnb, the reputation system erodes the very relationship that it seeks to evaluate. From the service provider's point of view, the reputation system becomes a form of surveillance: a "denunciation system" in which they may be publicly shamed at any moment and, in the case of Sharing Economy platforms, punished.

Sharing Economy reputation systems have become fronts for hierarchical and centralized disciplinary systems, which have nothing to do with notions of "peer-to-peer" reputation, "algorithmic regulation" or regulation with a "lighter touch" through ratings. We trust strangers on Sharing Economy platforms for the same reason we trust hotel employees and restaurant waiters: because they are in precarious jobs where customer complaints can lead to disciplinary action. The reputation system is a way to enforce "emotional labor"; service providers are compelled to manage their feelings and present the face that the platform demands, to become that "friend with a car" or that "neighbor helping neighbors." It's the fast food worker's "Have a nice day" taken to the next step.

■

Sharing Economy reputation systems do not solve the problem of trust. At best, they provide a disciplinary mechanism that keeps service providers smiling and efficient by virtue of erratic and inconsistent ratings. For service providers, reputation systems are a form of surveillance, mainly enacted by the most entitled and demanding customers on the platform. For the community, and for the notions of sharing which the Sharing Economy is supposed to be bringing back, reputation systems are turning us into a society of snitches, giving us the ability to casually turn in our fellow citizens to a strict and unaccountable form of discipline.

7. A Short History of Openness

The Sharing Economy is only the latest wave of digital technology to take inspiration from ideas of openness. The facts surrounding the movement will change rapidly, even by the time between the writing and publishing of this book. But there are forces that shape the development of this movement as they have shaped previous waves of digital revolution, and we can look to these other digital movements to understand where the Sharing Economy is likely to take us. This chapter and the next take a look at the broader digital environment from which the Sharing Economy has emerged, and the ideas from which it takes its inspiration.

Open source, open content, and open data: each of these promised to empower individuals while challenging the power of big corporations and governments. Just as the Sharing Economy claims to be on the side of regular people against hotel chains and "Big Taxi," so openness promised to be on the side of hobbyist coders against Microsoft, of living-room musicians against big record labels, and of bloggers against big media companies. But one by one these promises have been broken: instead of producing a more level playing field, openness has replaced one set of powerful institutions with another, often even more powerful, set. This chapter describes how ideals of digital openness have been repeatedly appropriated for private gain.

Brian Chesky writes that "At Airbnb, we are creating a door to an open world—where everyone's at home and can belong, anywhere." Openness is almost a synonym for sharing, for a kind of exchange that goes beyond straightforward market transactions; it is central both to the broader appeal of the Sharing Economy and to the story that Airbnb tells about itself. Chesky's words echo those of Mark Zuckerberg, who started a letter to potential Facebook investors this way: "Facebook was not originally created to be a company. It was built to accomplish a social mission—to make the world more open and connected . . . As people share more, they have access to more opinions from the people they trust about the products and services they use. This makes it easier to discover the best products and improve the quality and efficiency of their lives." Zuckerberg may have forgotten that his original Facebook was actually a "hot or not" web site allowing Harvard students to compare pictures of students and vote on which was hotter, but he remembers that openness and sharing appeal to the best in us.

■

Openness was central to the beginnings of the Internet. With the foundations created in university and government labs (DARPA), the source code for programs was shared among the researchers who made up the early Internet community. The early uses (email, Usenet) were built on a distributed network architecture with no central server; the early Internet was a non-commercial and decentralized environment. The basic protocols and standards on which the Internet was built were and are open. Not only were they open in their specification (anyone could implement them) but they were open in their philosophy; they were designed, for example, such that any computer could add itself to the network without having to ask permission of some administrator.

The early software that ran the Internet was also open: shared in a non-commercial fashion, largely among researchers and others in the university and government world. The World Wide Web was invented at CERN, and the first generation of web software was developed at government labs. The source code for these applications was not owned by individual companies, it was made available to anyone who wanted it as "open source."

Commercial use was forbidden on early government-funded precursors to the Internet, but the 1992 Scientific and Advanced-Technology Act allowed the US National Science Foundation to interconnect with commercial networks, and the mixture of commerce and non-commercial activity started. There was vociferous argument over the ethics of pursuing profit over the Internet, but digital commerce exploded. Digital openness, which

was initially a norm of the non-commercial world of researchers and enthusiasts cut off from the world of private property, was exposed to the profit
motive. Inevitably, things would change.

The Internet is often seen as a natural place for openness because files
and documents can be copied: I can give you a copy of a song, and still keep
a copy for myself, I can upload a video to YouTube and everyone can watch
it. If software or songs are made "open" they are no longer commodities
that can be privately owned: they are made free for others to use as they
wish, and so are taken out of the normal commercial realm of buying and of
selling. It seems like openness is an alternative to the commercial marketplace. But openness on the Internet co-exists with the market: YouTube is a
way of sharing content, but it is also a for-profit part of a for-profit company.
In these mixed environments, openness has two effects:

1. It disrupts existing markets. By cutting the price of a product
    or service to zero, for everyone and for any purpose, it under-
    mines the business of those who previously controlled access
    to that product or service. Making songs available for free on
    Napster was a threat to the business of the music labels and the
    main street music stores.

2. It creates new markets in complementary offerings. Comple-
    ments are products or services that go together, so that cutting
    the price of one increases demand for the other. File sharing in-
    creases the demand for Internet Service Providers, file sharing
    sites, and digital music players. These new markets are doppel-
    gängers—shadows that follow openness wherever it goes; new
    markets that spring up inevitably from the ruins of the old.

The disruption of existing markets appeals to those who want an alternative to the free market, and who see openness as a way to challenge existing
hierarchies and power imbalances in society. It's a vision adopted by Airbnb
when it speaks of its communities of "regular people, sharing the homes in
which they live" as an alternative to the mass-produced world of corporate
hotel chains.

But openness also attracts those who want to build bigger corporations.
Commercial interests have repeatedly used the non-commercial appeal of

openness as a front for their own very commercial agendas. The problem is, openness does not simply create new markets and new businesses to replace the old ones that they disrupt, it tends to create less-competitive markets and more powerful businesses.

The markets disrupted by openness are often traditional in structure, characterized by decreasing returns, with market power that is distributed and limited in scope. The payoff to building a bigger music store inevitably falls off and becomes uneconomic at some point, opening the space for specialist stores and competitors. Add too many new artists to a music label and it becomes impossible to promote them all, so music labels have to specialize and compete.

In contrast, constant fixed costs and zero marginal costs are "the baseline case" for information goods,[1] so digital environments are characterized by "increasing returns": the bigger you are, the bigger you get. The markets are likely to be oligopolistic, consisting of a few, big firms, each with significant market power. For several years Apple's iPod and Google's YouTube had no serious competitors.

Many of the sources of increasing returns for digital marketplaces are lumped under the term "network effects": each new user of a service makes that service more valuable. Social media companies obviously benefit from network effects: you join the social media platform where the people you want to meet hang out. But there are other, less obvious forms of increasing returns: Google learns from every search carried out on its platform and so has a continuing advantage over its rivals (such as they are); advertisers want to be on the search engine that most people frequent, so the leading search engine will attract the most advertising money to feed its further growth. Other network effects are familiar from the brick-and-mortar world: a successful corporate brand can communicate familiarity and dependability and so grow faster. Or, as is the case with Amazon, a growing business provides money that can be re-invested in building more efficient infrastructure, driving the next cycle of competitive advantage.

Not that network effects continue without limit. New technologies do come along to challenge existing ones such as music streaming companies challenging Apple's iTunes Store. Also, cultural instincts don't just bind us all together on Facebook, they drive us apart too. What teen wants to be on the same social networking site as their parents? So Snapchat and Instagram become the social networks for the next generation, and new entrants (Yoho, Whisper, WhatsApp, Kik) try to create new identities that will appeal to a new demographic. Faced with generational changes in tastes, the best thing that this generation's company can do is sometimes to buy its challengers, as Facebook has done by buying Instagram and WhatsApp.

Network effects are not unique to the Internet, but the Internet provides an environment in which they can become particularly powerful. For one thing, they are not obviously limited by national borders in the way that, for example, phone networks are. Successful companies can become international without leaving home: without even trying, Google can serve up search results to Australians as easily as to Californians; the technical challenge of streaming a movie to Paris is not much different to streaming it to New York. Again, there are limits imposed by the physical aspects of a business (Amazon needs to set up distribution centers), or the cultural (language, for example), or the legal (licensing restrictions, for example), but the potential for global reach is always there.

The examples in this chapter show how digital openness has served to create these doppelgänger markets far more than it has leveled the playing field between individuals and powerful institutions.

OPEN-SOURCE SOFTWARE

In 1991, Finnish student Linus Torvalds started work "just for fun" on the open-source operating system that was to become Linux, and it quickly became a phenomenon. Linux was trumpeted as a triumph of the loosely-coordinated amateur (that is, non-commercial) efforts of "hackers" (that is, people programming for fun rather than as a job), and in 1998 Eric S. Raymond started his famous essay *The Cathedral and the Bazaar* this way:

> Linux is subversive. Who would have thought even five years ago that a world-class operating system could coalesce as if by magic out of part-time hacking by several thousand developers scattered all over the planet, connected only by the tenuous strands of the Internet?[2]

The success of Linux and other open source software projects spurred a wave of optimism about a fundamentally new way of creating complex products by relying on networks of peers. Yochai Benkler made an academic case for peer networks in his essay "Coase's Penguin: Linux and the Nature of the Firm" and then in his influential book *The Wealth of Networks*, holding up Linux as the archetype of a new form of production that could reshape economies.[3] The traditional economy is driven, in this view, by markets and by hierarchical firms or state organizations, but Benkler saw a third possibility, which he labeled "commons-based peer production." "Commons-based" because the result is not owned by anyone; "peer production" because those who take part do so as peers. In "Coase's Penguin," Benkler describes the puzzle of why people contribute to Linux and other efforts:

> Programmers do not generally participate in a project because someone who is their boss instructed them, though some do. They do not generally participate in a project because someone offers them a price, though some participants do focus on long-term appropriation through money-oriented activities, like consulting or service contracts. But the critical mass of participation in projects cannot be explained by the direct presence of a command, a price, or even a future monetary return, particularly in the all-important microlevel decisions regarding selection of projects to which participants contribute. In other words, programmers participate in free software projects without following the normal signals generated by market-based, firm-based, or hybrid models.[4]

The success of Linux seems to validate Benkler's hopes for this new form of production. Despite having to compete against commercial operating systems produced by the world's largest technology companies such as Hewlett Packard, IBM, Sun, and of course Microsoft and Apple, the Linux Foundation can say "Today, Linux powers 98% of the world's super computers, most of the servers powering the Internet, the majority of financial trades worldwide and tens of millions of Android mobile phones and consumer devices. In short, Linux is everywhere."[5]

But as Linux has grown, it has changed. Each year the Linux Foundation issues a report on who writes the source code that makes up the Linux kernel, which is the heart of the operating system, and the 2015 report is clear about the evolving nature of this huge project. The Linux kernel now has about 20 million lines of code, which is about ten times larger than when Eric Raymond wrote his essay. The Linux kernel received nearly 100,000 separate contributions during the year 2014, from over 4,000 individual developers, but surprisingly only one in eight changes were from developers who are working "with no financial contribution from any company," and

> . . . well over 80% of all kernel development is demonstrably done by developers who are being paid for their work . . . the volume of contributions from unpaid developers has been in slow decline for many years. It was 14.6% in the 2012 version of this paper, and 13.6% in 2013; now it is 11.8% . . . more than half of our new developers are paid to work on the kernel from their very first patch."[6]

Linux is no longer the product of "part-time hacking." Most of the programmers who work on the project earn a good living for doing so, just as do those who work on proprietary software. The companies that sponsor and contribute to Linux do not do so out of the generosity of their hearts, they do so for solid commercial reasons.

Linux is no longer subversive. It has moved steadily away from being an outsider to taking its place as a comfortable part of the existing commercial world. In a way, if there was a revolution, Linux has won, but it's an Animal Farm victory. In winning, Linux has become like those it displaced· more professional, more structured, more carefully governed. Linux has not undermined powerful institutions and companies (although it has made some operating systems obsolete); instead, those institutions have learned to live happily with Linux, and even profit from it.

■

The story of Linux is repeated in the wider world of open-source software. Originally described as a "movement," and still seen by some in that light, open source has succeeded in challenging powerful institutions, only to put new powerful institutions in their place.

There was a time when it made sense in the software industry to contrast "open source initiatives" (Linux) with "closed source companies" (Microsoft being the preferred target), but now the biggest software companies as well as each new wave of startups mix open source and proprietary code in a pragmatic way, keeping valuable work in-house and collaborating on open-source projects for work that does not give the company a competitive advantage. Oracle and Microsoft were seen as "closed source" companies, but Oracle owns the Java programming language and the MySQL database, two of the most widely-used open source projects in the world, and Microsoft has made its ".NET" programming languages open source. Meanwhile companies that proclaim their openness, such as Google, keep key parts of their intellectual property under wraps. Like the Linux kernel, the open source world has become more professional over time. A 2014 study showed that half of all contributions to open source projects happen during working hours,[7] and in 2007 a PhD thesis showed that "paid developers are more likely to maintain critical parts of the code base" within open source projects.[8]

■

Even though the big Internet companies all run on a combination of open source software and proprietary code, the culture of many Silicon Valley companies seems to require a belief in the virtues of open-source computing, and of openness in general. Jonathan Rosenberg, Senior Vice President of Product Management, set out this belief in an email he sent to Google staff; it was received so well that Google reposted it on the company's official blog in December 2009.[9]

Rosenberg starts off by saying "At Google we believe that open systems win. They lead to more innovation, value, and freedom of choice for consumers, and a vibrant, profitable, and competitive ecosystem for businesses." The document is a passionate argument in favor of open standards and open source software and against proprietary approaches to software; in favor of baking a bigger pie for everyone rather than trying to get the biggest slice for yourself.

There is one exception to Rosenberg's argument, however, and eye-rolling is unavoidable here. It turns out that Google's commitment to openness does not extend to the software that runs its core businesses of search and advertising:

> Our goal is to keep the Internet open, which promotes
> choice and competition and keeps users and developers

from getting locked in. In many cases, most notably our search and ads products, opening up the code would not contribute to these goals and would actually hurt users. The search and advertising markets are already highly competitive with very low switching costs, so users and advertisers already have plenty of choice and are not locked in. Not to mention the fact that opening up these systems would allow people to "game" our algorithms to manipulate search and ads quality rankings, reducing our quality for everyone.

Rosenberg is understating the truth here in two ways. First, Google's continued dominance of the search audience argues against his contention of a highly competitive market; there are clearly major barriers to entry in the world of search. Second, in addition to the search and advertising products, Google has kept to itself the custom software it uses to run its massive data centers, including its home-built Google File System and Google Big Table software, and has also been closing off large parts of its Android smartphone operating system. The open systems that Rosenberg advocates serve as complements to closed "black box" algorithms (as law professor Frank Pasquale describes them in his recent book)[10] which are the key to Google's business.

Three years on, Rosenberg was an advisor to Google management, and found himself in "a world that has outstripped even his wildest expectations."[11] Drawing on stories from books like *Wikinomics*,[12] on the Government of Canada's Open Government Declaration, on the non-profit Khan Academy's video lectures, on PatientsLikeMe in healthcare and Google's mapping tools, as well as Google's own success with Android smartphones and the Chrome browser, Rosenberg believes that openness needs to go even further: "We must aim beyond even an open internet. Institutions in general must continue to embrace this ethos." Here is the ambition of Silicon Valley: to reshape the world in the Internet's image. Open institutions, open government, open access. It's the ambition that the Sharing Economy seeks to realize: to take the philosophy of openness and to reshape whole industries, and their relationship to government, but to keep something for themselves.

Rosenberg's ability to hold contradictory beliefs is symptomatic of Silicon Valley culture. He believes thoroughly in openness, congratulating himself and his industry on discovering a viewpoint that is "counter-intuitive to the traditionally trained MBA who is taught to generate a sustainable competitive advantage by creating a closed system, making it popular, then milking it through the product life cycle." That he can do so while mentioning in passing that the software that actually makes money for Google must, regretfully and incidentally, remain closed, is remarkable. But it is sadly typical of Silicon Valley's outlook.

■

There are many who still see open source software as a social movement rather than as a part of the commercial world, who believe in the liberating possibilities of open source software, and who cast a baleful glare towards the giants of Silicon Valley.[13] For example, in the fallout from the Snowden revelations about NSA spying on the Internet, computer security researcher Jacob Appelbaum gave a keynote about the surveillance state at the 29C3 ("Chaos Communication Congress") hacker conference in December 2012 and included this ringing encomium for open source development:

> It is possible to make a living making free software for freedom, instead of closed source proprietary malware for cops . . . Everyone that's worked on free software and open source software . . . these are things we should try to focus on . . . When we build free and open source software . . . we are enabling people to be free in ways that they were not. Literally, people who write free software are granting liberties.

Unfortunately, free and open source software is not an alternative to the surveillance technologies of the NSA. Openness does not align with liberty. Appelbaum's opponents in the US National Security Agency have also embraced open source software in order to carry out the monitoring that Appelbaum rightly decries. In the Snowden documents that Appelbaum helped to release, the NSA "Boundless Informant" program proclaims that it "leverages FOSS [Free and Open Source Software] technology," for example the Hadoop File System for storing massive amounts of data, MapReduce for running queries against that data, and the CloudBase database system.

The NSA is happy to use free software, but is not in the business of granting liberties.

The NSA is not only a user of free software, it is an active and enthusiastic member of the open source community, along with other parts of the US military. To take one relevant example: in 2008 the NSA created Accumulo, a data storage and retrieval system for big data. Derrick Harris at research company GigaOm describes Accumulo as "The technological linchpin to everything the NSA is doing from a data-analysis perspective;"[14] it is probably part of the Boundless Informant open source stack that stores and analyzes the Verizon FISA data.[15] After developing Accumulo, the NSA submitted it to the Apache Foundation, the organization that "provides support for the Apache Community of open-source software projects, which provide software products for the public good."

In short Accumulo, developed specifically for the purpose of spying on citizens and expanding the reach of the security state, is now nurtured and supported by the open source community.

OPEN CONTENT

The bursting of the dot-com bubble in 2000 put the brakes on many commercial Internet ambitions, but not for long. The second wave was "Web 2.0," or "the Web as platform," as influential publisher Tim O'Reilly described it. In the "Web 1.0" world of email and Usenet, content was distributed across a network of computers. In a Web 2.0 world, that content is hosted on a single farm of computers owned by a single organization, and is managed by that company's own software—what is often called a "software platform." All Facebook posts live on Facebook's servers, all tweets on Twitter's, all YouTube videos on Google's.

If there is an archetype for Web 2.0, in the way that Linux is an archetype for open-source software, it is surely Wikipedia, the remarkable encyclopedia that anyone can edit. Wikipedia is so identified with web-based collaboration that its name has been incorporated into book titles (*Wikinomics: How Mass Collaboration Changes Everything*) and related initiatives such as the leaked document site WikiLeaks. In Benkler's *The Wealth of Networks*, Wikipedia plays a prominent role as an exemplar of "commons-based peer production." But Wikipedia turned out to be more the exception than the rule. While there are other not-for-profit large-scale collaborative platforms

(OpenStreetMap, for example), no other non-commercial site has reached anything resembling Wikipedia's influence. As Sue Gardner, then Executive Director of the Wikimedia Foundation, wrote in 2011:

> Wikipedia represents the fulfilment of the original promise of the internet: that it's a kind of poster child for online collaboration in the public interest. Because back when the internet started, we figured it would be full of stuff like Wikipedia. Turns out we were mostly wrong: if you take a look at the world's most popular websites, it's hard not to notice that Wikipedia's the only site in the top 25 whose primary purpose is to provide a non-commercial public service.[16]

By 2015 that "top 25" could be extended to the top 50: in fact, the next non-commercial entry in the listings of highest-traffic web sites is an organization from that earlier age so disparaged by digital enthusiasts: the venerable British Broadcasting Corporation in 70th spot.

■

It turns out that being the owner of a Web 2.0 platform can be very profitable, but the idea that Web 2.0 platforms were a new and democratizing force that could bring about a more open and equal culture was still compelling for many. It's an appeal that still resonates in the "peer-to-peer" claims of Sharing Economy companies.

Commercial Web 2.0 platforms such as Amazon, Netflix, and iTunes may not be "open" in the sense that some of the content is controlled and licensed, but for the purposes of this book, we can consider Web 2.0 platforms to be inspired by ideas of "open content." In his influential 2006 book *The Long Tail*,[17] *Wired* magazine editor Chris Anderson tied the rise of Web 2.0 platforms like Amazon and Netflix to the same subversive and liberating visions invoked by open-source software. His idea is that the bricks-and-mortar world of Walmart, bookseller retail chains, and record labels represent "the world the blockbuster built" and have to build their business on the "short head" of high-volume products.[18] In contrast, online stores are not constrained by "the tyranny of geography." Amazon can present millions of books that are individually obscure, but which together make up the "Long Tail" of demand, while the biggest of "brick and mortar" bookstores is limited to a few hundred thousand. For Anderson, Amazon represents the return of variety and diversity after decades of homogenous blockbusters: "We are turning from a mass market back into a niche nation, defined not by geography but by interests."[19] In a Long Tail world there is no need for formal gatekeepers who select or restrict the works that can find their public; instead, Web 2.0 platforms will do it for us using crowd-sourced consumer reviews and recommender systems: "By combining infinite shelf space with real-time information about buying trends and public opinion . . . unlimited selection is revealing truths about what consumers want and how they want to get it."[20]

Amazon and Airbnb are similar in many ways. Both are, at least in part, software companies whose inventory is simply a set of entries in a database, accessed via a web site. Anything can go into the database: for Amazon's books it might be Harry Potter or a self-published obscurity, or anything in between. Airbnb's database for New York has included over a thousand hosts who have never had a review, and at least one host who listed over 100 properties. It is easy to pick a few items from such a database and spin a story of the kind of business it is. *The Long Tail* starts with the story of *Touching the Void*, a book that languished in obscurity until reviews by Amazon readers pushed it up the best seller lists—and we have already seen the stories that Airbnb builds around its hosts.

Beyond these structural similarities, there are parallels between Anderson's vision of "The Future of Business" and Airbnb's Shared City manifesto. Both evoke simpler, more personal, pre-industrial times: "Cities are the original sharing platforms . . ." writes Brian Chesky, "but over time they began to feel mass-produced. We lived closer together, but drifted further apart. But sharing in cities is back, and we want to help build this future."[21] Both Anderson and Chesky select the most uniform aspects of bricks-and-mortar culture as their reference (the chain bookstores, the chain hotels).

Given these parallels, looking at how the industries identified in Anderson's *Long Tail* have developed helps us to see how the Sharing Economy is likely to evolve. And it turns out that, a decade after Anderson published his ideas, the "era of the hit" is not over after all: blockbusters are alive and well.

One of the most thorough looks at how the entertainment industry has actually developed over the last two decades is provided by Anita Elberse in her book *Blockbusters*.[22]

The companies that own the Web 2.0 platforms themselves are blockbusters. There are several factors that make many digital markets "winner-take-all" in structure. Amazon is not just the biggest online bookseller in the USA, it is the biggest by a massive margin. And digital markets are often global: Walmart may be huge in the US but its attempts to expand around the world have met with only patchy success, but Amazon is the leading online retailer in major markets throughout the world; other online services such as Netflix and iTunes are similarly global.

Also, as Elberse shows, the major digital platforms such as Amazon and iTunes have decided to build blockbuster products into their businesses in a big way. When Lady Gaga decided to pursue a massive launch strategy for her 2011 album *Born This Way*, she partnered with Amazon to sell 440,000 copies of the album at a discounted price, to take its sales over a million units in the first week.[23] Three years later Apple famously provided everyone with a copy of U2's *Songs of Innocence* in their iTunes music folder whether we wanted it or not, and Netflix is investing heavily in its own blockbuster content: mass-market TV series that it owns.

The focus on blockbusters extends beyond individual promotions. Google CEO Eric Schmidt, who wrote an enthusiastic blurb on the cover of *The Long Tail*, changed his mind within two years. In 2008 he said "although the tail is very interesting and we enable it, the vast majority of the revenue remains in the head. And this is a lesson that businesses have to learn. While you can have a long tail strategy, you better have a head, because that's where all the revenue is." Elberse quotes Schmidt as admitting "it's probable that the Internet will lead to larger blockbusters and more concentration of brands . . . . [W]hen you get everybody together they still like to have one superstar. It's no longer a US superstar, it's a global superstar. So that means global brands, global businesses, global sports figures, global celebrities."[24]

Overall, after looking at patterns across multiple cultural industries, Elberse concludes that "As demand shifts from offline retailers with limited shelf space to online channels with much larger assortments, the sales distribution is not getting fatter in the tail. On the contrary, as time goes on and consumers buy more goods online, the tail is getting longer but decidedly thinner. And the importance of individual bestsellers is not diminishing over time. Instead, it is growing."[25]

The technology that promised to undermine mass production and bring in a new area of personalized "niche culture" has instead found itself returning to the blockbuster. There have been conflicts, notably between Amazon and the major book publishers, but these are disputes over who gets to keep the money generated largely by authors and artists.

Open source promised to create a democratized alternative to the world of commercial software but instead found itself a part of the commercial landscape. Web 2.0 platforms promised to create a more egalitarian world where artists can connect directly to a global audience, but have ended up giving us more blockbusters.

■

Just as open-source programmers make their code freely accessible to others, so many in the technology world pushed back against other forms of enclosure in the cultural world. Copyright was the most prominent legal mechanism for restricting the distribution of cultural content, and the appropriation by the big record labels of most of the proceeds from the music business made them a target for opposition. The story of Napster's rise and fall is well known, followed by a proliferation of BitTorrent-based file-sharing sites for films, TV shows, and music. Some celebrated the rise of the "pirates," who saw themselves as populist opponents of big business, just as the free/libre open source hackers saw themselves as opponents of Microsoft and other proprietary software companies. Companies such as Google tried to walk a fence between the two camps: copyright-violating music videos were one of the drivers of YouTube's success but Google also wanted to make money off YouTube and that demanded co-operation.

The issues around copyright, culture, and digital technologies have been explored in countless books and articles so here I will focus on just a few parts of the story that have parallels with the Sharing Economy.

In his 2008 book *Remix*, law professor and influential open culture advocate Lawrence Lessig argues in favor of more liberal sharing of cultural works. His book adopts a golden-age view of history similar to those of Chris Anderson and Brian Chesky described above. There was a time, writes Lessig, when amateurs and professionals alike both consumed and created culture (in suitably binary terms he calls these "Read" and "Write" activities). But then came the mass-production world of the 20th century: "Never before in the history of human culture had the production of culture been as professionalized. Never before had its production been as concentrated."[26] The 21st Century, driven by digital technologies, promises a revival of participatory culture, a swing of the pendulum back to a more healthy balance. Healthy because the Internet "enables a wider range of people to speak"[27] and gives a new literacy to amateurs, who can "create in contexts that before only professionals ever knew."[28]

Lessig advocates what he calls "hybrid economies," where Internet platforms enable sharing and selling to coexist side by side. It is a vision with parallels to the way that open source has come to exist alongside proprietary software, and it finds echoes in the Sharing Economy, where people make "a little extra money" rather than having full-time jobs. And just as Lawrence Lessig argues that it is time to jettison "a regime of copyright built for a radically different technological age,"[29] so Sharing Economy advocates argue that the laws surrounding taxis and short-term rentals are outdated, made obsolete by new technology.

But just as Web 2.0 platforms have found that blockbuster strategies still make sense, so Lessig's promotion of participatory platforms has delivered less than it promises when it comes to democratization. There is a difference between open source software and open culture: in the world of software development many of those who contribute to open source projects have a steady income from their programming work (whether it is for open source contributions directly, or for complementary activities). In cultural industries the situation is different: it's not obvious where artists will make money if their work is made open. As a result, cultural creators, some of whom were entranced by the example of open source and the possibilities digital distribution offered for connecting directly with their audiences, have become increasingly disillusioned with the Web 2.0 world. In 2008 activist singer Billy Bragg wrote a *New York Times* op-ed piece about his experience with Michael Birch, CEO of social network Bebo, who had just sold that business to AOL for $850 million. When Birch approached Bragg to help set up Bebo he had big plans for musicians:

> He was hoping to expand his business by hosting music and wanted my advice on how to construct an artist-centered

environment where musicians could post original songs without fear of losing control over their work. Following our talks, Mr. Birch told the press that he wanted Bebo to be a site that worked for artists and held their interests first and foremost.

In our discussions, we largely ignored the elephant in the room: the issue of whether he ought to consider paying some kind of royalties to the artists. After all, wasn't he using their music to draw members—and advertising—to his business? Social-networking sites like Bebo argue that they have no money to distribute—their value is their membership. Well, last week Michael Birch realized the value of his membership. I'm sure he'll be rewarding those technicians and accountants who helped him achieve this success. Perhaps he should also consider the contribution of his artists.

Copyright was the tool of the major record labels to appropriate the money in the cultural world, but anti-copyright can also be used to expropriate. YouTube and iTunes both benefited from cheap (or even free) source material. Making "content" free is good for the digital platforms, not so good for the artists.

One of the most articulate analyses of how the anti-copyright movement has lost touch with those it claims to support is delivered by filmmaker and activist Astra Taylor in her 2014 book, *The People's Platform*.[30] As someone who makes a living from her art, Taylor has grown increasingly skeptical of those who identify artistic creation with amateurism, and who advocate making artistic creations available for free to gain exposure, looking for money-making opportunities elsewhere (concerts, conferences, T-shirts, consulting depending on your kind of creation). Opposition to copyright conveniently pushes questions of payment to one side, but those who make the arguments are often not short of a penny or two. Law professor Yochai Benkler tells us that "money isn't always the best motivator," and media professor and successful author of copyrighted books Clay Shirky reminds us that "the essence of amateurism is intrinsic motivation: to be an amateur is to do something for the love of it." A publication of the Harvard Business School argues that a decline in industry profitability "won't hurt production because artists' unique motivations will keep them churning out music even if they are operating at a loss."[31]

Taylor's book vividly captures the problem for artists in a world of openness and sharing. When she found her documentary film *Examined Life* posted online soon after its premiere she wrote "a pleasant note that began in a tone of gratitude, thanking the various uploaders for their enthusiasm and support of the project. Then I told them that the movie had been quite costly to produce and we were about to release it in theaters and to home viewers. I'd like a few months, I went on, to try to recover some of the film's expenses by charging people to see it . . . Would they mind, I wondered, removing the clips in the interim?" Of the two people who replied to her note, one told her that "since my [Taylor's] film was about philosophy and since philosophy . . . belongs to everyone in the world, my film does too." The other said essentially the same thing, but with more expletives.[32] The attitude to artists' payment brings Bertolt Brecht to mind: "Amongst the highly placed / It is considered low to talk about food. / The fact is: they have / Already eaten."

Creators (or is that "content producers"?) who look to Internet platforms as an alternative to the established industry will largely find themselves as disappointed as Billy Bragg and Astra Taylor. A recent example is the relationship between Google and independent musicians. Cellist Zoë Keating had built a YouTube channel as a promotional vehicle to build an audience, and used YouTube's Content ID system to claim a portion of advertising revenues from videos that feature her music. But Google is changing its revenue model for YouTube, and told Keating that if she wanted to continue using Content ID she would have to sign a new services agreement, committing her not to release music elsewhere before she releases it on YouTube, to running ads on all her videos, and to numerous other rules.[33] The content may be open, but the platform itself is not.

The rise of the amateur, of openness, and of free culture has not been at the expense of the blockbuster, but instead has led to a "missing middle." Those who look to make a living in a modest way from their art (or from their role in the creative process as booksellers, editors, and so on) have found themselves on the outside of all these changes. As Andrew Franklin of independent publisher Profile said in 2014:

> The large bestselling authors are taking a bigger and bigger share of the market. Just as in every branch of late

post-industrial capitalism, the rich are getting richer. New authors and struggling authors and mid-list authors are finding it harder. This [is] bad news for the average writer: they get paid less so that publishing houses can hold on to bestsellers with higher advances.[34]

The Web 2.0 platforms in the cultural industry have taken advantage of the winner-take-all tendencies of digital markets to take money from each and every transaction (by advertising or by direct sales) and have used their position, standing between the consumer and the service provider, to build enormous market power over service providers.[35] The dispute is often presented as one between scrappy startups and big corporate incumbents (Airbnb versus chain hotels in particular) and yet history suggests that these big players will find a way to coexist. Instead, those who are more likely to be hit are the smaller bed & breakfasts and independent hotels. And the new entrants, those who have the promise of easy access to consumers dangled in front of them, may find that the platform they depend on takes the lion's share of the money.

■

In addition to open-source software and open cultural content, many claims about the benefits of digital openness have centered on the changes it has brought to public debate and journalism. Glenn Reynolds' book on blogging is called *An Army of Davids: How Markets and Technology Empower Ordinary People to Beat Big Media, Big Government, and Other Goliaths.*[36] Newspapers have suffered, and citizen journalism in the form of blogs and social media commentary have become more prominent. But here too, the rise of the amateur and the embrace of openness have not led to the promised upending of powerful entrenched industries, or to the democratization of debate.

The last sentence of Matthew Hindman's *The Myth of Digital Democracy* is "It may be easier to speak in cyberspace, but it remains difficult to be heard."[37] The book was one of the first that actually collected and analyzed large data sets to investigate online trends in consumption as well as production. Hindman looked at the links among three million American political web pages together with data showing how Google leads its users to political sites and concluded that "communities of Web sites on different political topics are each dominated by a small set of highly successful sites." The scale of online concentration is so profound, he argues, that claims the Internet "democratizes" politics are misleading. For example, when it comes to blogs, "the top blogs are now the most widely read sources of political commentary in the United States," but these widely read bloggers are very few in number (a few dozen) and they are "overwhelmingly . . . well-educated white male professionals." The kind of voices that get heard in political discussion are the same kind that were heard through offline media, only perhaps more so. "The vigorous online debate that blogs provide may be, on balance, a good thing for US democracy. But as many continue to celebrate the democratic nature of blogs, it is important to acknowledge that many voices are left out."

Hindman's data on patterns of concentration in [American] online and traditional news media lead him to conclude that online media is even more concentrated (a few outlets get a larger share of the traffic) than many offline industries, particularly radio. The biggest story is, as in cultural production, "the missing middle," a phrase Hindman coined. He writes:

> From the beginning, the Internet has been portrayed as a media Robin Hood—robbing audience from the big print and broadcast outlets and giving it to the little guys. But the data . . . suggest that audiences are moving in both directions. On the one hand, the news market in cyberspace seems even more concentrated on the top ten or twenty outlets than print media is. On the other, the tiniest outlets have indeed earned a substantial portion of the total eyeballs . . . . It is the middle-class outlets that have seen relative decline in the online world. Moreover, it is overwhelmingly smaller, local media organizations that have lost out to national sources.[38]

The distinction between Hindman and Anderson's Long Tail comes down to comparisons. *The Long Tail* compared online platforms to large chain stores and big-box stores such as Walmart or the now-defunct Blockbuster video, Tower Records, or Borders books, but Hindman compares the online ecosystem to a more complete range of non-digital national and local media. As a result, he catches a key aspect of the comparison that Anderson misses: variety in a world subject to "the tyranny of geography" was always supplied by a variety of institutions, each capable of working at different scales. In the world of books, variety was supplied by a combination of chain stores, specialist bookstores who focused on one genre or another (especially in big cities), independent stores, and second-hand stores, whereas in the digital world winner-take-all market structures are more common. By looking only at the big chains and missing these smaller institutions, Anderson guaranteed that his comparisons would show the digital world to be more diverse and full of variety.

OPEN DATA

Other movements and businesses have been built around digital openness and sharing, such as open access publishing for research journals, open source hardware, and open education (including massively open online courses or "MOOCs"). Here I will look at only one other openness movement, which is that for Open Government Data, or Open Data for short.

The campaign for Open Data has many of the same qualities as other openness initiatives. It combines non-profit activities such as "civic hacking" with for-profit companies; it appeals to the civil liberties ideals of government transparency but also advocates free-market outcomes; it claims to focus on empowering the powerless, but too often empowers the already-empowered.

Many would trace the origins of the open government data movement to Carl Malamud's efforts to make available public domain information such as laws and regulations from various levels of government, and to put the US Securities and Exchange Commission's EDGAR database online. The common arguments for making government data open are expressed by the UK Open Knowledge Foundation:[39] increasing transparency (citizens need to know what their government is doing), releasing social and commercial value (driving the creation of innovative businesses and services), and encouraging participation and engagement (in an echo of Lessig's Remix, making a full "read/write" society).

The open data movement got a big boost when it was identified by Tim O'Reilly as the basis of an initiative he called "Government 2.0." This, he said, "is the initiative to make government data open to the public using Web-based technologies." O'Reilly describes the move to open data as "government as platform": open data—provided in such a way that programmers can write software to read it, analyze it, and transform it—will be the platform on which new transparency initiatives and innovative businesses can build.

Government 2.0 got a big boost in the US from Barack Obama's early memo on transparency and open government, and the setting up of the data.gov web site. The UK established data.gov.uk and tied it to David Cameron's "Big Society" initiative. Even Canada's notoriously secretive Conservative government undertook an open data initiative, and many cities have opened up data feeds. Sounds great? Well yes and no.

The rhetoric of open data, as with other openness movements, draws heavily on the efforts by private citizens and non-profit groups to make government more accountable. It has a strong civil liberties flavor, with talk of citizen engagement and of citizens' rights ("giving citizens access to data that is theirs"), participatory society, collaborative democracy, transparency, and so on. In a collection of essays called *Open Government*,[40] the examples almost all deal with citizen access to the US government's inner workings: campaign contributions, lobbying data, congressional votes, legislative proceedings, federal government contracts and spending, court proceedings. It describes efforts by non-commercial groups such as opensecrets.org, maplight.org, followthemoney.org, govtrack.us, and so on to use this data to enforce greater accountability. This is all fine and good—although practitioners in those groups recognize that access to information is just one step in an arms race and that those who want to hide information will now look for ways to do so.

But the open data movement has a second agenda: it demands that data be made open not only to citizens, but also to private companies: the Open Knowledge Foundation defines open data as "any content, information or data that people are free to use, re-use and redistribute—without any legal, technological or social restriction."[41]

As with open source and open content, open data affects existing power structures in subtle ways. A well-known cautionary example comes from India. In the state of Tamil Nadu, near the town of Marakkanam, right next to a reserved forest, lies a plot of contested land. Records say this three-acre plot belongs to a member of the Mudaliar caste, but lower-caste Dalits living nearby claim it should be part of the reserved forest, which is not privately owned, and that the Mudaliars have pulled a fast one, using their influence in the local bureaucracy to fix the land records. The Dalits also claim that older records will bear out their claim. Complicating the case, officials say that boundaries between land parcels in the area are often difficult to ascertain.

According to development economist Bhuvaneswari Raman,[42] the Dalit claim was sideswiped when the Tamil Nadu government undertook a program to standardize, digitize, and centralize land records. The program, pushed by the World Bank as a pro-poor, pro-transparency initiative, was undertaken to capitalize on the boom of nearby Chennai. The absence of clear land titles had made extensive land purchases time consuming and expensive, and this was a bottleneck to large-scale development projects. As part of the program, the Tamil Nadu government declared that the digitized records would be the only evidence admissible in court for land claims, so the older records and less precise data that formed the basis of the Dalit claims lost any footing they had, and their claim was sunk.

A new generation of land developers grew up alongside the digitized records, firms who had the resources, skills, and information to make efficient use of this new resource. These developers lobbied effectively for records and spatial data to be made open, and then used their advantages to displace smaller developers who, as Raman writes, "relied on their knowledge of local histories and relationships to assemble land for development." The effects went far beyond the three-acre plot near Marakkanan; newly visible master plans became used as "the reference point to label legal and illegal spaces and as a justification for evicting the poor from their economic and residential spaces. The "pro-poor" initiative turned out to be anything but, and Tamil Nadu was not alone in running an open data project that made life harder for the poor. Neighboring Karnataka's Bhoomi (or "land") e-governance program has had similar effects: Raman and her colleagues concluded that "the digitization of land records led to increased corruption, much more bribes and substantially increased time taken for land transactions. At another level, it facilitated very large players in the land markets to capture vast quantities of land at a time when Bangalore experiences a boom in the land market."[43] The story is another case of the "missing middle," where small businesses with local expertise are displaced, thanks to digital technologies, by fewer and bigger companies with the resources and expertise to make the most of formalized data sets.

When commerce is mentioned by open data proponents, they tend to use the language of entrepreneurship and innovation, contrast the new firms with the aging business models they seek to replace, and they often present commercial use as a complement to civic use.

Michael Gurstein, a leading light in the field of community informatics who has been constructively raising concerns about how open data may "empower the empowered" for some time, argues that the skills and resources needed to make "effective use" are complements to data.[44] He quotes from a study of who uses the British mySociety TheyWorkForYou.com open government initiative:

> People above the age of 54 tend to be over-represented, while those younger than 45 are under-represented in comparison to the Internet population. In terms of demographics there is a strong male bias and a strong overrepresentation of people with a university degree that also translates into strong participation from high income groups . . . . One in five users (21%) of the site has not been politically active within the last year.

After attending a conference on open government data, Gurstein comments in a blog post that:

> This attempt to enhance democratic participation has ended up providing an additional opportunity for those who already, because of their income, education, and overall conventional characteristics of higher status (age, gender etc.) have the means to communicate with and influence politicians. The additional information and an additional communications channel thus has the effect of reinforcing patterns of opportunity that are already there rather than widening the base of participation and influence.[45]

Kentaro Toyama, an expert in the use of information technology for development, argues that "in contexts where literacy and social capital are unevenly distributed, technology tends to amplify inequalities rather than reduce them."[46] An email account cannot make you more connected unless you have some existing social network to build on.

Development studies scholar Kevin Donovan sees similarities between open data efforts and James Scott's book *Seeing Like a State*.[47] Open standards and structured, machine-readable data are key parts of the open data program, and for Donovan this formalization and standardization is "far more value-laden than typically considered." Open data programs, like the state, seek to "make society legible through simplification." Standardized data, like the state, "operate[s] over a multitude of communities and attempt[s] to eliminate cultural norms through standardization." He writes:

> Eliminating illegibility in this way reduces the public's political autonomy because it enables powerful entities to act on a greater scale. Scott argued, "A thoroughly legible society eliminates local monopolies of information and creates a kind of national transparency through the uniformity of codes, identities, statistics, regulations and measures. At the same time it is likely to create new positional advantages for those at the apex who have the knowledge and access to easily decipher the new state-created format."[48]

Open data undermines the power of those who benefit from "the idiosyncrasies and complexities of communities . . . . Local residents [who] understand the complexity of their community due to prolonged exposure." The Bhoomi land records program is an example of this: it explicitly devalues informal knowledge of particular places and histories, making it legally irrelevant; in the brave new world of open data such knowledge is trumped by the ability to make effective queries of the "open land records." The valuing of technological facility over idiosyncratic and informal knowledge is baked right in to open data efforts.

More encouragingly, Donovan looks at how some "data geeks" recognized their own myopia in the Map Kibera project, which started as a community-mapping project to trace the massive Nairobi slum. Some questioned the need for the project as "locals [already] knew their surroundings intimately." Making mapping information available would more likely benefit external parties than the residents themselves.

The problems the project seeks to address are what Donovan calls "wicked problems: ill-defined, tangled, and resistant to technological fixes." However,

> Although it began as an example of misdiagnosing a wicked problem (Kibera's poverty and marginalization) as a tame one (insufficient information availability), Map Kibera has admirably grown beyond a reductionist approach; it has expanded to include other forms of activity such as citizen reporting, and has taken steps to ensure local ownership of the project. The project has moved beyond a technological goal to a set of social goals. Its list of sponsors, interestingly, includes only non-commercial organizations.

Donovan contrasts Map Kibera's evolution with that of more narrowly technological mapping projects, such as Google's Map Maker initiatives, which have been accused of unethical "exploitation of open communities."[49] The danger of such projects is that, by eliminating the illegibility that privileges local knowledge over outsider knowledge, they may allow the already powerful to gain access to community knowledge that was previously hidden from them: to "see like a slum."

When it comes to development programs, Donovan concludes, open data is not enough and should not be the primary focus. Instead, transparency must be linked with deliberative development: effecting social change cannot avoid the need to actually address underlying dynamics of power.

One of the most valuable complements to open data is other data: a bus schedule is more valuable if you can combine it with a map. This combinatorial aspect of open data raises problems for government-collected data, as legal scholars Teresa Scassa and Lisa M. Campbell highlighted, because data protection legislation "typically requires that information collected for specific purposes should not be used for other purposes without consent."[50]

Scassa and Campbell look at how "even relatively low quality spatial data may attract the application of data protection or privacy law, particularly when it is matched or combined with other data sets." They look, for example, at Ottawa Police's crime mapping tool, which is a map of calls for police assistance provided through a collaboration between Ottawa Police and Public Engines, a US company. If insurance companies make decisions about rates or insurability based on the crime-mapping data, or if security companies use it to target specific areas for marketing campaigns, then this site could be violating those conditions.

The faith in markets sometimes goes further among open data advocates. It's not just that open data *can* create new markets, there is a substantial portion of the push for open data that is explicitly seeking to create new markets as an alternative to providing government services. Political scientist Jo Bates has highlighted the way in which open government data programs can be used as a form of privatization and deregulation: a deliberate attempt to create new markets in Public Sector Information (PSI) reuse instead of providing government services. Here is a summarizing quotation:

> [T]he current "transparency agenda" [of the UK government, supported by prominent Open data advocates] should be recognised as an initiative that also aims to enable the marketisation of public services, and this is something that is not readily apparent to the general observer. Further, whilst democratic ends are claimed in the desire to enable "the public" to hold "the state" to account via these measures, there is an issue in utilising a dichotomy between the state and a notion of "the public" which does not differentiate between citizens and commercial interests . . . . The construction . . . encourages those attracted to civic engagement into an embrace of solidarity with profit seeking interests, distanced from the ever suspect notion of the state.[51]

Here is the kind of activity that now comes under "open data" initiatives (again from Bates):

> [T]here has been significant lobbying by the financial industry to get better access to UK weather data so that it is able to compete in this [weather risk management] market. Groups such as the Lighthill Risk Network, of which Lloyds of London are a member, have lobbied government for better weather data so that they can develop

risk based weather products. Similarly, the insurance industry has requested real time information on the pretext that they might respond more quickly to extreme weather events such as flooding. My own research and the recent announcement suggest that these demands have been met enthusiastically by well placed policy makers in national government who are keen to develop a UK weather derivatives market.

Weather risk management might seem like an odd industry, but Bates reports that "This weather risk management market far outweighs the USA's commercial weather products market which in 2000 was estimated at approximately $500 million a year," touching over $45 billion in 2005–06.

Welcoming corporate involvement in open data activities leads to new Amazons and Apples, while undermining the community activism that is the movement's strong point. One of the leading companies in the open data space is Palantir Technologies. It was highlighted by the civic-minded Code for America; it sponsored O'Reilly's Gov 2.0 summit and adopts his "Government as a Platform" terminology, and was an early partner of USAid's Food Security Open Data Challenge.[52] Palantir received early funding from the CIA's In-Q-Tel venture capital arm and from Peter Thiel's Founders Fund, both organizations known for their deep commitment to openness and equality. Peter Thiel is Palantir's Chairman of the Board: perhaps he will be pursuing open data projects for the secretive Bilderberg Group, on whose Steering Committee he sits?

It would be nice to think that the shift to open data might undermine some vested interests without re-enacting *Animal Farm*, but the prospects are not bright.

One lesson of cultural economics is that creative works for which there is significant demand in a small market can be swamped by near-zero-marginal cost exports from large markets. It is more profitable for TV stations in smaller markets to broadcast cheap American shows than it is to broadcast more expensive home-grown material, *even in cases where the latter would draw a bigger audience*, because cultural producers seek to cover their costs in their home market and typically sell at discounted rates elsewhere.[53]

To maintain cultural diversity in the face of winner-take-all markets, governments in smaller countries have designed a toolbox of interventions.

The contents include production subsidies, broadcast quotas, spending rules, national ownership, and competition policy. In general, such measures have received support from those with a left-leaning outlook.

Unfortunately, the open data movement demands that data be provided without borders and in a uniform way: machine processable, available to anyone, and license-free. It mandates non-discriminatory licensing, focuses on standards-based formats, and generally insists that data be accessible to rich and poor alike, like justice and the Ritz. It insists that any measures governments would like to take to favor, for example, non-commercial users or local users, be taken off the table. For open data to be a public good, it must be accompanied by social changes. If the goal of the movement is to promote equality it will need far more emphasis on experimentation in standards, licensing, and selective provision of data at all levels of government, otherwise what is a potentially valuable public resource will simply be plundered by those with the digital skills and resources to make most use of it.

■

Many successful open movements grow in a consistent pattern.

The movement starts by appealing to egalitarian ideals, and relies on claims that openness can redress the balance with powerful institutions such as "incumbent" corporations or the state.

As an openness movement grows, the smart money learns how to work with it. Sometimes that smart money comes from those who seemed to be threatened: IBM was an establishment software company with its own operating system, which learned to love Linux, and the music industry learns to put ads on (and in) YouTube music videos. So businesses grow around the open commons.

Big companies are often better placed to influence the development of the movement than the amateurs who appear in the stories. Alliances with such companies ("Blockbuster strategies," in Anita Elberse's phrase) can be tempting for openness initiatives, and are often accompanied by a change in language. Visions of community are replaced by arguments that openness provides a better experience for consumers or is a more efficient production method. In the Open Data world, arguments for citizen engagement get put to one side in favor of arguments about new consumer services (Google Maps, real-estate listings); Linux's goal of providing users with more control over their computing environment takes second place to powering Wall Street and the US security state.

The same pattern happens with online platforms. EBay is the ancestor of Sharing Economy companies, and many people still think of it as "everybody's garage sale," but the company itself now describes its history in three phases.[54] The first is the garage sale phase, and the second was of professional small vendors making a living from the marketplace. That too has been superseded as the major brands now use eBay. The auction model that lent the site its informal, bartering atmosphere has long gone; most of the purchases are of new goods rather than second hand. As with Sharing Economy companies, the belief that free-market economics and commons-based, or community-based social exchange are compatible, means that commercial success and the ambition to grow eat away the very characteristics that gave them their early appeal.

This new world can be good for us in our role as consumers, but it is bad for producers and distributers who are trying to make money from their work, and who now become portrayed as obstacles to progress. Open Source developers are often in a relatively good space, in that they can get paid for working in the new businesses that surround open source software, but for journalists, photographers, and filmmakers: the message for them is that they have to give up the idea that they somehow deserve to be paid for their work. The new world is best of all for the Web 2.0 platform owners, who have every reason not to ask themselves whether what they have delivered fits with what they promised.

8. Open Wide

Silicon Valley is deeply committed to the idea that sharing and commerce go together. Beyond the Sharing Economy, there are many examples, some of which we saw in Chapter 7: Lawrence Lessig's idea of the "hybrid economy"[1] relies on amateurs and professionals working side by side, often on for-profit platforms; Social Enterprises are organizations that apply commercial strategies to maximize improvements in human and environmental well-being; Benefit Corporations such as Etsy, the online craft trading marketplace, are firms "that want to consider society and the environment in addition to profit in their decision making process."

The related idea of social entrepreneurship uses markets to scale up efforts to create social good. Groups such as Markets for Good (a wing of the Bill and Melinda Gates Foundation) and Google.org, the charitable arm of Google, put these ideas into practice.

Steven Berlin Johnson's idea of "peer progressives" was mentioned in Chapter 1. It highlights both for-profit and not-for-profit peer-to-peer networks as a framework for solving social problems, and seeks to position digital platforms and their communities for social good.[2]

Pierre Omidyar is one of the most vocal proponents of the social enterprise model. Omidyar founded eBay, one of the direct ancestors of the Sharing Economy. eBay took what was a neighborhood activity (the yard sale) and scaled it up by putting it on the Internet, with massive success. eBay made Pierre Omidyar a billionaire and he has put that money to active use. Together with his wife Pam Omidyar, he created the Omidyar Network, which blurs the line between giving and investing (it calls itself "a philanthropic investment firm") and the line between profit and social good (it invests in "entrepreneurs who share our commitment to advancing social good"). It is "dedicated to harnessing the power of markets to create opportunity for people to improve their lives."

A common thread of these initiatives, many of which are linked to successful technology entrepreneurs, is that they insist entrepreneurship (rather than, for example, service) is the right way to solve social problems. They believe profit and social good can not only coexist, but can benefit each other so long as the motivations of those in charge are pure.

In the world outside Silicon Valley, views about the effects of markets on other forms of social interaction are more mixed. Two traditions reach back to the 18th century and the ideas of Adam Smith. One sees the market as civilizing, harnessing Smith's belief that "It is not from the benevolence of the butcher, the brewer, or the baker that we expect our dinner, but from their regard to their own interest." Another sees the market as corrupting and prefers a different quote from Adam Smith: "People of the same trade seldom meet together, even for merriment and diversion, but the conversation ends in a conspiracy against the public, or in some contrivance to raise prices." Along another dimension, some see the market as "feeble" in its effects on society, neither particularly civilizing nor destructive, while others, like Omidyar, see markets as mechanisms for bringing about desired social and political change.[3]

This chapter looks at how efforts to combine profit and sharing have worked out in two arenas that are particularly important to the Sharing Economy: on the Internet and in cities.

CROWDING OUT

Sharing Economy exchanges are supposed to have two components to them. "Economy" refers to a market exchange between a service provider and a consumer, but "sharing" invokes a more personal and empathetic exchange, like neighbors helping neighbors. Money may be involved, but the exchange is about more than the money, it's about connections and it's about community.

Chapter 4 referred to the common trope among technology commentators and Silicon Valley entrepreneurs to describe history in three states. An age of personal exchange and civic involvement is followed by an era of alienating mass consumption and mass production. That is followed in turn by a resurgence of civic and community-based involvement driven by new technologies. It's an arc that pulls from some well-respected research on the late–20th century fall-off in civic involvement, most notably Robert Putnam's *Bowling Alone*, but which too often ends up as a caricature.[4] Here is Brian Chesky's version:

> Cities used to be generally villages, and everyone was essentially kind of like an entrepreneur. You were either a farmer, or you worked in the city as a blacksmith, or you had some kind of trade. And then the Industrial Revolution happened . . . [World War II followed, and] suddenly cities became more and more mass-produced. And we stopped trusting our neighbors.[5]

Even following this collapse of community, non-commercial activities are so much a part of the fabric of our daily lives that it is easy not to notice them, but our neighborhoods and cities continue to depend on civic action, and those who think about profit and sharing in the digital world can learn a lot from our cities and culture. A few years ago Clay Shirky wrote that it had taken 100 million hours to create Wikipedia and wondered what we could do with this newly discovered "cognitive surplus."[6] It's an impressive number, but like so many big numbers it is less impressive when put in perspective. To take one example, Canadians volunteered over 2.1 billion hours in 2010 alone, and there is no reason to suppose that Canada is more volunteer-minded than other countries.[7] That's the equivalent of over 1 million full-time jobs, or twenty complete Wikipedias, spent in hospitals and with sports teams and charitable and arts organizations. Practices of non-commercial sharing and collaboration are still pervasive in our cities, and much of what we call "culture" has long been marked by a combination of voluntary sharing and monetary work, from sports to the arts to the social practices of our everyday lives.

In a simplistic economic view, money is interchangeable with other motivations, so the idea of adding monetary incentives to encourage and amplify social exchanges sounds obvious. It's a style of argument that was pursued most actively by Nobel prize–winning economist Gary Becker, one of the most influential economists of the 20th century.

But in social exchanges, as Cyndi Lauper sang, money changes everything. In a famous study called *The Gift Relationship*, Richard Titmuss compared the American and British systems of blood donation and concluded that the introduction of monetary incentives in the US had lowered the frequency of donations, because "allowing a market in blood changes the social understanding of blood donation from 'a gift of life' to a mere cash equivalent."[8,9] Giving blood for nothing is something you can feel good about; giving blood for money is not. Instead of increasing the incentive to perform this social act, money "crowded out" the intrinsic motives that had led people to donate.

Titmuss showed that monetary incentives also lowered the quality of donated blood. People giving blood for social reasons will naturally avoid giving if they do not meet the blood system's requirements, but people giving for money are more likely to give even if their blood may be dangerous to recipients. Screening becomes far more important.

There are many other examples where money and gifts are not interchangeable. Sending flowers after a date means one thing, leaving a $50 bill means something else. Offering someone money to step ahead of them in a supermarket queue is unlikely to be successful. Paying money for votes is incompatible with the democratic process.

The "Ultimatum Game," a simple two-player exercise that illustrates cultural notions of fairness, shows why alienation increases along with the money involved. In this game, a pot of $100 is assigned to one player, who must make a take-it-or-leave-it offer of a portion of the pot to a second player. The size of the offer is up to the first player. If the second player accepts the offer then both take their portion of the pot, but if the second player rejects the offer then the pot must be returned and both players are left penniless. It turns out that many second players reject small offers, even though it means losing money, rather than see the first player get away with being greedy. Ideas of fairness cause people to turn their backs on what would, in other circumstances, be a good offer ($10 for free!).

Sharing Economy companies ignore the ways that money crowds out social exchange.

Uber is well-known for its "surge pricing" approach to dealing with supply and demand. Some critics object to it, and customers faced with high fares have been quick to record their displeasure, but economists[10] as well as Uber itself are quick to explain, often as if to a slow child, that it's just the natural law of supply and demand:

> With surge pricing, Uber rates increase to get more cars on the road and ensure reliability during the busiest times. When enough cars are on the road, prices go back down to normal levels.[11]

In their defense, Uber's surge pricing is far from new, even in the world of transit. Bus fares and train fares are more expensive at peak times in many cities; and airlines adjust pricing depending on how many seats they want to sell. But Uber, and too many economists, are blind to a different aspect of the debate, which is that surge pricing on New Year's Eve or at rush hour is one thing, but surge pricing during snow storms is something else.

At times of emergency we as a community rely on people pulling together to get us through the crisis: we expect people to check on their neighbors (for free), to help people who are stuck (without charging!) and to generally pitch in and be community-minded. We expect people to share their time and their possessions.

Emphasizing monetary incentives during a crisis crowds out community motives. If my neighbor and I help push your car out of a snowbank without payment then we're just doing the right thing, but if my neighbor is being paid and I'm doing it for free, then I'm just being a mug. There is a reason that profiting from emergencies is called "price gouging" and it is because the broader situation demands a community-driven response that the monetary incentives of supply and demand only undermine, regardless of its impact on the number of Uber vehicles it gets on the road.

At times of crisis, surge pricing may put more cars on the street, but they are not available to those who cannot afford the prices. We object to surge pricing at such a time for the same reason that we would object to lifeboats being made available only for first-class passengers on the Titanic: at times of emergency, equitable access is a strong requirement.[12] Uber is deaf to such arguments, as might be expected from a company founded by a follower of Ayn Rand.

Even Uber had to back down after a 2014 hostage crisis in Sydney's central business district, a tragedy that left three people dead. During the confusion of the early stages of the crisis, as people fled the center of the city, Uber hiked prices by up to a factor of four, at one point charging a minimum fare of $100.[13] Initially the company stood by its policy on Twitter, explaining that "Fares have increased to encourage more drivers to come online & pick up passengers in the area," before reversing the increase in the face of criticism. Until the vocal reaction from Sydney residents prompted an apology, the company was unable to see why the Economics 101 logic of supply-and-demand is inappropriate at a time of civic crisis.

Snowstorms are another example of a community crisis, and in the winter of 2014–15 Uber rates sometimes surged up to seven or eight times the normal price. In the USA, New York and Washington told Uber that its practices violated price gouging laws, and the company agreed to limit its surge pricing during emergencies across the country.[14] Uber has no idea about sharing and community. Its insistence that all exchanges reduce to market transactions is an ideological flaw; it exemplifies the implicit political agendas that often hide behind the apps and algorithms of Sharing Economy business models, and should make us take their claims to be responsible self-regulators with a pinch of salt. The fact that a strong government stance succeeded in changing the company's behavior reminds us that there is nothing inevitable about the way that the Sharing Economy will evolve.

COMMONS IN THE CITY

David Harvey never once mentions digital technologies in his book *Rebel Cities*,[15] but his analysis is full of lessons for thinking about the Sharing Economy.

Harvey writes about the role of commons in the city. He uses the word "commons" in an everyday sense, to mean anything owned in a shared or communal fashion and so out of the bounds of private property, which is a broader definition than the technical one used by some academics.[16] A city park is a commons, and in the digital world the code that makes up an open source project is a commons. As a Marxist, Harvey adopts a dialectical perspective: commons are not good or bad, but "questions of the common . . . are contradictory and therefore always contested. Behind these contestations lie conflicting social and political interests."[17] These conflicting interests are too often overlooked or assumed away in the Silicon Valley perspective where markets and social goods go together, but they are the heart of the matter when it comes to culture, online or offline.

The Sharing Economy appeals to many people, disenchanted with both the centralized bureaucracy of the state and the pervasive commodification of the market, who are on the lookout for alternative models of organization and collaboration, new models for democratic and collective living. Built around the act of sharing, the concept of the commons offers tantalizing visions of co-operative and non-authoritarian patterns of collaboration.

But managing commons in a sustainable fashion has proven difficult, particularly at large scale, which is why many commons have been discarded, replaced legitimately or illegitimately by private resources managed as commodities (agricultural enclosure, carbon permits, tradable fishing quotas), or by public resources managed by a central authority (roads, public hygiene). Still, urban commons (in the city) and digital commons (online) are spaces where new models of production and collaboration are being played out: continual sources of hope, and of hype.

Commons and community are tangled. You can't have a common without a community to tend it, and you can't have a community without a common to manage. In other words, a common is whatever a community forms around. There are many ways of keeping commons healthy, and Elinor Ostrom won a Nobel Prize for pioneering the study of commons management and building a framework to analyze the diverse institutions and practices that have evolved. But the practice of tending a common is, by definition, collective rather than private and shared rather than commodified: it is off-limits to the logic of private property and market exchange.[18] Ostrom's Nobel Prize lecture was titled "Beyond Markets and States."

Most of us are familiar with environmental commons: clean air, fresh water, silence, or fish stocks—scarce resources, collectively owned. Many aspects of culture are commons as well, but with a twist: environmental commons must be carefully managed and conserved, but cultural commons are not obviously depleted by use—they are "non-rival," at least up to a point: my listening to a song does not interfere with your ability to listen to it; consumption does not "use up" the resource. More often than not, the challenge with cultural commons is to ensure a sufficient level of production or community participation, rather than to worry about overconsumption.

Our cities are rife with cultural commons that have elements of shared ownership and participation. Examples include parks, sidewalks, streetscapes, community sports, and Business Improvement Areas. Other examples are more nebulous but no less important: the energy of Manhattan, the "cafe culture" of Rome, the Catalan history and distinctive architectural environment of Barcelona, the unique symbolic meaning of post–Cold War Berlin, the focal role of Tahrir Square during the 2011 Egyptian uprising, or of New York's Zucotti Park during the Occupy movement in 2012.

Cities are sites where people of all sorts and classes mingle. The social, collective production of culture is much of what makes a city a city: Harvey quotes Hardt and Negri: "the metropolis [is] a factory for the production of the common."

Commercial cultural industries play an increasingly important role in the economy: "The number of workers engaged in cultural activities and production has increased considerably over the past few decades."[19] But culture is distinct from commodities like shirts and shoes[20] in that commerce is just the tip of the cultural iceberg. Under the water, the mass of cultural activity is a non-commercial commons: we participate in cultural activities as amateurs for reasons of fun, personal growth, belief in the importance of the common purpose, or other intrinsic motives. The health of neighborhood sports, artistic, and creative programs is driven largely by non-commercial activities and motivations. Commerce is never entirely absent—people make money from giving music lessons, selling books, and so on—but it is only above the waterline that the language becomes unapologetically and pervasively that of business, and we speak of "cultural industries," the cultural marketplace, and call sports teams and movie productions "franchises."

Many cultural activities have taken root on Internet platforms and in open source projects, and have a similar iceberg structure: many people take part for fun, some make a living, and a few people make fortunes. The commons around which communities form are among the most dramatic features of the Internet landscape. Examples include the source code of the Webkit browser; the syntax of the Python programming language; the content of Wikipedia; the geographical data of Open Street Map; the ratings and comments that make reputation systems work; the book reviews and ratings on Amazon, GoodReads, and LibraryThing; the contributions to the Ravelry knitting and crocheting community; the message threads of forums such as 2+2 (online poker), Reddit, 4chan, Something Awful, and GardenWeb; the questions, answers, and user feedback on Q&A sites like Stack Overflow, Server Fault, and Quora.

Labeling culture and computing as commons does not complete their description: when it comes to commons, there is variety in scope of access, in ownership, and in management. Looked at closely, commons reveal rich combinations of practices that resist generalization.[21] Here is a short tour around some of that variety.

Cultural commons are more often open-access than commons of easily-exhausted resources simply because they are not exhausted by use, but not all cultural commons are open. Wikipedia and Times Square might be open to all, but access to Angie's List, Ravelry, and community gardens is restricted to the community that tends these commons. At Stack Overflow anyone can read the answers, but you must be a member in order to post questions, and there is a complex set of permissions depending on your contribution level: the more you contribute, the more you can do on the site. City center streetscapes are open to all, but the infrastructure is the responsibility of government, the store windows the private responsibility of shop owners, the ambience the outcome of citizen behavior, and business associations have particular interest and say in the standards and practices of the area.

This variety of practices is a sign that commons are complex, and potentially vulnerable. While the openness of Wikipedia and Linux are the foundation myths of the Sharing Economy, the internal management of these commons has become more complex over time, displaying a steady accretion of formal procedures as well as hierarchies of responsibility and influence. Controversial pages are locked down on Wikipedia by a complex protection policy, while changes to Linux kernel code must now make it through levels of committers and maintainers if they are to be accepted.

Not all public spaces are commons. As Harvey writes: "Public goods and spaces in the city have always been a matter of state power and public administration: sanitation, public health, education, paved streets,"[22] but the dividing line can be fluid. Some spaces (like Tahrir Square) are transformed from public space to commons (collectively owned by those who occupy them) at times of crisis: "transformed by social action into the commons of revolutionary movement."[23] Other spaces are transformed from commons to public spaces when they become essential services and when universal access is a priority; for example, education and welfare used to be provided by churches in many communities.

Some commons, like worker-owned and buyer-owned co-operatives, are owned by the community that tends them, but many cultural commons don't have a clear owner. A distinguishing feature of many Web 2.0 digital commons is that they are tended by a community, but are ultimately owned by a single entity: the value of TripAdvisor may lie in the content provided by users, but TripAdvisor itself is owned by its shareholders and investors.

There is continual experimentation in the institutions and practices for managing commons. Some institutions are informal (norms of behavior, informally enforced by the community itself), while others are more formal (elected councils, appointed officials, and so on). With their practices of non-commodified sharing, it is tempting to associate commons with egalitarian and loosely progressive ideals, and for many people a belief in open, cultural commons is linked to their political beliefs. But the "egalitarian = commons" equation is too simple: libertarians see the commons as an alternative to state regulation just as socialists and liberals see the commons as an alternative to the market. Harvey writes, concerning gated communities, "The ultra-rich, after all, are just as fiercely protective of their residential commons as anyone."[24] A prestigious and conservative golf club may be a common owned by its members; collective ownership of workplaces exists for law firms as well as worker co-operatives.

COMMONS AND CAPITAL

Tending the commons is inherently collective and non-commodified, but "the common, even—and particularly—when it cannot be enclosed, can always be traded upon even though it is not in itself a commodity."[25] Going back to Chapter 3 and my experience in Rome, the ambience of Trastevere is a commons: a collective product of the citizens who live and work in the area, and the buildings they have inherited and maintain. Many residents trade on that commons, offering restaurants and gift shops for the tourists it attracts.

It's often undesirable to keep money out of the commons completely. The financial possibilities of "trading on the commons" are often part of what sustains a community and hence its common. If there was no money to be made from tourists, Trastevere would have a difficult time sustaining its character. Individual members of the community are often instrumental in maintaining the value of a common while profiting by trading on the commons, and will seek to control the ways in which money is made from it. As another example from a different sphere, literary culture has been maintained by a complex ecosystem of authors and readers, publishers and booksellers, reviewers and editors, agents and distributors—many of whom make money from their work as well as contributing to the commons.

It is one of the oddities of the economics of cultural goods that they are simultaneously one-of-a-kind (one novel is not a perfect replacement for any other novel) and commodities (there is a "market for books"). There is money to be made from monopoly goods ("monopoly rents"), and the more distinctive the cultural good, the more it attracts capital. Bestselling books make money for their author and their publisher because there is no easy substitute.

There is a tension at the heart of trading on the commons. The more a community is successful in creating a healthy commons—the more it creates something distinctive, something unique—the more the commons attracts capital, which seeks to turn it into a commodity that can be bought and sold.

Successful commons are the product of distance from the market, but are continually pulled toward it. The idea that those who disapprove of commerce should wholeheartedly embrace the commons, and that "open source," for example, is a countercultural response to proprietary software, is yet another appealing idea we have already seen turns out to be too simple. Similarly, the Sharing Economy belief in the natural synergy of commons and commerce turns out to be simplistic and self-serving; the relationship between commons and capital is fraught with contradiction.

Let's get more specific. Here are three contradictions between commons and commerce: alienation, erosion, and distortion.

ALIENATION

Alienation is very similar to the crowding out of social motives discussed above. It appears when some contributors get paid, while others do not, or when the owner of a privately owned common sees it as a source of profit, or when the creativity and commitments of cultural producers are appropriated for the benefit of others.

The potential conflict of interest is present at even small scales. The venue owner who provides a space for musicians to play in exchange for money is both tending the musical commons and making money from it, and there are constant tensions around these dual roles in cultural communities between musicians, bar owners, and patrons.

Even when a common is not directly diminished by use, it can still be endangered when capital makes too much money off it, as the community increasingly feels like they are working for an undeserving entity and may turn their back on the labors of tending the commons.

Here is an example from the Sharing Economy. Couchsurfing is a site for travelers and for people hosting travelers, which pioneered the use of the Internet for casual travel before Airbnb. It lets you "stay with locals in every country on earth. Travel like a local, stay in someone's home and experience the world in a way money can't buy." In its early days Couchsurfing was a non-profit organization that focused on building community among young backpackers, but in August 2011 Couchsurfing reorganized itself into a for-profit corporation and accepted $7.6 million from the Omidyar Network and others.[26] The action led to widespread alienation of many members who had not only contributed to the health of the community, but who had even helped to build the software that runs the Couchsurfing site.

The community aspect of Couchsurfing has deteriorated as its market valuation has grown. As a non-profit, Couchsurfing get-togethers were "art gatherings, bonfires, a weekly meetup at a bar, cafe gatherings, potlucks,"[27] and the result of that community was an impressive record of safety for meetings among strangers, highlighted by Clay Shirky in his book *Cognitive Surplus*. But the health of Couchsurfing was not the result of its technology; it was the result of the local communities of members. As a commenter at Quora writes: "The old Couchsurfing thrived with a very haphazard and under-funded management structure precisely because local volunteers around the world believed they were part of a cause bigger than profit. Local collectives were highly tied to their local communities .... The technical architecture of the new systems is much better, but paradoxically the 'professional' product development process fixes things that were broken on purpose. In other words, Couchsurfing evolved around certain quirks and inefficient processes that actually became critical to the health of the social trust platform."

The alienation of Couchsurfing community members is clear[28] and the commons aspect of the organization has been damaged. As commons advocate David Bollier has written, the changes reflect the crowding out of one set of ethics by another as commerce has replaced sharing:

> Since its corporatization, the site's cultural ethic and vibe shifted. This was inevitable once venture capital investors became involved because VCs generally want to earn some serious return on investment. And that requires advertising, cross-branding promotions, discount deals with various travel companies, etc. In other words, a new ethic, a new set of implicit relationships with people, a hyper-awareness of marketing identity. Yet the absence of all the familiar marketing come-ons and market relationships was precisely what Couchsurfers treasured.[29]

Contrast the story of Couchsurfing to a venerable effort that has remained resolutely non-profit. At over 100 years old, youth hostelling organizations are still going strong around the world. Hostelling International currently provides 35 million overnight stays a year through more than 4,000 hostels in over 80 countries. People do trade on the commons of hostels—some people work in the hosteling organizations, others are paid to run the hostels themselves—but the money they make is seen to be compatible with the aims of tending the commons: the sudden injection of millions of dollars from venture capitalists would be a whole different order of magnitude.

Couchsurfing is far from unique. Chapter 5 showed how Zipcar failed to sustain a community feel once it scaled up its commercial efforts, and how Lyft's community-focused model also collapsed as it looked to monetary incentives to recruit drivers and as it raised venture capital to compete with Uber. Successful music and cultural festivals often have a year or two of being alternative and cool, before the monopoly rents that the festival generates become incompatible with the community spirit of many festivals, and the corporate world moves in; counter-cultural movements typically have a short lifetime before being absorbed into the commercial mainstream. It is often better to think in terms of moments than movements when evaluating the success of non-commercial initiatives.

Other large online communities have experienced a similar dollar-shock. The owners of book-reading community site GoodReads sold the site to Amazon in 2013, triggering a backlash among its reader base who have collectively provided much of the value that the site holds. A couple of weeks later, academic reference manager site Mendeley brought down the wrath of its own user base by selling itself to Elsevier: the contrast between Mendeley's language of openness and community and its sale to a company with a reputation for resisting open access publication at every turn was too much for some. These are far from the first. Early collaborative sites like IMDB (sold to Amazon) and database of music CD track titles CDDB (now owned by Sony Corporation) were treated as commons for some time, then sold off for profit, alienating many of their users.

New waves of capital must reconfigure the commercial and non-commercial environment, disrupting those who currently make money from trading on the commons. The invaders, seeking access to the value of a commons, highlight the contradictions in the existing system, portraying small-scale money as a source of inefficiency, and as Luddite opposition to progress.

Techno-enthusiasts labeled booksellers and publishers "gatekeepers" and "incumbents," portraying them as parasites on the commons of literary culture, exploiting and profiting from writers and readers while controlling access to the marketplace. Those who seek to make money out of new music distribution models portray the existing rentiers as dinosaur profiteers. But the best booksellers and publishers are flamekeepers as well as gatekeepers, commoners as well as monopolistic incumbents. And the new capital is not just a friend of the author and reader, it has its own commercial agenda as well. As Clay Shirky wrote, "Institutions will try to preserve the problem to which they are the solution," but the corollary is that new institutions will try to create new problems to which they are the solution.[30]

Both sides of debates over intellectual property and cultural production—around the legitimacy of pirate sites or record labels, for example—acknowledge the conflict between capital and commons by portraying opponents as money-grabbers, while appealing to the health of the commons using the language of community. Cultural production is always "about" something, but never "about" the money: the script demands that each side must avoid talking about its own commercial motives.

When it comes to debating the cultural commons, Hollywood suddenly finds that it values the efforts of the lowly camera operators and technicians; software platform owners appeal to openness but are silent regarding their own commercial incentives (advertising revenue, for example). Examples abound on the web sites of Sharing Economy companies: "Couchsurfers share their lives with the people they encounter, fostering cultural exchange and mutual respect," "Our community is comprised of users, passionate and eager to explore and enrich the world through the sharing of space. We invite you to join the movement and become part of our story" (Airbnb); "Welcome to the TaskRabbit community, a marketplace dedicated to empowering people to do what they love." For the owners of Zipcar, the company "isn't just about the concept of car sharing; it's about the people who make it a reality: a team that works hard, members who believe, and organizations that are making conscious decisions for the future." They may believe it's not about the money, but they didn't mind selling to Avis when the price was right even if it alienated the community that they talk about so affectionately.

■

Microfinance is the practice of making small loans to poor people in developing countries whose lack of collateral had previously made access to credit impossible, apart from loan sharks who charge extortionate rates of interest. The leading light was Mohammed Yunus, who set up his Grameen Bank in 1976. Grameen Bank pioneered a form of group-based credit: by loaning to small groups, largely to groups of women, Yunus found loan repayment rates were high because peer pressure within the group ensured that members kept to their repayment commitments.

The Grameen Bank's success led to a Nobel Peace Prize for Mohammed Yunus, and sparked a broad interest in microfinance. In 2006 a debate erupted in the world of microfinance between "pure do-gooders and profit-minded do-gooders," and notably between Mohammed Yunus and Pierre Omidyar. The Grameen Bank is a for-profit institution but not a public company: it is owned by the borrowers themselves, so that profits are returned to the borrowers. Omidyar had other ideas:

Yunus is now seen by Omidyar and many others as the archetypal founder, too wedded to his original vision. In recent years, younger and nimbler players have been taking microfinance—their preferred term—toward the idea of building a fully commercial, profit-making sector. This conflict, between pure do-gooders and profit-minded do-gooders, has come to define the current debate in the microfinance world.[31]

A few years later Hugh Sinclair, who spent several years working for microfinance institutions, compellingly described his disillusionment and anger at the way the industry was going in his book *Confessions of a Microfinance Heretic*.[32] Sinclair claims that, as money flooded into the microfinance institutions, they became like the loan sharks they replaced.

At the center of his book is the Lift Above Poverty Organization (LAPO), a Nigerian microfinance institution (MFI) that charged deceptive and high interest rates, which was audited by the brother of the CEO, and that siphoned money into many already wealthy pockets. LAPO was for several years a major partner of "peer-to-peer" lender Kiva, until Kiva cut ties in 2010.[33] The episode highlighted a fact that was worrying some observers: "peer-to-peer" lending is not actually peer-to-peer; instead, Kiva works with intermediary partners that in turn make loans that were not, as many thought, interest-free.[34]

As microfinance grew in scale it has spawned a web of interacting operations. Microfinance funds invest in microfinance institutions that are rated by microfinance rating agencies, and that make loans through other partners. Principal-agent problems become pervasive and, without a regulatory framework, there were incentives everywhere that not only enabled corruption but, Sinclair argues, pushed participants to keep a lid on stories of corruption—to try to fix them quietly rather than to risk the reputation of the broader industry. Taking a charity and turning it into a bank is, as Sinclair says, a great way to build assets and then capitalize on them.

The Omidyar Network was a force behind the transformation of microfinance into a market-driven industry. More specifically, Omidyar was a big donor to Unitus, a microfinance fund which was embroiled in a 2010 scandal involving Indian MFI SKS, set up as a "social enterprise" by Vikram Akula, winner of the World Economic Forum's "Young Global Leader" award. There was controversy in 2010 when SKS went public, raising $350 million in its IPO, following which Unitus backed out of microfinance.[35] "In charity circles, people wondered about the motives of the Unitus board members, at least four of whom had invested in SKS Microfinance themselves and thus would reap profits from the I.P.O."[36] More controversy followed in 2012 when it was revealed that:

> More than 200 poor, debt-ridden residents of Andhra Pradesh killed themselves in late 2010, according to media reports compiled by the government of the south Indian state. The state blamed microfinance companies—which give small loans intended to lift up the very poor—for fueling a frenzy of overindebtedness and then pressuring borrowers so relentlessly that some took their own lives.[37]

The companies, including market leader SKS Microfinance, denied it. However, internal documents obtained by the Associated Press, as well as interviews with more than a dozen current and former employees, independent researchers, and videotaped testimony from the families of the dead, show top SKS officials had information implicating company employees in some of the suicides.

Sinclair concludes that "Frankly, I think the only means to rein in these groups is to formally regulate them."[38] He also notes that "Impact Investing," which is the Omidyar Network's current emphasis, has similar problems: "I do not believe there are panaceas for poverty reduction—it is hard work and requires a number of tools used wisely and collaboratively."[39] As sharing and commerce have conflicting goals, using markets to scale up social action can destroy the very thing that made it special in the first place.

Microfinance operates at the border between charity and business. The founders of GlobalGiving, an Omidyar-funded[40] "Internet-based service focused on making international philanthropy more efficient and high impact" have also experienced how uncomfortable this border can be and describe their experience in a chapter of a recent book. GlobalGiving set out to use technology and capital to scale up charitable giving, just as Omidyar had set out to use capital and commerce to scale up microfinance. Believing in Omidyar's vision of "market-based efforts that catalyze economic and social change," GlobalGiving adopted a "hybrid model" involving a parallel company (ManyFutures) that provided a technology platform to support its charitable work. But ManyFutures never made money, so the funding transfer ended up going from GlobalGiving to ManyFutures rather than the other way round, and controversy ensued. As with microfinance, the tantalizing idea that capital and sharing are natural complements went wrong.

EROSION

In addition to alienating the community, capital may erode the commons on which it seeks to capitalize. Alienation comes from a clash of motivations among those who tend the commons or build the community, but sometimes the actions of capital erode the commons itself.

Trading on the commons is a contradiction when the interests of those trading on the commons are incompatible with those who tend the commons. Cultural commons may not be scarce resources that can be used up, like fish stocks, but they can still be degraded by certain kinds of commercial activity.

Gentrification is an example. Harvey writes,

> A community group that struggles to maintain ethnic diversity in its neighborhood and protect against gentrification may suddenly find its property values (and taxes) rising as real estate agents market the "character" of their neighborhood to the wealthy as multicultural, street-lively, and diverse. By the time the market has done its destructive work, not only have the original residents been dispossessed of that common which they had created (often being forced out by rising rents and property taxes), but the common itself becomes so debased as to be unrecognizable.[41]

Capital demands uniqueness as it demands homogenization. For global capital to make money from a city's uniqueness it must be able to fit that city into its worldwide operations. Hotel chains need to be able to build their (preferably standardized) hotels; charter companies need airports; marketing departments need messages that are recognizable across the world. The more distinct a city is, the more there is pressure to squeeze it into the homogenizing templates of global tourism and global trade. The rise of Barcelona to prominence among the cities of Europe has been "in part based on its steady amassing of symbolic capital and its accumulation of marks of distinction"[42] from its architectural heritage to its Catalan history. These unique qualities are a source of rents for the tourist industry, which brings homogenizing commodification in its wake, so that "The later phases of waterfront development look like every other in the western world: the stupefying congestion of the traffic leads to pressures to put boulevards through parts of the old city, multinational stores replace local shops . . . and Barcelona loses some of its marks of distinction."[43]

Airbnb erodes the commons by gentrification of its biggest markets, which are the world's major tourist destinations. Harvey's comments about hotels apply to Airbnb also: Barcelona loses its marks of distinction as residents are driven out by the proliferation of rental apartments. Even when the company pays taxes on behalf of its hosts it refuses to give to the city governments the names and addresses of those hosts, making it almost impossible for democratically elected city governments to manage the impact of tourism on some their most valuable neighborhoods. Airbnb also demands homogenization: it operates in 34,000 cities and chafes at the inconsistency of regulations; but each city is different and the inconsistency, or variety, of regulations is a feature, not a bug.

The ideas of urbanist Jane Jacobs have been a prolific source of ideas about the value of commons in our daily lives, but technology organizations such as Code for America, who seek to combine Jacobs' ideas with software and work "to change the way cities work through technology and public service" are pursuing a contradiction. They seek to force the uniqueness of individual cities into standardized frameworks in order to build software that works across many cities. The very idea of a one-size-fits-all solution to bottom-up city innovation is flawed, because every application that is successfully implemented in a large number of cities erodes the uniqueness that makes the cities distinct. Beyond this, the notion of welcoming "civic startups" as somehow different from other money-making enterprises ignores the conflicting demands of sharing and money-making, and will lead to the erosion of civic commons.

There is a recursive nature to the commons. Collective management demands trust and the maintenance of reputation, but trust itself is a shared resource that requires tending, so informal management regimes are themselves commons (hence the language of "self-organization"). A common may be managed by a common. Just as a common resource is shared in a non-commercial fashion, so the tasks of monitoring and enforcing community norms are shared, in a non-commercial fashion, among those who have a stake in the health of the underlying commons.

Sharing Economy companies use software reputation systems to manage "marketplace reputation" as a common. The reputation system itself, with all the evaluations and ratings that populate it, becomes a valuable common resource. Individual ratings of hosts on Airbnb contribute to the non-commercial collective tending of trustworthy information about the standards of accommodations. As with any other commons, market driven motivations are anathema to fair ratings. If a host pays you to give a high rating you are automatically eroding the value of the reputation system, and a gamed reputation system undermines the value of the whole site, and the community of hosts and guests with it.

DISTORTION

As capital is attracted to a successful common, the nature of the common itself becomes a matter for dispute. Harvey gives as an example the reconstruction of an historical dock area of Liverpool: "The initial erasure of all mention of the slave trade in the reconstruction of Albert Dock in Liverpool generated protests on the part of the excluded population of Caribbean background."[44] Arguments that swirled around the reconstruction of Berlin after reunification had similar strands of exclusion and inclusion as competing camps sought to shape the culture and meaning of the city. "The Turkish population, many of whom are now Berlin-born, have suffered many indignities, and have largely been forced out from the city center. Their contribution to Berlin as a city is ignored." Another source of dispute was "the collection of international modernist architects brought in by the multinationals (largely in opposition to local architects) to dominate the Potsdamer Platz." Berliners were caught between the frying pan of a globalized aesthetic (the "Disneyfication of the Berlin Wall"[45]) and the fire of a "parochial nationalism," with the potential for "a virulent rejection of foreigners and immigrants."[46] Capital "must wade into the culture wars" if it is to pursue its desire for the monopoly rents that are at stake "through interventions in the field of culture, history, heritage, aesthetics, and meanings."[47]

Open Data is a digital commons that is being distorted. The Omidyar Network is deeply involved in the Open Government Partnership at the international level, in Code for America in the USA, and is the first major investor in the UK Open Data Institute. At Code for America, which describes itself as a new kind of public service, Omidyar has funded an Accelerator arm that invests in startups, conveniently augmenting the idea of "service" with the contradictory idea of "entrepreneurship" and blurring the boundaries between those who want to make money from government contracts and those who want to contribute to a stronger civic space. As described in Chapter 7, the Open Data initiative has been colonized by major financial interests: the major conferences have been sponsored by the big software companies. What was once an initiative focused on the release of data for civic use—a contribution to government transparency—becomes instead a handover of civic resources to the data brokers and insurance companies who can use it to optimize their business models.

In 2012 Change.org, a web site that hosts petitions and that made its name thanks to the actions of many progressive organizations that ran campaigns on the site, joined Couchsurfing as a ".org" site with a for-profit motive—a misleading presentation of the organization's nature. In May 2013 it took venture capital from the Omidyar Network and started allowing "corporate advertising, Republican Party solicitations, astroturf campaigns, anti-abortion or anti-union ads and other controversial sponsorships."[48] The change in mission was described by Lindsay Beyerstein in *In These Times* and Ryan Grim of the *Huffington Post*.[49,50] The Omidyar/ Change.org press release uses the standard language of social entrepreneurs' blandly inspirational and content-free. Every challenge is a problem, rather than a conflict.

> "Social enterprises can play an instrumental role in solving some of the world's biggest problems," Rattray said. "This funding will help us continue to expand our empowerment tools internationally while innovating on new products with the potential for disruptive social impact."

As a final example of the distortion of a commons, consider peer-to-peer lending company Lending Club. Set up in 2007, it is now the leader in a wave of innovations that Rachel Botsman describes with typical enthusiasm:

> [A] new generation of person-to-person and crowd-driven funding, lending, currency and investment services that will decentralize and democratize finance, money and banking . . . It is a subject I am passionate about. How can we shift banking back to being a trusted pillar of society? How can we create monetary systems where the real benefits flow back to individuals, not the big financial mega stores? How can we create financial access to underserved communities?[51]

The Lending Club model takes the idea of microfinanced, socially-driven investments, and applies it to personal loans. Here is *The Economist*'s take on how it works:

> Fans compare peer-to-peer lenders to other pioneers of the "sharing economy." Like Uber with cars and Airbnb with accommodation, the newcomers are making available a commodity they do not provide themselves: in this case, money. Instead of a bank intermediating between savers and borrowers, the two parties deal with each other directly. The platforms do the credit-scoring and make a profit from arrangement fees, not from the spread between lending and deposit rates.[52]

Like other areas of the Sharing Economy, Lending Club seeks to appeal to both heart and wallet. The *New York Times* describes its "blend of altruism and yield" this way:

> By cutting banks out of the process, borrowers typically got a lower interest rate than they would have paid on a credit card or a loan without collateral. And individual lenders earned higher returns—averaging in the high single

digits—than they would have received by parking their money in a savings account or a certificate of deposit.[53]

Like other areas of the Sharing Economy, peer-to-peer lending is booming. *The Economist* continues:

> The sector has grown rapidly: the five biggest platforms for consumer lending—Lending Club, Prosper and SoFi, all based in San Francisco, and Zopa and RateSetter in London—have so far issued nearly 1m loans between them and are generating more at the rate of well over $10 billion a year . . . Those loans are still dwarfed by the $3 trillion of consumer debt outstanding in America alone. But the sector is doubling its lending roughly every nine months, and almost everyone expects it to go on growing rapidly.

If it all sounds too good to be true, that's because it is. By qualifying loan applicants, Lending Club is managing a commons resource for lenders. Once it became clear that Lending Club was a source of potential borrowers, big financial firms realized they could take advantage of this commons. Hedge funds were the first institutions to join the opportunity and now "big financial firms, not small investors, dominate lending on the two platforms [Lending Club and its competitor Prosper]."[54] While peer-to-peer loans were primarily "fractional," in that several small lenders would combine to fund a loan, by March 2015 "65% of the more than $3 billion loans on the two platforms [Prosper and Lending Club] came from investors snatching up whole loans, which are almost always made by institutional investors rather than individuals."[55]

Lending Club's evolution is similar to that of eBay, discussed in Chapter 7. Starting as a marketplace for individuals, eBay has ended up as another way for major chains to reach customers. Both companies adopted a blockbuster strategy, partnering with big organizations at the expense of their original model.

High profile partnerships, such as Lending Club's April 2015 partnership with Citigroup to make $150 million in loans available, emphasize how much the so-called disrupter has come to feel at home among the establishment, and how completely the promise of avoiding the banking system has morphed into just another wing of that system.[56] Peer-to-peer lending marketplaces have transformed themselves into "loan originators and underwriters for traditional banks,"[57] and left any notion of financial "democratization" far behind. Recently, the peer-to-peer lending companies have rebranded themselves as "marketplace lending" companies.

The major institutions now take up not only the majority of the loans, but they take the best ones. When investing is done by computers, those with the best computers get to make the best loans, so the big institutions take the pick of the crop, leaving the original Lending Club audience of individual investors with the bottom of the barrel.

Some of Wall Street's biggest names have joined the marketplace lenders as board members and investors, and investment banks vied to manage Lending Club's initial public offering in December 2014.[58]

When peer-to-peer lending advocate Jonathan McMillan attended the industry conference LendIt 2015 he found that "The initial idea of connecting borrowers and lenders directly has been abandoned. Now, hedge-funds, asset managers and banks are using marketplace lending as a supplier of loans in their chase for yield . . . . Asset managers have started to securitize marketplace loans into asset-backed securities, and hedge-funds use large amounts of borrowed money to leverage their investments. Some investors are already talking about the need to create credit default swaps for marketplace loans."[59]

■

The problems of alienation, erosion, and distortion all sharpen as the scale of financial involvement grows. Sharing Economy advocates who seek to recapture the egalitarian, sustainable, and community focus that inspired many to join the movement can do so only by avoiding the temptations of believing in a technological fix for society, powered by venture capital and free markets. Instead of scaling up efforts around sharing, the involvement of capital only leads to broken promises.

9. What's Yours is Mine

In a few short years the Sharing Economy has gone from the generosity of "what's mine is yours" to the self interest of "what's yours is mine", as the non-commercial values invoked by the phrase "sharing economy" have been left behind or reduced to public relations exercises.

The main impulse that drove the writing of this book was a sense of betrayal: that what started as an appeal to community, person-to-person connections, sustainability, and sharing, has become the playground of billionaires, Wall Street, and venture capitalists extending their free-market values ever further into our personal lives. The promise of a more personal alternative to a corporate world is instead driving a harsher form of capitalism: deregulation, new forms of entitled consumerism, and a new world of precarious work. There is a lot of talk of democratization and networks, but what's happened instead is a separation of risk (spread among the service providers and customers) from reward, which accrues to the platform owners. Despite the claims of ecological sustainability embodied in ideas like "access over ownership" and the re-use of excess capacity, the on-demand sector is instead encouraging a new form of privileged consumption: "lifestyle as a service."

What is particularly sad is that many well-intentioned people, who hold a misplaced faith in the intrinsic abilities of the Internet to promote egalitarian community and trust, have unwittingly aided and abetted this accumulation of private fortune, and the construction of new and exploitative forms of employment.

TRENDS

The tension between capital and commons in the Sharing Economy, set out in Chapter 8, has stretched to breaking point as the money pouring into the sector turned from a trickle to a flood.

Take Airbnb, which for all its faults maintains an aura of the original ideas of sharing. While the ridesharing and on-demand companies may be creating precarious forms of work, Airbnb hosts are not, in general, in the same category. And there is a role for a low-intensity form of travel in which people share accommodations and swap homes. The travelers' urge to engage in cheap, personal forms of travel outside the mainstream have taken different forms at different times: Youth Hostelling, informal sharing of holiday homes, my childhood holidays with Miss Whitaker, and Couchsurfing are all examples of this impulse. But Airbnb's mandate is to take these impulses and scale them up through its platform: in taking this path, Airbnb risks eroding the culture from which it has grown.

Airbnb keeps up its talk of community, but it continues to promote the acquisitive instincts of its hosts. Despite the sepia-tinted photos on the Airbnb web site, the company's business is no longer built on strangers sharing home cooking around a dining table; it is built on "whole home" rentals in which the host and guest may never meet (perhaps even major hotel chains) as the company follows its path of growth. At the same time, Airbnb insists that these hosts do not need the regulation (and costs) that go with professionalism.

The Toronto neighborhood of Kensington highlights the contradictions of Airbnb. Here is how the Globe and Mail describes it:

> In Toronto, Kensington stands out as a utopian, bohemian, urban space. That's why it features prominently in tourism marketing. That's why a film, television or video shoot is there every day, trying to capture the cultural diversity to which Toronto and Canada usually aspire. [1]

As Airbnb builds the aura of Kensington Market into its marketing materials, a local community group reports "complaints from at least 30 tenants about landlords using questionable tactics to bully renters out of their homes, often converting the apartments into short-term rental units."

Local houses for sale are advertised as "Airbnb-ready". And activist group Fairbnb (for whom I have supplied data) claims:

> Airbnb has 131 active listings in Kensington. On Craigslist, 12 apartments are for rent in the area. Fairbnb's analysis found 68 Airbnb units are owned by 21 hosts, all of whom have multiple listings within or near the neighborhood. [2]

In a recent initiative, the company has announced its intention to move into the lucrative world of business travel, but only hosts offering "entire homes" will be allowed to participate, and these hosts are encouraged to offer an increased level of professionalism. We can expect to see more professionalism, less personal contact, and to see Airbnb partnering with other travel giants

The picture of small-scale, intimate exchanges is a key to the environmental sustainability claims of Sharing Economy companies, but such claims increasingly read as the selective truths of company marketing departments. Airbnb trumpets its environmental impact by comparing the energy use of Airbnb travelers to the impact of the same number of people staying in hotels, but when it comes to economic impact, it compares its impact to the same number of people staying at home. Uber and Lyft compare their environmental impact to people driving private cars rather than to people riding buses or taking the subway. They claim that their relatively small car-pooling operations demonstrate their commitment to the environment, but avoid talking about their impact on congestion and average driving speed in New York City.[3]

There are many sectors of the Sharing Economy that I have not covered in detail, because they have remained relatively small to date, and increasingly look like they will remain so. The community nature of these has also been exaggerated. The leading player in the pet services world, DogVacay, is mentioned routinely in Sharing Economy articles, and as of early 2017 had signed up 60,000 sitters. The site may look to build a community feel but researcher Giana Eckhardt, building on her experience researching Zipcar (see Chapter 4) suggests that its success is more likely to rely on another mechanism for establishing trust, saying that "In the sharing economy, consumers look toward these companies to provide the type of big-brother surveillance that is needed to overcome trust issues, and this effect is amplified when a living creature is involved."[4]

Social dining is a sector that may yet break out. Feastly and VizEat and EatWith and the other twenty or so startups in this space invite people to dine in homes, connect with hosts, share stories, and enjoy homemade cuisine, portraying their exchanges as part of the informal private sphere. And up to a point, that's appropriate: there has always been a place for food as a commons-based sharing experience, as a way to meet new people; there is a long history of dining clubs organized within social circles. As a low-intensity, largely uncommercial activity (perhaps like the five million or so Americans that take part in book clubs) it does not need regulation.

Where it will go wrong is if one of these companies succeeds in taking it global, guided by venture capitalists with previous experience, building a big business in the social dining sector by taking a fee for each meal and by encouraging hosts to see it as a money-making opportunity. The history of successful Sharing Economy companies tells us how that is likely to go. A breakout company in the sector is likely to have a business model that positions the meals as private exchanges, claiming that the meals arranged through their platform have no need for health and safety inspectors, and should not have to charge sales tax. At the same time, it will encourage vendors to build businesses on the platform, and look to take a slice of each business. It may even adopt a blockbuster strategy and look for big partners to team up with. And to the extent that they become successful they will have undermined the premise of their venture. Intimacy scaled up is no longer intimacy.

■

Uber has continued its meteoric rise during 2015 and 2016, and together with Airbnb its growth has been taken as a demonstration of the superiority of this emerging form of company, in which employees are replaced by contractors and managers are replaced by reputation systems. Tim O'Reilly writes that this demonstrates "the way that networks trump traditional forms of corporate organization,"[5] and he generally welcomes the inevitable rise of these technology-driven firms. But the allure of the seamless app experience covers a multitude of less savory but no less important behind-the-scenes factors in driving the success of these businesses. Technology does bring new efficiencies, but it also serves as an opportunity to build new business models that externalize costs, by restructuring regulations that balance the interests of companies and the communities in which they live, or that balance the interests of companies and service providers.

Airbnb's relentless promotion of tourism over every other aspect of a city's well-being shows that its commitment to cities and to communities stops as soon as its bank account is challenged. While the company is prepared to make some compromises with local governments, such as collecting hospitality taxes, one thing it steadfastly refuses to do is to share its list of hosts with local government. In this way, Airbnb hobbles any attempt to limit the density of Airbnb rentals in popular districts or to avoid the gentrification that accompanies a sudden influx of tourists, and it leads the company into repeated conflicts with city governments In places such as Barcelona and Amsterdam, where tourism is a mixed blessing. It also hobbles realistic investigations of the company's impact on affordable housing, community zoning rules. Airbnb makes its money by imposing a whole series of costs on the communities in which it operates.

Uber's ability to provide value to its consumers comes not only from its technology but also, as we saw in Chapter 4, from its ability to externalize costs. Beyond this, the company keeps costs down by running at a loss in order to foster growth. It's a common thread throughout the Sharing Economy.

Section 230 of the Communications Decency Act says that "No provider or user of an interactive computer service shall be treated as the publisher or speaker of any information provided by another information content provider."[6] The law means that bloggers are not legally responsible for what commenters write on their site, that YouTube is not legally responsible for videos that users upload, Facebook is not responsible for what its users post, and so on. But the law has repeatedly been interpreted broadly, extending protection to all kinds of online platforms,[7] and Sharing Economy companies have argued that the law means that they are not responsible for the actions of their service providers, or for what goes on between service providers and customers. Presenting themselves as marketplaces, as technology companies, and not as service providers, allows the claim that Section 230 applies to them. Taxi companies may be responsible for taxi rides, but if you're a ridesharing provider you don't want that expense; hotels and B&Bs may be responsible for what happens to their guests, but if you're Airbnb you don't want that kind of liability.

It may seem far-fetched that a company like Uber, which is now experimenting with taking roughly 30% of the fare for each ride and which includes a $1 "safety fee" in its price, has no responsibility when things go wrong on that ride, and when Uber was designated as a Transportation Network Company in California, the question was left open.[8] But for Sharing Economy companies Section 230 is a good start until courts show otherwise. Legislators such as New York State Senator Liz Krueger are frustrated by the law. Speaking about Airbnb she said:

> We have not been able to find a way as a state government
> to say, "Airbnb, we know you're breaking laws, and we're
> going to stop you." So, frankly, these companies look at
> me and go, "You're a fly on the wall. We don't care. You
> can't do anything to us. Yes, you can go after the people
> who illegally rent out the apartments. You can go after the
> people who illegally rent as tourists. But us, the ones who
> as their business model are actively encouraging and sup-
> porting illegal activity—there's nothing you can do to us."[9]

Successful Sharing Economy companies avoid the expense of ensuring safety. They do state publicly their commitment to safety and make some gestures in that direction—Airbnb chose to give free smoke alarms to hosts, Uber claims to have a safety inspection on its vehicles—but they also do what they can to avoid municipal rules such as fire inspections for bed & breakfasts, and they make sure they are not on the hook if things go wrong.

Successful Sharing Economy companies also avoid the expense of providing universal access provisions. In Chapter 4 we saw Uber and Lyft claim that access for the disabled is not their problem; suggestions that Airbnb's platform inadvertently enables the propagation of racial profiling have met with the same response.

Successful Sharing Economy companies avoid the expense of wages by keeping their service providers off the payroll, and classifying them instead as independent contractors, often called "1099 workers" after the

US tax form they have to fill in. As part of this move, the companies avoid paying benefits, avoid paying for equipment, avoid paying for idle time and travel time, avoid insuring against injury, and avoid any pension obligations.

More than a decade ago, Amazon successfully avoided being responsible for sales tax in most states for many years, giving it a natural price advantage over "brick and mortar" stores, and the major Internet companies such as Google and Apple have become expert at routing business through low-tax subsidiaries in Ireland or Luxembourg to minimize their tax burdens.

Successful Sharing Economy companies have learned from these efforts. Taxi passengers in Toronto pay sales tax to the province of Ontario, the taxi driver pays tax on their earnings, and the taxi company (if there is one) also pays taxes. Uber passengers pay their fee to Uber BV, an Uber subsidiary in the Netherlands, so that Uber pays no taxes. Uber also leaves the question of taxes on the driver's income to the drivers, knowing full well that many cash-strapped drivers will avoid paying taxes if possible. Airbnb makes claims about its willingness to pay tourist taxes on behalf of its hosts when needed, and to encourage its hosts to register with the city if required, but example after example (see Chapter 3) shows that they have done so in a self-interested way that continues to leave cities frustrated.

Successful Sharing Economy companies have learned how to minimize insurance costs. Uber and Lyft started by arguing that no commercial insurance was necessary for private rides, and ever since have made efforts to minimize the coverage they provide in the face of demands from cities. Pushing insurance requirements onto drivers without demanding verification, knowing that many will be tempted to avoid the expense of full insurance, is one path. In many locations, for example, gaps persist for when drivers are using the app but are not driving customers.

Successful Sharing Economy companies have not been able to shirk all these responsibilities, but they have taken an approach inspired by Peter Thiel, an investor in several of the leading players. Foreseeing problems with financial regulations, Thiel's company PayPal pioneered an aggressive approach to the problem: raise a boatload of money, expand quickly, and present lawmakers with a fait accompli. Here is the future, deal with it.

Sharing Economy companies' price advantage, the reason for so much investor interest in the sector, and the reason for the correspondingly massive market valuations of the leading players, is not just a product of the efficiencies of their technology, it's also a product of their ability to circumvent or change regulations. It's why Uber and Airbnb have invested heavily in high-profile and well-connected lobbyists at the national level, and make intensive lobbying efforts in key cities. Here is Bloomberg's Karen Weise on Uber's impressive lobbying efforts in Portland:

> Over the past year, Uber built one of the largest and most successful lobbying forces in the country, with a presence in almost every statehouse. It has 250 lobbyists and 29 lobbying firms registered in capitols around the nation, at least a third more than Wal-Mart Stores. That doesn't count municipal lobbyists. In Portland, the 28th-largest city in the U.S., 10 people would ultimately register to lobby on Uber's behalf. They'd become a constant force in City Hall. City officials say they'd never seen anything on this scale.[10]

Tim O'Reilly writes that "The discussion around companies like Uber and Airbnb is too narrow. The issue isn't just employment, but a huge economic shift led by software and connectedness." But to see the issue as one of software and connectedness is also too narrow: it's also about power, money, and influence.

∎

The language of peer-to-peer trust, so prominent in many stories, is now falling to one side. Reputation systems are a front for companies being able to "deactivate" users and to impose their own discipline: Airbnb ejects hosts from its platform when it is politically expedient (as recently happened in Los Angeles[11]), and Uber fires drivers at executives' whim.

The Sharing Economy has become an opportunity to take decision-making powers out of the reach of elected bodies and place them in new extravagantly glass-walled but still opaque San Francisco boardrooms. Expensive lobbyists are arguing to officials in Washington that the new companies can regulate the behavior of their service providers better than governments, that algorithms provide better guarantees than old-fashioned rules, and that the free market will ensure that the algorithmically enhanced companies will exert their influence in responsible and socially-beneficial ways.

The effectiveness of reputation systems and algorithmic ratings systems in providing a solid basis for trust is exaggerated in the Sharing Economy world.

Sites that rely on algorithmic ratings have run into problems of fairness and of proper process, for example marketplace lending company Lending Club. By becoming a new way to qualify potential borrowers, the marketplace lending companies are entering into the area of credit scoring. Data scientist Cathy O'Neil argues that one reason Lending Club and others can bring such value to big financial institutions is that they provide a way to bypass credit scoring regulations, such as the Federal Trade Commission's Equal Credit Opportunities Act (ECOA) that prohibits credit discrimination on the basis of race, color, religion and other factors and the Fair Credit Reporting Act (FCRA). In their early days Lending Club and other marketplace lending companies argued that they do not provide loans, just as Uber does not provide rides, Handy does not provide cleaning services, and Airbnb does not provide accommodation. As a result, their business model fell into a regulatory gap.[12] Since then, and particularly since a significant rate of defaults in 2008, the Securities and Exchange Commission has stepped in to require a little more accountability, but important parts of its model remain outside the scope of practical regulation.

Just as Airbnb has a search algorithm that implicitly ranks hosts, and just as Uber uses its detailed data on everyone on its platform to govern the behavior of its drivers, so Lending Club uses a proprietary mathematical model to score potential borrowers, and it rejects about 90% of applicants.[13] The input includes data purchased from data brokers such as Acxiom or Experian; early stage models in the peer-to-peer lending world looked at social media profiles; other factors such as web browsing habits, employment histories: anything they can get their hands on. But this appetite for data can easily (and perhaps inadvertently) run into the ECOA and FCRA provisions. Indicators that align with race and other factors for discrimination can be used, and those who are refused loans have no way of finding out the reason for their denial or appealing a Lending Club decision: the algorithm becomes a black box into which neither regulators nor those who are assessed and rated by it can see.[14]

PUSHING BACK

Faced with the influence and ambition of the Sharing Economy, an increasing number of groups have found their voices and are pushing back. In Europe, where Airbnb makes the majority of its revenue and where Uber is pushing to grow, there were two significant developments in June 2015 alone. The most dramatic was the taxi drivers' protests in France: Uber's UberPOP service (the equivalent of its UberX service in North America) was declared illegal in 2014, but Uber instructed its drivers to keep operating while it appealed the ruling. Taxi drivers' frustrated confrontations with riot police pushed the Paris government to clamp down on the service.[15] Uber has followed the same pattern in other countries: in August it stated that it would support drivers fined by police in Costa Rica, an act that has an unpleasant resonance in a part of the world where American companies have taken active part in challenging and even overthrowing local governments.[16]

Meanwhile Barcelona elected a new mayor, radical activist Ada Colau who stood as a leader of an anti-eviction group called Mortgage Victims' Platform. One of the issues of her campaign is tourism: the annual number of tourists now outnumbers the number of residents by four times, and "persistent issues with noise, illegal tourist flats and rising real estate prices have led weary residents to draw battle lines in recent years against the seemingly never-ending tide of camera-toting, beer-swilling visitors."[17] Colau vowed to stop Barcelona "ending up like Venice," a city where locals have been pushed out by tourists. In this environment, Airbnb's bland assurances of the opportunity to "live like a local," its continued reminders of the money that it brings to the city, and its complete refusal to consider any civic role in shaping the supply of tourist apartments sounds an off note.

In the US too, there has been resistance to Sharing Economy incursions.

The independent contractor status of Uber and the on-demand cleaning services have drawn legal challenges. Chapter 5 described how the issue affected cleaning services Homejoy and Handy, but let's take a broader look. In Canada, if cleaners were on the payroll then the company would have to pay taxes, employment insurance contributions, and Canada Pension Plan contributions: by classifying them as independent contractors all these onerous costs are eliminated. Kevin Hipkins of Molly Maid, an Ontario cleaning services company with about 1,200 employees, claims that "If we could wave a magic wand, we could bring down our costs by about 30%, and avoid all this messy tax stuff. Taxation is a moral responsibility, I think we are creating a culture of tax cheats."[18]

The way Sharing Economy platforms work, paying taxes is left to the cleaners, and of course there is a temptation for low-paid service workers to postpone or minimize the tax being paid. Services such as cleaning have long been part of the informal economy, done for cash. What's different now is that people are building billion dollar businesses on this informal model. Molly Maid's Hipkins believes "there's a difference when it's a small under-the-table arrangement between a client and individual cleaner, versus a large US company, with millions in market capitalization."

In October 2014, two former Handy cleaners took the company to court, Reporter Kevin Montgomery writes: "The suit alleges that the company refuses workers minimum wages, paid breaks, overtime pay, and withholds tips, amongst other violations. Workers also claim the startup, which has raised $45.7 million in funding, imposes onerous demands on workers, including instructing them on "how to use the bathroom."[19]

Sharing Economy platforms have grown more quickly than would otherwise be possible, because they claim that their service providers are not employees. They can offer cheaper services because they don't need to provide benefits, or pay them when there is no work to be done. But there is a challenge for the platforms: despite claiming that they do not provide cleaning services, Handy wants to establish a successful brand, and that means they have to control what they (don't) deliver. The IRS rules have a twenty-point test for whether a worker is an employee, but the gist of it is that:

> The general rule is that an individual is an independent contractor if you, the person for whom the services are performed, have the right to control or direct only the result of the work and not the means and methods of accomplishing the result.

Ellen Huet followed the case, which is not yet settled, and writes:

> Contractors, however, come with specific limitations.
> You can't tell contractors how to do their job—not what
> to wear, how much to charge, what to say to customers,
> what materials to use. For startups that want to ensure
> a smooth, branded customer experience, that's a serious
> hindrance.[20]

It's not an argument that is unique to Sharing Economy companies. After a long series of court cases, a federal appeals court in Oakland found that FedEx misclassified its drivers from 2000 to 2007 as independent contractors, a decision leading to a $228 million payout.[21] Also in California, short-haul truck drivers who worked for a logistics company got a $2.2 million settlement when they were found to be employees rather than independent contractors.[22]

Boston lawyer Shannon Liss-Riordan has led the charge around employment status in the Sharing Economy. In her case against Uber she pointed to the strict guidelines that Uber drivers must follow if they want to stay on the platform, such as taking 90% of assignments and keeping a customer rating above a certain mark, and to the ability of Uber to dismiss ("deactivate") drivers. "Just because your services are dispatched through a smartphone doesn't make you a technology company . . . You're a car service, and you have the responsibilities of being an employer of the people driving the cars."[23] Liss-Riordan has also taken up cases against Lyft, Handy, Homejoy, and Instacart.

In June 2015, the California Labor Commissioner's Office ordered Uber to reimburse one of its drivers, Barbara Ann Berwick, just over $4,000 in costs, deciding that Berwick was an employee of the company.[24] The company will appeal the ruling, but it is a positive sign for Liss-Riordan's cases against Uber and Lyft, which, as of May 2015, are headed to a jury trial. The employment status argument will no doubt drag on for a long time, and may well end up in a gray area where Sharing Economy workers will fall into a number of buckets, depending on hours worked and exclusivity.

Being an employee is not a simple either-or status: employment is a bundle of rights and responsibilities, and there is a spectrum of employment relationships in active use throughout the economy. According to law professor Sanjukta Paul, we can think about these rights without needing to directly address the thorny question of employment status. Her particular example is about Uber drivers' right to bargain with their employer. Uber provides the functions of a "hiring hall", which "coordinate[s] short-term employment in industries where jobs are by nature seasonal, fluctuating, or short-term, and where employers have a need to find workers for jobs on short-notice".[25] Uber claims that the riders are employers, and that their "driver-partners" are providing the work. But, as Paul points out, antitrust law forbids sellers of a commodity from coordinating to fix a price; if independent drivers set a common price (as Uber does), that would be illegal. The fact that Uber has been able to carry out this price coordination across supposedly independent drivers shows that "Uber is operating a virtual, for-profit hiring hall, and it is doing so on terms that would not be allowed to workers themselves."

Paul suggests that this problem can be resolved by permitting Uber drivers to 'engage in collective action in their bargains with the firm that sets prices in the services they perform". That is, Uber drivers should have collective bargaining rights regardless of their status as employees.

Airbnb has met opposition on several fronts. A high-profile confrontation in New York led to the formation of Share Better, a coalition of tenants' groups, neighborhood associations, affordable housing advocates, elected officials, and hotel workers who have banded together to challenge the impact of Airbnb on the city, and the issue has reached a high profile within the city council. A similar group, ShareBetter SF, has set up in San Francisco, and in Los Angeles the influential community and anti-poverty advocacy group LAANE has adopted the short-term rental issue in its housing actions; there are similar coalitions forming elsewhere.

■

Along with this pushback, social scientists and legal scholars have been looking at the questions raised by the Sharing Economy.

In one of the first legal articles on the subject, Vanessa Katz identified the main challenge to regulating Sharing Economy platforms as the three-party nature of transactions, in which customers buy services (at least formally) from service providers, through a platform that takes a more or less active role in the transaction.[26] Who, in such a scenario, bears what responsibility? Katz looks to the principle of "least cost avoider" to apportion responsibility: it serves the social good if the responsibility is given to "the party who can adopt precautions against a given risk at the lowest cost". In many cases, this is the platform. Even though in some cases these platforms may be (or may claim to be) intermediaries in a transaction—remember those license agreement claims such as "Uber is not a provider of transportation services"—they may still bear indirect liability. The platform companies have often pointed to Section 230 of the CDA to disclaim liability (see above), but Katz argues that the more a platform is involved in the transaction, the more liability it should take on. She identifies the Digital Millennium Copyright Act, the law that requires Google to take copyright-violating videos off YouTube when a copyright holder lodges a complaint, as one model, and for platforms even more involved in the service she suggests an active "duty to monitor" the service provided. This kind of spectrum is increasingly being adopted by cities as they push back against platform companies. Katz also points out that Sharing Economy companies raise new risks: privacy and data-handling, and the fairness of reputation systems. The increasing publicity around race-based discrimination taking place through the platforms and their rating systems has made these questions more relevant than ever.

In an article that positions Uber and Airbnb as "the new public accomodations", Aaron Belzer and Nancy Leong look at one specific challenge on Katz's list: the responsibility to provide non-discriminatory services. Providers of public accommodations, like hotels, restaurants, and taxi services, are not permitted to discriminate on the grounds of attributes such as race or religion. But if Sharing Economy platforms maintain they are not the providers, what happens to these "public accommodation" protections?

Belzer and Leong argue that Sharing Economy platforms meet the requirements to be classed as providers of public accommodations and that their internet roots do not provide an escape clause:

> Although internet platforms are integral to their operation, SEBs (Sharing Economy Businesses) are nonetheless intimately linked to physical places that function like public accommodations in the traditional economy. A SEB's online platform is the only way of accessing its physical aspects—that is, Airbnb's website is the only way of gaining

access to a physical rental, and Uber's app is the only way of summoning a physical car. . . For our purposes, it is unnecessary to determine whether a website *must* have a link to something in the physical world: SEB platforms do, and that is sufficient to establish that they are public accommodations.[27]

Focusing again on the American case, Belzer and Leong carry on to argue that Title II of the 1964 Civil Rights Act, which addressed discrimination in commerce, should apply to lodging platforms such as Airbnb and delivery companies such as Instacart, just as they apply to more "physical" businesses. They also argue for transparency by Sharing Economy platforms about their business as a way of monitoring compliance.[28]

Belzer and Leong's assertion that platforms should be held accountable is welcome. Too many observers have been distracted by the typical terms and conditions of Sharing Economy platforms. In an October 28, 2016 employment tribunal in London, Judge A.M. Snelson said what should be obvious when discussing Uber and its drivers:[29]

The notion that Uber in London is a mosaic of 30,000 small businesses linked by a common "platform" is to our minds faintly ridiculous. In each case, the "business" consists of a man [sic] with a car seeking to make a living by driving it. (Paragraph 90)

And also:

Any organization (a) running an enterprise at the heart of which is the function of carrying people in motor cars from where they are to where they want to be… but (c) requiring drivers and passengers to agree, as a matter of contract, that it does not provide transportation services, … merits, we think, a degree of skepticism. (Paragraph 87)

Ryan Calo and Alex Rosenblat address Katz's "new risks" in a working paper called "The Taking Economy: Uber, Information, and Power", discussed in Chapter 4.[30] Their concern is that the detailed and extensive data that Uber has collected about the behavior of its drivers and customers, about the details of each ride, give the company many opportunities to manipulate the market. Following the revelations of early 2017 about Uber's Greyball program (to deceive city regulators) and Hell program (to track Lyft drivers) such concerns are anything but far-fetched. Like Belzer and Leong, Calo and Rosenblat emphasize that transparency on the part of Sharing Economy platforms, which the platform owners so stoutly and consistently resist, is an important first step to keeping them in line.

As to regulating Uber, the authors emphasize the concept of fiduciary duty. Some commercial relationships place the customer in a vulnerable position relative to a service provider, as with a bank, financial advisor, or medical practitioner. In these cases the service provider is bound to act in their customer's interest: to act as a fiduciary. The law around fiduciaries is well developed, and extending the concept to Sharing Economy platforms may provide a legal lever to rein in some of the excesses of their behavior.

■

The changes brought on by the rapid growth and focus of the Sharing Economy giants has led even supportive organizations to wonder about its future. OuiShare is a French-based global community built around ideas of collaboration, and with a strong technological focus. It was one of the leading organizations promoting the Sharing Economy in its early years, but the theme for its 2015 conference was "Lost in Transition?" Neal Gorenflo of non-profit Shareable writes that the theme "brought the elephant in everybody's room to the fore—the gaping contradiction between the utopian possibilities and the hyper-capitalist realities of the sharing economy."[31]

If the newly-skeptical OuiShare attendees are going to find a way to convert the Sharing Economy into something useful, something that actually delivers on the promise of community and human-scale exchange, it must leave aside its identification with technology. There are few signs that it will do so; Gorenflo reports that the "blockchain" technology underlying Bitcoin is the new thing: "Everybody was talking about the blockchain from keynotes to side conversations." To look for a technical fix, a designed-in mechanism for solving social problems, will only end up going down the same path. Bitcoin itself has already cycled through the familiar trajectory of rebellious alternative, promising a currency independent of the state, through to a venture-capital-funded investment vehicle in which 0.1% of the participants own 50% of the coins.

The debate needs to move away from its exclusive focus on technology companies. It needs to recognize that there are no easy fixes for complex social problems and even less so for the real conflicts and injustices that permeate society. The Sharing Economy's complete neglect of the history of collaborative and co-operative movements is one of the reasons it has been so easy for business to co-opt.

People who support the ideas behind sharing can do better working with cities than allying with venture capitalists. Cities have been innovative in many non-commercial sharing initiatives. In transit there are the car-sharing and widely-imitated bike-sharing initiatives of Paris; there are new ideas around public transit; new initiatives around green taxi services. One of the benefits of city-level initiatives is that citizens can take the best from other places and lobby for adoption in their home town, so that cities can learn from each other.

Evgeny Morozov calls the idea that technology provides a fix for complex social problems "solutionism," and it is unfortunately endemic among those who promote the Sharing Economy.[32] What is called for is a little modesty on the part of those who identify with new technologies. It's not a question of whether technology is good or bad, but that technology is not an answer to complex social questions. If technologists were prepared to accept that technology can play a helpful but secondary role in social movements, we might get somewhere. But the naiveté of twenty-six-year old CEOs, the hubris of their venture capital advisers, and the narrowness of vision of the hacktivists, still fighting the battle of the 1990s and promoting open source, do not bode well.

Bibliography

Airbnb. "Airbnb Economic Impact." *The Airbnb Blog - Belong Anywhere*. Accessed May 9, 2015. http://blog.airbnb.com/economic-impact-airbnb/.

——. "Airbnb's Economic Impact on New York City," *The Airbnb Blog - Belong Anywhere*. Accessed May 9, 2015. http://blog.airbnb.com/airbnbs-economic-impact-nyc-community/.

——. "Building Trust with a New Review System," July 10, 2014. http://blog.airbnb.com/building-trust-new-review-system/.

——. "One Way Forward: After the Crash, Keeping the Roof Overhead, Airbnb Stories." *Airbnb*. Accessed May 9, 2015. https://www.airbnb.com/stories/new-york/one-way-forward.

——. "Organizing in 100 Cities: The Airbnb Host Movement." *Airbnb Citizen: San Francisco*, November 5, 2015. https://san-francisco.airbnbcitizen.com/organizing-in-100-cities-the-airbnb-host-movement/.

——. "Sandy's Impact: Opening Doors in a Time of Need, Airbnb Stories." *Airbnb*. Accessed May 9, 2015. https://www.airbnb.com/stories/new-york/sandys-impact.

"Airbnb in the City." The Office of New York State Attorney General Eric T. Schneiderman, October 16, 2014. http://www.ag.ny.gov/pdfs/Airbnb%20report.pdf.

"Alex." "Happy New Year!" *Uber Global*, December 30, 2013. http://newsroom.uber.com/2013/12/happy-new-year/.

Anderson, Chris. *The Long Tail: Why the Future of Business Is Selling Less of More*. New York, New York: Hyperion, 2006.

"Andrew." "Three Septembers of uberX in New York City." *Uber Company Blog*, October 29, 2014. http://blog.uber.com/nyc-three-septembers-uberX.

——. "What Does a Typical New York uberX Partner Earn in a Week?" *Uber Company Blog*, December 1, 2014. http://blog.uber.com/how-much-nyc-uberX-partner-drivers-earn-per-week.

Asay, Matt. "For 50 Percent of Developers, Open Source Is a 9-to-5 Job," September 2, 2014. http://www.techrepublic.com/article/for-50-percent-of-developers-open-source-is-a-9-to-5-job/.

——. "The Effects of Commercialization on Open-Source Communities," March 4, 2008. http://www.cnet.com/news/the-effects-of-commercialization-on-open-source-communities.

Associated Press. "SKS Under Spotlight in Suicides." *Wall Street Journal*, February 24, 2012, sec. World News. http://www.wsj.com/articles/SB10001424052970203918304577242602296683134.

Baker, Dean. "Ubernomics." *CEPR "Beat the Press" blog*, January 23, 2015. http://www.cepr.net/blogs/beat-the-press/ubernomics.

Baker, Michael B. "Barclays: Airbnb Usage To Surpass Hotel Cos., But Not For Business Travel." *Business Travel News*, January 16, 2015. http://www.businesstravelnews.com/Hotel-News-Barclays-Airbnb-Usage-To-Surpass-Hotel-Cos-But-Not-For-Business-Travel.

Baker, Vicky. "Not-for-Profit Couchsurfing Becomes a Company (with a Conscience)." *The Guardian*, August 26, 2011. http://www.theguardian.com/travel/2011/aug/26/couchsurfing-investment-budget-travel.

Banjo, Shelly. "Citgroup Has Finally Thrown Its Lot in with Online Lending." *Quartz*, April 14, 2015. http://qz.com/383160/citgroup-has-finally-thrown-its-lot-in-with-online-lending/.

———. "Wall Street Is Hogging the Peer-to-Peer Lending Market." *Quartz*, March 4, 2015. http://qz.com/355848/wall-street-is-hogging-the-peer-to-peer-lending-market/.

Barbrook, Richard, and Andy Cameron. "The Californian Ideology." *Mute*, August 1995. http://www.imaginaryfutures.net/2007/04/17/the-californian-ideology-2/.

Bardhi, Fleura, and Giana M. Eckhardt. "Access-Based Consumption: The Case of Car Sharing." *Journal of Consumer Research* 39 (December 2012): 881–898.

Bates, Jo. "'This Is What Modern Deregulation Looks Like': Co-Optation and Contestation in the Shaping of the UK's Open Government Data Initiative" 8, no. 2 (2012). http://ci-journal.net/index.php/ciej/article/view/845/916.

Belzer, Aaron, and Nancy Leong. "The New Public Accommodations." *Georgetown Law Journal* 105 (February 1, 2016). https://papers.ssrn.com/abstract=2687486.

Benjamin, Solomon, Bhuvaneswari Raman, P. Rajan, and B. Manjunath. "Bhoomi: 'E-Governance', Or, An Anti-Politics Machine Necessary to Globalize Bangalore?" CASUM-M Working Paper. Bangalore: International Institute of Information Technology, 2005.

Benkler, Yochai. "Coase's Penguin, or Linux and the Nature of the Firm." *Computing Research Repository* cs.CY/0109 (2001).

———. *The Wealth of Networks: How Social Production Transforms Markets and Freedom*. New Haven; London: Yale University Press, 2006.

Bercovici, Jeff. "Uber's Ratings Terrorize Drivers And Trick Riders. Why Not Fix Them?" *Forbes*, August 14, 2014. http://www.forbes.com/sites/jeffbercovici/2014/08/14/what-are-we-actually-rating-when-we-rate-other-people/.

Berdou, Evangelia. "Managing the Bazaar: Commercialization and Peripheral Participation in Mature, Community-Led Free/Open Source Software Projects." London School of Economics and Political Science, 2007. http://flosshub.org/sites/flosshub.org/files/PhD_Berdou.pdf.

Berman, Mark. "Why Uber Will Limit Its Surge Pricing during the Snow Emergency." *The Washington Post*, January 26, 2015. http://www.washingtonpost.com/news/post-nation/wp/2015/01/26/why-uber-will-limit-its-surge-pricing-during-the-snow-emergency/.

Beyerstein, Lindsay. "Change.org Quietly Changing Course." *In These Times*, October 23, 2012. http://inthesetimes.com/duly-noted/entry/14070/change.org_quietly_changing_course.

Bhuiyan, Johana. "Uber Sought To Hire Opposition Researcher To 'Weaponize Facts.'" *BuzzFeed*, November 20, 2014. http://www.buzzfeed.com/johanabhuiyan/uber-sought-to-hire-opposition-researcher-to-weaponize-facts.

——. "What Uber Drivers Really Make (According To Their Pay Stubs)." *BuzzFeed*, November 19, 2014. http://www.buzzfeed.com/johanabhuiyan/what-uber-drivers-really-make-according-to-their-pay-stubs.

Bhuiyan, Johana, and Charlie Warzel. "'God View': Uber Investigates Its Top New York Executive For Privacy Violations." *BuzzFeed*. Accessed May 23, 2015. http://www.buzzfeed.com/johanabhuiyan/uber-is-investigating-its-top-new-york-executive-for-privacy.

Biddle, Sam. "Here Are the Internal Documents That Prove Uber Is a Money Loser." *Gawker*, August 5, 2015. http://gawker.com/here-are-the-internal-documents-that-prove-uber-is-a-mo-1704234157.

——. "Uber Calls Woman's 20-Mile Nightmare Abduction an 'Inefficient Route.'" *Valleywag*, October 14, 2014. http://valleywag.gawker.com/uber-calls-womans-20-mile-nightmare-abduction-an-ineff-1645819700.

——. "Uber Driver: Here's How We Get Around Background Checks." *Valleywag*, June 27, 2014. http://valleywag.gawker.com/uber-driver-heres-how-we-get-around-background-checks-1596902249.

Bingham, Jonathan. "The Sharing Economy: Q&A With Airbnb's Chip Conley," April 10, 2015. http://www.realbusiness.com/2015/04/trendspotting/the-sharing-economy-qa-with-airbnbs-chip-conley/.

Bisby, Adam. "'Airbnb for Dogs': Do Pet Services Go a Step Too Far in Today's Sharing Economy?" *The Globe and Mail*, July 9, 2015. http://www.theglobeandmail.com/life/relationships/dog-sharing-an-uber-contentious-extension-of-sharing-economy/article25391657/.

Bollier, David. "Lessons from the Corporatization of Couchsurfing," February 14, 2014. http://bollier.org/blog/lessons-corporatization-couchsurfing.

Booth, Robert. "Uber Whistleblower Exposes Breach in Driver-Approval Process." *The Guardian*, June 15, 2015. http://www.theguardian.com/technology/2015/jun/12/uber-whistleblower-exposes-breach-driver-approval-process.

Botsman, Rachel. "Collaborative Finance: By the People, For the People." *Collaborative Consumption*, July 31, 2014. http://www.collaborativeconsumption.com/2014/07/31/collaborative-finance-by-the-people-for-the-people/.

——. "The Sharing Economy Lacks A Shared Definition." *Co.Exist*, November 21, 2013. http://www.fastcoexist.com/3022028/the-sharing-economy-lacks-a-shared-definition.

——. "Transcript of 'The Currency of the New Economy Is Trust.'" TED talk, September 2012. http://www.ted.com/talks/rachel_botsman_the_currency_of_the_new_economy_is_trust/transcript.

——. "Welcome to the New Reputation Economy." *Wired*, September 2012. http://www.wired.co.uk/magazine/archive/2012/09/features/welcome-to-the-new-reputation-economy.

Botsman, Rachel, and Roo Rogers. *What's Mine Is Yours: The Rise of Collaborative Consumption*. Harper Business, 2010.

Bowles, Nellie. "Tech Titans on Income Inequality and Their 'Stingy, Stingy' Industry." *Re/Code*, May 31, 2014. http://recode.net/2014/05/31/tech-titans-on-income-inequality-and-their-stingy-stingy-industry/.

Bradshaw, Tim. "Lunch with the FT: Brian Chesky," December 26, 2014. http://www.ft.com/intl/cms/s/0/fd685212-8768-11e4-bc7c-00144feabdc0.html?siteedition=intl#axzz3UxDunrnM.

Brooks, David. "The Evolution of Trust." *The New York Times*, June 30, 2014. http://www.nytimes.com/2014/07/01/opinion/david-brooks-the-evolution-of-trust.html.

Bruce, Chris. "Uber Miami Accused of Coaching Drivers to Circumvent Airport Laws." *Autoblog*, November 14, 2014. http://www.autoblog.com/2014/11/14/uber-coaching-airport-drivers-violate-rules/.

Bulajewski, Mike. "The Cult of Sharing," August 5, 2014. http://www.mrteacup.org/post/the-cult-of-sharing.html.

Burkhardt, Paul, and Chris Waring. "An NSA Big Graph Experiment," May 20, 2013. http://www.pdl.cmu.edu/SDI/2013/slides/big_graph_nsa_rd_2013_56002v1.pdf.

California Public Utilities Commission. "Transportation Network Companies." Accessed May 22, 2015. http://www.cpuc.ca.gov/PUC/Enforcement/TNC/.

Calo, Ryan, and Alex Rosenblat. "The Taking Economy: Uber, Information, and Power." SSRN Scholarly Paper. Rochester, NY: Social Science Research Network, March 9, 2017. https://papers.ssrn.com/abstract=2929643.

Carhart, Kevin. "The Ten Ninety Nihilists," November 6, 2013. https://libcom.org/blog/ten-ninety-nihilists-06112013.

Carson, Biz. "Lyft Tripled Its Rides in 2016." *Business Insider*, January 5, 2017. http://www.businessinsider.com/lyft-tripled-its-rides-in-2016-2017-1.

CBC News. "Airbnb Renters Who Trashed Calgary House Used Fake Credit Cards to Fuel Party," May 7, 2015. http://www.cbc.ca/1.3065243.

Chesky, Brian. "Shared City," March 26, 2014. https://medium.com/@bchesky/shared-city-db9746750a3a.

———. "Who We Are, What We Stand for," October 3, 2013. http://blog.airbnb.com/who-we-are/.

Chesters, Graeme, and David Smith. "The Neglected Art of Hitch-Hiking: Risk, Trust and Sustainability" 6, no. 3 (2001). http://www.socresonline.org.uk/6/3/chesters.html.

Chu, Patrick. "Fedex's $228 Million Settlement Could Dent Uber, Lyft, Postmates, Homejoy, Caviar and Other San Francisco Companies Using Low-Cost Independent Contractors for Labor." *San Francisco Business Times*, June 16, 2015. http://www.bizjournals.com/sanfrancisco/morning_call/2015/06/fedex-settlement-uber-lyft-caviar-homejoy-labor.html.

Clampet, Jason. "Airbnb CEO Responds to Illegal Rentals Story." *Skift*, January 11, 2013. http://skift.com/2013/01/11/airbnb-responds-to-illegal-rentals-story-first-of-all-its-not-illegal-everywhere/.

Clark, Shelby. "A Transition at Peers to Create Greater Impact," December 11, 2014. http://blog.peers.org/post/104965337094/a-transition.

Clemons, Eric. "What An Antitrust Case Against Google Might Look Like." *TechCrunch*. Accessed May 17, 2015. http://social.techcrunch.com/2009/03/01/what-an-antitrust-case-against-google-might-look-like/.

CNBC.com staff. "Uber's $90K Salary Could Disrupt the Taxi Business," May 28, 2014. http://www.cnbc.com/id/101710406.

Coca, Nithin. "The Rise and Fall of Couchsurfing." *NithinCoca.com*, March 27, 2013. http://www.nithincoca.com/2013/03/27/the-rise-and-fall-of-couchsurfing/.

Coleman, E. Gabriella. *Coding Freedom: The Ethics and Aesthetics of Hacking.* Princeton University Press, 2012.

Corbet, Jonathan, Greg Kroah-Hartman, and Amanda McPherson. "Who Writes Linux: Linux Kernel Development: How Fast It Is Going, Who Is Doing It, What They Are Doing, and Who Is Sponsoring It." The Linux Foundation, 2015. http://www.linuxfoundation.org/publications/linux-foundation/who-writes-linux-2015.

Cortese, Amy. "Loans That Avoid Banks? Maybe Not." *The New York Times,* May 3, 2014. http://www.nytimes.com/2014/05/04/business/loans-that-avoid-banks-maybe-not.html.

Coscarelli, Joe. "Airbnb Poster-Child Was Evicted for Airbnb-Ing a Converted Barn She Didn't Own." *Daily Intelligencer.* Accessed May 9, 2015. http://nymag.com/daily/intelligencer/2014/10/airbnb-poster-child-shell-evicted-for-airbnbing.html.

"Craig." "An Uber Impact: 20,000 Jobs Created on the Uber Platform Every Month." *Uber,* May 27, 2014. http://blog.uber.com/uberimpact.

Cresci, Elena. "Uber Offers Free Rides after Backlash over Surge Pricing during Sydney Siege." *The Guardian,* December 15, 2014 http://www.theguardian.com/technology/2014/dec/15/uber-offers-free-rides-after-backlash-over-surge-pricing during-sydney-siege.

Crunchbase. "TaskRabbit." *CrunchBase.* Accessed June 19, 2015. https://www.crunchbase.com/organization/taskrabbit.

Cushing, Ellen. "Uber Employees Warned a San Francisco Magazine Writer That Executives Might Snoop on Her." Accessed May 23, 2015. http://www.modernluxury.com/san-francisco/story/uber-employees-warned-san-francisco-magazine-writer-executives-might-snoop-her.

Daalen, Robin van. "Airbnb to Collect Tourist Taxes in Amsterdam," December 18, 2014. http://blogs.wsj.com/digits/2014/12/18/airbnb-to-collect-tourist-taxes-in-amsterdam/.

Dale, Daniel. "Council Votes to Overhaul Toronto Taxi Industry." *The Toronto Star,* February 19, 2014. http://www.thestar.com/news/city_hall/2014/02/19/council_votes_to_overhaul_toronto_taxi_industry.html.

Davies, Evan. "Digital Marketplaces." *The Bottom Line, with Evan Davies.* British Broadcasting Corporation, October 19, 2013. http://www.bbc.co.uk/programmes/b03ctfp4.

Davies, Lizzy. "Activists Vow to Buy Abandoned Cinema and Save Rome's Bohemian Soul." *The Guardian,* Accessed May 10, 2015. http://www.theguardian.com/world/2014/sep/13/rome-student-occupation-activists-save-artistic-soul-trastevere.

DeAmicis, Carmel. "On the Way to $220M in Funding, Instacart Quietly Changed Its Business Model," January 14, 2015. https://gigaom.com/2015/01/14/on-the-way-to-220m-in-funding-instacart-quietly-changed-its-business-model/.

———. "Uber Starts Directly Leasing Cars in Program That Could Appeal to Short-Term Drivers." *Re/Code,* July 29, 2015. http://recode.net/2015/07/29/uber-offers-revised-car-leasing-program-that-could-be-more-appealing-for-drivers/.

Dellarocas, C., and C. A. Wood. "The Sound of Silence in Online Feedback: Estimating Trading Risks in the Presence of Reporting Bias" 54, no. 3 (2008): 460–476.

Dempsey, Paul Stephen. "Taxi Industry Regulation, Deregulation, and Reregulation: The Paradox of Market Failure." *University of Denver College of Law, Transportation Law Journal* 24, no. 1 (1996): 73–120.

DePillis, Lydia. "At the Uber for Home Cleaning, Workers Pay a Price for Convenience," September 10, 2014. http://www.washingtonpost.com/news/storyline/wp/2014/09/10/at-the-uber-for-home-cleaning-workers-pay-a-price-for-convenience/.

D'Onfro, Jillian. "Uber CEO Founded The Company Because He Wanted To Be A 'Baller In San Francisco.'" *Business Insider*. Accessed May 22, 2015. http://www.businessinsider.com/why-travis-kalanick-founded-uber-2013-11.

Donovan, Kevin. "Seeing Like a Slum: Towards Open, Deliberative Development." SSRN Scholarly Paper. Rochester, NY: Social Science Research Network, April 26, 2012. http://papers.ssrn.com/abstract=2045556.

Dubinsky, Zach, Mark Gollom, and John Rieti. "Cab Driving Riskier than Police Work." *CBC*, May 3, 2012. http://www.cbc.ca/1.1258776.

DutchNews.nl. "Amsterdam Airbnb Fines Mount Up, Top €500,000." *DutchNews.nl*, March 2, 2017. http://www.dutchnews.nl/news/archives/2017/03/amsterdam-airbnb-fines-mount-up-top-e500000/.

Dyer, Zach. "Uber Says It Will Support Drivers Fined by Police in Costa Rica -." *Tico Times | Costa Rica Information | Travel | Real Estate | Hotel*, August 22, 2015. http://www.ticotimes.net/2015/08/22/uber-says-will-support-drivers-fined-police-costa-rica.

Edelman, Benjamin, and Michael Luca. *Digital Discrimination: The Case of Airbnb .com*, 2014.

E.J. Dickson. "Gross, Sexist French Uber Campaign Features 'Sexy Girl' Drivers." *The Daily Dot*, October 22, 2014. http://www.dailydot.com/business/uber-france-sexism/.

Elberse, Anita. *Blockbusters: Hit-Making, Risk-Taking, and the Big Business of Entertainment*. Henry Holt and Co., 2013.

———. "Should You Invest in the Long Tail?" *Harvard Business Review* 86, no. 7/8 (August 2008): 88–96.

Elberse, Anita, and Felix Oberholzer-Gee. "Superstars and Underdogs: An Examination of the Long Tail Phenomenon in Video Sales." *Marketing Science Institute* 4 (2007): 49–72.

Electronic Frontier Foundation. *Airbnb, Inc. v. Schneiderman*, 2013. https://www.eff.org/cases/airbnb-inc-v-eric-schneiderman.

———. "Section 230 Protections." *Electronic Frontier Foundation*. Accessed June 26, 2015. https://www.eff.org/issues/bloggers/legal/liability/230.

Erbentraut, Joseph. "Here's What The People Delivering Your Instacart Groceries Really Think." *The Huffington Post*, February 2, 2015. http://www.huffingtonpost.com/2015/02/02/instacart-workers_n_6548822.html.

Essers, Loek. "Amsterdam Using Airbnb Listing Service to Identify Illegal Rentals," February 4, 2013. http://www.itworld.com/article/2716001/it-management/amsterdam-using-airbnb-listing-service-to-identify-illegal-rentals.html.

Farmer, F. Randall, and Bryce Glass. *Building Web Reputation Systems*. O'Reilly Media, 2010.

Fenske, Sarah. "After Our Uber Exposé, Their PR Team Tried to Dupe Us." *L.A. Weekly*, October 29, 2014. http://www.laweekly.com/news/after-our-uber-expos-their-pr-team-tried-to-dupe-us-5177453.

Ferguson, Jordan. "Recent Transportation Network Company Ordinances." Best Best and Krieger LLP, October 30, 2014. http://www.bbknowledge.com/california-public-utilities-commission-cpuc/recent-transportation-network-company-ordinances-in-austin-houston-and-washington-d-c-display-variety-of-regulatory-approaches/.

Fernholtz, Tim. "Is Uber Costing New Yorkers $1.2 Billion Worth of Lost Time?" *Quartz*, July 10, 2015. http://qz.com/449600/uber-is-slowing-down-new-york-city-but-slowing-down-uber-wont-fix-the-problem/.

Fink, Erica. "Uber-Nasty? Staff Submits 5,560 Fake Ride Requests." *CNNMoney*, August 11, 2014. http://money.cnn.com/2014/08/11/technology/uber-fake-ride-requests-lyft/index.html.

Flamm, Matthew. "Strange Bedfellows in Airbnb Dispute." *Crain's New York Business*. Accessed May 9, 2015. http://www.crainsnewyork.com/article/20131013/HOSPITALITY_TOURISM/310139970/strange-bedfellows-in-airbnb-dispute.

Fourcade, Marion, and Kieran Healy. "Moral Views of Market Society." *Annual Review of Sociology* 33, no. 14 (August 2007): 1–27.

Fowler, Geoffrey A., and Evelyn M. Rusli. "Don't Talk to Strangers, Unless You Plan to Share Your Mac-and-Cheese," January 14, 2013. http://www.wsj.com/articles/SB10001424127887323689604578222662518578442.

Fowler, Susan. "Reflecting on One Very, Very Strange Year at Uber." *Susan J. Fowler*, February 19, 2017. https://www.susanjfowler.com/blog/2017/2/19/reflecting-on-one-very-strange-year-at-uber

Fradkin, Andrey. "Search Frictions and the Dsign of Online Marketplaces." Working Paper, November 2014. http://andreyfradkin.com/assets/Fradkin_JMP_Sep2014.pdf.

French, Jason, Sam Schechner, and Matthias Verbergt. "How Airbnb Is Taking Over Paris." *WSJ*. Accessed July 7, 2015. http://graphics.wsj.com/how-airbnb-is-taking-over-paris.

Friedman, Thomas L. "And Now for a Bit of Good News . . ." *The New York Times*, July 19, 2014. http://www.nytimes.com/2014/07/20/opinion/sunday/thomas-l-friedman-and-now-for-a-bit-of-good-news.html.

Friedman, Uri. "Airbnb CEO: Cities Are Becoming Villages." *The Atlantic*, June 29, 2014. http://www.theatlantic.com/international/archive/2014/06/airbnb-ceo-cities-are-becoming-villages/373676/.

"From the People, for the People." *The Economist*, May 9, 2015. http://www.economist.com/news/special-report/21650289-will-financial-democracy-work-downturn-people-people.

Gambetta, Diego, and Michael Bacharach. "Trust in Signs." In *Trust in Society*, 148–184, n.d.

Gannes, Liz. "Competition Brings Lyft, Sidecar and Uber Closer to Cloning Each Other." *AllThingsD*. Accessed May 22, 2015. http://allthingsd.com/20131116/competition-brings-lyft-sidecar-and-uber-closer-to-cloning-each-other-and-cabs/.

——. "Lyft Sells Zimride Carpool Service to Rental-Car Giant Enterprise." *AllThingsD*, July 12, 2013. http://allthingsd.com/20130712/lyft-sells-zimride-carpool-service-to-rental-car-giant-enterprise/.

——. "Zimride Turns Regular Cars Into Taxis With New Ride-Sharing App, Lyft," May 22, 2012. http://allthingsd.com/20120522/zimride-turns-regular-cars-into-taxis-with-new-ride-sharing-app-lyft/.

Gans, Joshua. "Is Uber Really in a Fight to the Death?" *Digitopoly*, November 25, 2014. http://www.digitopoly.org/2014/11/25/is-uber-really-in-a-fight-to-the-death/.

Gansky, Lisa. *The Mesh: Why the Future of Business Is Sharing.* Portfolio / Penguin, 2010.

Gardner, Sue. "Wikipedia at 10: A Web Pioneer Worth Defending." *The Guardian.* Accessed May 15, 2015. http://www.theguardian.com/commentisfree/cifamerica/2011/jan/12/wikipedia-internet.

Ge, Yanbo, Christopher R. Knittel, Don MacKenzie, and Stephen Zoepf. "Racial and Gender Discrimination in Transportation Network Companies." Working Paper. National Bureau of Economic Research, October 2016. doi:10.3386/w22776.

Geist, Michael. "Popular yet Controversial App-Based Car Service Has No Privacy Policy Specific to Canada." *The Toronto Star,* November 21, 2014. http://www.thestar.com/business/2014/11/21/why_uber_has_a_canadian_privacy_problem.html.

Geron, Tomio. "California Becomes First State To Regulate Ridesharing Services Lyft, Sidecar, UberX." *Forbes,* September 19, 2013. http://www.forbes.com/sites/tomiogeron/2013/09/19/california-becomes-first-state-to-regulate-ridesharing-services-lyft-sidecar-uberx/.

——. "Startup Homejoy Works With Public Sector To Find Home Cleaners," September 3, 2013. http://www.forbes.com/sites/tomiogeron/2013/09/03/startup-homejoy-works-with-cities-to-find-workers/.

Gorenflo, Neal. "OuiShare Fest Finds Itself While Lost in Transition." *Shareable,* May 29, 2015. http://www.shareable.net/blog/ouishare-fest-finds-itself-while-lost-in-transition.

Grant, Peter S., and Chris Wood. *Blockbusters and Trade Wars: Popular Culture in a Globalized World.* Douglas and McIntyre Ltd., 2004.

Grim, Ryan. "Change.org Changing: Site To Drop Progressive Litmus Test For Campaigns, Say Internal Documents." *Huffington Post,* October 22, 2012. http://today.yougov.com/huffingtonpostwidget/live/webpollsmall1.html?topic=politics.

Griswold, Alison. "In Search of Uber's Unicorn." *Slate,* October 27, 2014. http://www.slate.com/articles/business/moneybox/2014/10/uber_driver_salary_the_ride_sharing_company_says_its_drivers_make_great.html.

——. "Paris Is Blaming Airbnb for Population Declines in the Heart of the City." *Quartz,* January 5, 2017. https://qz.com/877344/paris-is-blaming-airbnb-for-population-declines-in-the-heart-of-the-city/.

Guendelsberger, Emily. "I Was an Undercover Uber Driver." *Philadelphia Citypaper.* May 7, 2015. https://infogr.am/uber_numbers-1179.

Gurstein, Michael. "Are the Open Data Warriors Fighting for Robin Hood or the Sheriff?" *Gurstein's Community Informatics,* July 3, 2011. https://gurstein.wordpress.com/2011/07/03/are-the-open-data-warriors-fighting-for-robin-hood-or-the-sheriff-some-reflections-on-okcon-2011-and-the-emerging-data-divide/.

Gurstein, Michael. "Open Data: Empowering the Empowered or Effective Data Use for Everyone?" *First Monday* 16, no. 2 (January 23, 2011). http://firstmonday.org/ojs/index.php/fm/article/view/3316.

Gustin, Sam. "Lyft-Off: Car-Sharing Start-Up Raises $60 Million Led by Andreessen Horowitz," May 2013. http://business.time.com/2013/05/23/lyft-off-car-sharing-startup-raises-60-million-led-by-andreessen-horowitz/.

Hall, Jonathan, and Alan Krueger. "An Analysis of the Labor Market for Uber's Driver-Partners in the United States," January 22, 2015. https://s3.amazonaws.com/uber-static/comms/PDF/Uber_Driver-Partners_Hall_Kreuger_2015.pdf.

Handy. "Be a Professional with Handy!" *Handy Company Web Site.* Accessed June 19, 2015. https://www.handy.com/apply.

Handy Corporation. "About Us." *Handy Website.* Accessed July 10, 2015. http://www.handy.com/about.

Handybook. "Handybook Raises $30 Million in Series B Led by Revolution Growth," June 11, 2014. http://www.prnewswire.com/news-releases/handybook-raises-30-million-in-series-b-led-by-revolution-growth-262693731.html.

Hannak, Anniko, Claudia Wagner, David Garcia, Markus Strohmaier, and Christo Wilson. "Bias in Online Freelance Marketplaces: Evidence from TaskRabbit." New York University Law School, 2016. http://datworkshop.org.

Hantman, David. "Good News from Amsterdam," June 3, 2013. http://publicpolicy.airbnb.com/good-news-from-amsterdam/.

———. "More Good News in Amsterdam," February 13, 2014. http://publicpolicy.airbnb.com/good-news-amsterdammeer-goed-nieuws-uit-amsterdam/.

———. *New York: The next Steps,* 2013. http://publicpolicy.airbnb.com/new-york-next-steps/.

Haque, Umair. "The Servitude Bubble — Bad Words." *Medium,* June 8, 2015. https://medium.com/bad-words/the-servitude-bubble o9o998c437c6.

Harris, Derrick. "Under the Covers of the NSA's Big Data Effort," June 7, 2013. https://gigaom.com/2013/06/07/under-the-covers-of-the-nsas-big-data-effort/.

Harvey, David. *Rebel Cities: From the Right to the City to the Urban Revolution.* New York: Verso, 2012.

Haverkort, Heleen. "Airbnb Is Allowed in Amsterdam," June 7, 2013. http://www.nu.nl/economie/3494485/airbnb-mag-wel-in-amsterdam.html.

Hill, Kashmir. "'God View': Uber Allegedly Stalked Users For Party-Goers' Viewing Pleasure." *Forbes,* October 3, 2014. http://www.forbes.com/sites/kashmirhill/2014/10/03/god-view-uber-allegedly-stalked-users-for-party-goers-viewing-pleasure/.

———. "Meet the Lawyer Taking on Uber and the Rest of the on-Demand Economy." *Fusion,* April 16, 2015. http://fusion.net/story/118401/meet-the-lawyer-taking-on-uber-and-the-on-demand-economy/.

Hindman, Matthew. *The Myth of Digital Democracy.* Princeton University Press, 2008.

Hirsch, Todd. "Taxi Trouble: Disruptive Technology Claims Another Victim." *The Globe and Mail,* November 21, 2014. http://www.theglobeandmail.com/report-on-business/economy/economic-insight/taxi-trouble-disruptive-technology-claims-another-unadapting-victim/article21675184/.

Horan, Hubert. "Can Uber Ever Deliver? Part One – Understanding Uber's Bleak Operating Economics." *Naked Capitalism,* November 30, 2016. http://www.nakedcapitalism.com/2016/11/can-uber-ever-deliver-part-one-understanding-ubers-bleak-operating-economics.html.

Hornig, Frank. "Darth Vader vs. Death Strip: Berlin Wall Sinks into Cold War Disneyland." *Spiegel Online,* August 8, 2011, sec. International. http://www.spiegel.de/international/spiegel/darth-vader-vs-death-strip-berlin-wall-sinks-into-cold-war-disneyland-a-778941.html.

Huet, Ellen. "Apps Let Users Hire House Cleaners, Handymen without Talking." *SFGate,* February 11, 2014. http://www.sfgate.com/technology/article/Apps-let-users-hire-house-cleaners-handymen-5219729.php.

——. "Contractor or Employee? Silicon Valley's Branding Dilemma," November 18, 2014. http://www.forbes.com/sites/ellenhuet/2014/11/18/contractor-or-employee-silicon-valleys-branding-dilemma/.

——. "Uber Now Taking Its Biggest UberX Commission Ever -- 25 Percent." *Forbes,* September 22, 2014. http://www.forbes.com/sites/ellenhuet/2014/09/22/uber-now-taking-its-biggest-uberx-commission-ever-25-percent/.

——. "Uber's 'F' Rating At Better Business Bureau Isn't For Surge Pricing -- Just For Unresponsiveness." *Forbes,* October 14, 2014. http://www.forbes.com/sites/ellenhuet/2014/10/14/ubers-f-rating-at-better-business-bureau-isnt-for-surge-pricing-just-for-unresponsiveness/.

Hutt, Katherine. "The Truth About BBB and Uber: 10 Facts You Should Know." *BBB Consumer News and Opinion Blog,* October 13, 2014. http://www.bbb.org/blog/2014/10/the-truth-about-bbb-and-uber-10-facts-you-should-know/.

Internet Association. "The Internet Association Files Amicus Brief to Quash the NYAG Subpoena against Airbnb." Press Release, November 8, 2013. http://internetassociation.org/11082013airbnbamicusbrief/.

Isaac, Mike. "How Uber Deceives the Authorities Worldwide." *The New York Times,* March 3, 2017. https://www.nytimes.com/2017/03/03/technology/uber-greyball-program-evade-authorities.html.

Isaac, Mike, and Natasha Singer. "California Says Uber Driver Is Employee, Not a Contractor." *The New York Times,* June 17, 2015. http://www.nytimes.com/2015/06/18/business/uber-contests-california-labor-ruling-that-says-drivers-should-be-employees.html.

Jacobs, Steven. "Handybook Rebrands As Handy, Says It Grew 10x in Past 9 Months." *Streetfight: Inside the Business of Hyperlocal,* September 16, 2014. http://streetfightmag.com/2014/09/16/handybook-rebrands-as-handy-says-it-grew-ten-times-in-past-nine-months/.

Johnson, Steven. *Future Perfect: The Case for Progress in a Networked Age.* Riverhead, 2012.

Jordan, Jeff. "Unpacking the Grocery Stack," n.d. http://jeff.a16z.com/2014/06/16/unpacking-the-grocery-stack/.

Kalanick, Travis. "A Leader for the Uber Campaign." *Uber,* August 19, 2014. http://blog.uber.com/davidplouffe.

——. "Celebrating Cities: A New Look and Feel for Uber." *Uber Global,* February 2, 2016. https://newsroom.uber.com/celebrating-cities-a-new-look-and-feel-for-uber/.

——. "Uber Policy White Paper 1.0." *Uber,* April 12, 2013. http://blog.uber.com/2013/04/12/uber-policy-white-paper-1-0/.

Kalanick, Travis, and Kara Swisher. Uber CEO: We're in a Political Battle with an "Assh*le," May 28, 2014. http://mashable.com/2014/05/28/travis-kalanick-co-founder-and-ceo-of-uber/.

Kane, Kat. "The Big Hidden Problem With Uber? Insincere 5-Star Ratings." *WIRED,* March 19, 2015. http://www.wired.com/2015/03/bogus-uber-reviews/.

Kassam, Ashifa. "Barcelona's Tourist Hordes Are Target for Radical New Mayor Ada Colau." *The Guardian,* June 13, 2015. http://www.theguardian.com/world/2015/jun/13/ada-colau-barcelona-spain-mayor-targets-tourists.

——. "Naked Italians Spark Protests against Antics of Drunken Tourists in Barcelona," August 12, 2014. http://www.theguardian.com/world/2014/aug/21/naked-italians-protests-drunken-tourists-barcelona.

Katz, Vanessa. "Regulating the Sharing Economy." *Berkeley Technology Law Journal* 30, no. 4 (November 29, 2015): 1067. doi:http://dx.doi.org/10.15779/Z38HG45.

Keating, Zoë. "What Should I Do about Youtube?" Accessed May 17, 2015. http://zoekeating.tumblr.com/post/108898194009/what-should-i-do-about-youtube.

Kell, John. "Avis to Buy Car-Sharing Service Zipcar," January 22013. http://www.wsj.com/articles/SB10001424127887324374004578217121433322386.

Kiva. "Kiva - Lift Above Poverty Organization (LAPO)." *Kiva*, April 17, 2012. http://www.kiva.org/partners/20#LAPOupdate.

Koch, Alison. "Omidyar/Hewlett Press Release - GlobalGiving," August 2, 2005. http://www.globalgiving.org/aboutus/media/omidyar_hewlett2.html.

Krueger, Liz. "On Behalf of Regular New Yorkers, Sen. Krueger Responds to Airbnb's 'Three Principles.'" Accessed May 8, 2015. http://www.nysenate.gov/press-release/behalf-regular-new-yorkers-sen-krueger-responds-airbnbs-three-principles.

Kuchler, Hannah. "Airbnb to Collect and Remit Taxes for Hosts in Paris." *Financial Times*, August 25, 2015. http://www.ft.com/intl/cms/s/0/e2ab8028-4b4b-11e5-9b5d-89a026fda5c9.html?siteedition=uk#axzz3kEBZAOWj.

Laband, David N. "An Economics Lesson at the Baggage Carousel." *Wall Street Journal*, January 9, 2014, sec. Opinion. http://www.wsj.com/articles/SB10001424052702303848104579308820544892490.

Lapowsky, Issie. "Believe It: Co-Working Space Startup WeWork Is Now Worth $5B." *WIRED*, December 16, 2014. http://www.wired.com/2014/12/wework-valuation/.

Lathrop, Daniel, and Laurel Ruma, eds. *Open Government: [Collaboration, Transparency, and Participation in Practice]*. 1st ed. Theory in Practice. Beijing ; Cambridge [Mass.]: O'Reilly, 2010.

Lawler, Ryan. *Mr. Kalanick Goes to Washington: How Uber Won in DC*, Dec 42012. http://techcrunch.com/2012/12/04/mr-kalanick-goes-to-washington-how-uber-won-in-dc.

Lecuyer, Mathias, Max Tucker, and Augustin Chaintreau. "Improving the Transparency of the Sharing Economy." Perth, Australia. Accessed April 8, 2017. http://mathias.lecuyer.me/assets/assets/www2017airbnb.pdf.

Legal Information Institute. "47 U.S. Code § 230 - Protection for Private Blocking and Screening of Offensive Material." Cornell University Law School. Accessed June 26, 2015. https://www.law.cornell.edu/uscode/text/47/230.

Leisy, Craig. "TAXICAB DEREGULATION AND REREGULATION IN SEATTLE: LESSONS LEARNED," 2001. http://sfcda.org/CPUC/Seattle_DeReg.pdf.

Leonard, Andrew. "The Sharing Economy Gets Greedy," July 31, 2013. http://www.salon.com/2013/07/31/the_sharing_economy_gets_greedy/.

Lessig, Lawrence. *Remix: Making Art and Commerce Thrive in the Hybrid Economy*. New York: Penguin Press, 2008.

Levy, Ari, and Dakin Campbell. "EBay-Style Loans Lure Summers to Mack in Wall Street Asset Craze." *Bloomberg.com*, August 27, 2013. http://www.bloomberg.com/news/articles/2013-08-27/ebay-style-loans-lure-summers-to-mack-in-wall-street-asset-craze.

LeWeb. *Douglas Atkin - Airbnb - LeWeb London 2013*. Accessed August 28, 2015. https://www.youtube.com/watch?v=cp2Hlp2TP-M.

Lewis, Peter. "Couchsurfing: The Meltdown Continues." *Our Mechanical Brain*, March 20, 2013. https://mechanicalbrain.wordpress.com/2013/03/20/couchsurfing-the-meltdown-continues/.

Lieber, Ron. "Airbnb Horror Story Points to Need for Precautions." *The New York Times*, August 14, 2015. http://www.nytimes.com/2015/08/15/your-money/airbnb-horror-story-points-to-need-for-precautions.html.

Linksvayer, Mike. "CC as a Hybrid Organization and a Tool for Hybrids - Creative Commons," June 8, 2009. https://creativecommons.org/weblog/entry/15046.

LoGiurato, Brett. "This Is The One Law Airbnb's Opponents Desperately Want To Change." *Business Insider*, April 22, 2014. http://www.businessinsider.com/airbnb-illegal-law-case-2014-4.

Lopez, Linette. "Billionaire Hedge-Fund Manager Says Uber Told Him It Might Cut Driver Pay 'because We Can.'" *Business Insider*, May 18, 2015. http://www.businessinsider.com/uber-cfo-because-we-can-2015-5.

Lu, Vanessa. "Do Companies like Uber, Handy Fuel Underground Economy?" *Toronto Star*, February 23, 2015. http://www.thestar.com/business/economy/2015/02/23/do-companies-like-uber-handy-fuel-underground-economy.html.

MacQueen, Graeme. *The 2001 Anthrax Deception: The Case for a Domestic Conspiracy.* Atlanta, GA: Clarity Press, Inc, 2014.

Manjoo, Farhad. "Grocery Deliveries in Sharing Economy." *The New York Times*, May 21, 2014. http://www.nytimes.com/2014/05/22/technology/personaltech/online-grocery-start-up-takes-page-from-sharing-services.html.

Maron, Mikel. "We Need to Stop Google's Exploitation of Open Communities." *Brain Off*. Accessed May 20, 2015. http://brainoff.com/weblog/2011/04/11/1635.

Marosevic, Zeljka. "Is the Mid-List, 'publishing's Experimental Laboratory,' Disappearing?" *Melville House Books.* Accessed May 17, 2015. http://www.mhpbooks.com/is-the-mid-list-publishings-experimental-laboratory-disappearing/.

Marritz, Ilya. *Two True Stories from the Airbnb Wars.* Accessed May 9, 2015. http://www.wnyc.org/story/two-true-stories-airbnb-wars/?utm_source=sharedUrl&utm_medium=metatag&utm_campaign=sharedUrl.

Marwick, Alice E. *Status Update: Celebrity, Publicity, & Branding in the Social Media Age.* Yale University Press, 2013.

McFarland, Matt. "Uber's Remarkable Growth Could End the Era of Poorly Paid Cab Drivers." *The Washington Post*, May 27, 2014. http://www.washingtonpost.com/blogs/innovations/wp/2014/05/27/ubers-remarkable-growth-could-end-the-era-of-poorly-paid-cab-drivers/.

McMillan, Jonathan. "Peer-To-Peer Lending Is Dead." *The End of Banking*, April 18, 2015. http://www.endofbanking.org/jonathan-mcmillan-visits-lendit/.

Meelen, Toon, and Koen Frenken. "Stop Saying Uber Is Part Of The Sharing Economy." *Co.Exist*, January 24, 2015. http://www.fastcoexist.com/3040863/stop-saying-uber-is-part-of-the-sharing-economy.

Mesh, Aaron. "City Commissioner Nick Fish Berates Airbnb Lobbyist," December 22, 2014. http://www.wweek.com/portland/blog-32614-video_city_commissioner_nick_fish_berates_airbnb_lobbyist.html.

Mintz, Corey. "Residents of Toronto's Kensington Market Concerned as Airbnb Moves in." *The Globe and Mail*, April 28, 2017. http://www.theglobeandmail.com/news/toronto/residents-of-torontos-kensington-market-concerned-as-airbnb-moves-in/article34851601/.

Montgomery, Kevin. "Handy Sued for Being a Hellscape of Labor Code Violations," November 122014. http://valleywag.gawker.com/handy-sued-for-being-a-hellscape-of-labor-code-violatio-1657889316.

Morozov, Evgeny. *To Save Everything, Click Here*. PublicAffairs, 2013.

Naughton, John. "Meet Tech's New Concierge Economy, Where Serfs Deliver Stuff to Rich Folk." *The Guardian*, December 28, 2014. http://www.theguardian.com/commentisfree/2014/dec/28/uber-amazon-tech-concierge-economy.

Newcomer, Eric. "Uber, Lifting Financial Veil, Says Sales Growth Outpaces Losses." *Bloomberg.com*, April 14, 2017. https://www.bloomberg.com/news/articles/2017-04-14/embattled-uber-reports-strong-sales-growth-as-losses-continue.

News, Dutch. "Amsterdammers Break Airbnb Rules: Long Lets with Too Many People," August 30, 2014. http://www.dutchnews.nl/news/archives/2014/08/amsterdammers_break_airbnb_rul/.

———. "Amsterdammers Can Rent Their Homes to Tourists via Airbnb after All," January 17, 2014. http://www.dutchnews.nl/news/archives/2014/01/amsterdammers_can_rent_their_h/.

Njus, Elliot. "Airbnb to Block Portland Users from Listing Multiple Properties." *OregonLive.com*, January 24, 2017. http://www.oregonlive.com/front-porch/index.ssf/2017/01/airbnb_to_block_portland_users.html.

———. "Portland Legalizes Airbnb-Style Short-Term Rentals," July 30, 2014. http://www.oregonlive.com/front-porch/index.ssf/2014/07/portland_legalizes_airbnb-styl.html.

Norris, Clive. "The Sociological Implications of Smart Surveillance Systems." *Criminologia*, November 11, 2011. http://criminologia.de/2011/12/vortrag-von-clive-norris-the-sociological-implications-of-smart-surveillance-system/.

Norris, Clive, Nigel Fielding, Charles Kemp, and Jane Fielding. "Black and Blue: An Analysis of the Influence of Race on Being Stopped by the Police." *The British Journal of Sociology* 43, no. 2 (June 1, 1992): 207–24. doi:10.2307/591465.

Nosko, Chris, and Steven Tadelis. "The Limits of Reputation in Platform Markets: An Empirical Analysis and Field Experiment." Working Paper. NBER Working Paper. National Bureau of Economic Research, January 2015. http://www.nber.org/papers/w20830.

O'Keefe, Brian, and Marty Jones. "How Uber Plays the Tax Shell Game." *Fortune*, October 22, 2015. http://fortune.com/2015/10/22/uber-tax-shell/.

O'Neill, Maura, and Kat Townsend. "Food Security Open Data Challenge | USAID Impact." *USAid Blog*. Accessed May 20, 2015. http://blog.usaid.gov/2012/05/food-security-open-data-challenge/.

Open Knowledge Foundation. "What Is Open?" Open Knowledge Foundation. Accessed May 18, 2015. https://okfn.org/opendata/.

O'Reilly, Tim. "Networks and the Nature of the Firm: The Discussion around Companies like Uber and Airbnb Is Too Narrow. The Issue Isn't Just Employment, but a Huge Economic Shift Led by Software and Connectedness., The Evolution of Platforms, Networked Platforms for Physical World Services, The Franchise of One, From Decentralization to Recentralization, Key Lessons, Uberisation of Education." *Medium*, August 14, 2015. https://medium.com/the-wtf-economy/networks-and-the-nature-of-the-firm-28790b6afdcc.

Ostrom, Elinor. *Governing the Commons: The Evolution of Institutions for Collective Action*. The Cambridge Series on the Political Economy of Institutions. Cambridge University Press, 1990.

Owyang, Jeremiah. "The Collaborative Sharing Economy Has Created 17 Billion-Dollar Companies (and 10 Unicorns)." *Web Strategist*. Accessed June 21, 2015. http://www.web-strategist.com/blog/2015/06/04/the-collaborative-sharing-economy-has-created-17-billion-dollar-companies-and-10-unicorns/.

Paris, Jon Henley in. "Electric 'Boris Cars' Are Coming to London – How Do They Work in Paris?" *The Guardian*. Accessed May 23, 2015. http://www.theguardian.com/cities/2014/jul/09/electric-boris-car-source-london-how-work-paris-autolib.

Pasquale, Frank. *The Black Box Society: The Secret Algorithms That Control Money and Information*. Cambridge: Harvard University Press, 2015.

Paul, Sanjukta. "Uber as For-Profit Hiring Hall: A Price-Fixing Paradox and Its Implications." SSRN Scholarly Paper. Rochester, NY: Social Science Research Network, August 2, 2016. https://papers.ssrn.com/abstract=2817653.

Peck, Adam. "Uber's New Delivery Service Only Caters To D.C's White Neighborhoods." *ThinkProgress*, August 19, 2014. http://thinkprogress.org/economy/2014/08/19/3473323/uber-is-making-life-a-little-bit-easier-for-washington-dcs-white-people/.

Peltier, Dan. "Airbnb Faces Big Fines in Portland If Hosts Don't Get City Permits," February 23, 2015. http://skift.com/2015/02/23/airbnb-faces-big-fines-in-portland-if-hosts-dont-get-city-permits/.

Peterson, Andrea. "The Missing Data Point from Uber's Driver Analysis: How Far They Drive." *The Washington Post*, January 22, 2015. http://www.washingtonpost.com/blogs/the-switch/wp/2015/01/22/the-missing-data-point-from-ubers-driver-analysis-how-far-they-drive/.

Peterson, Latoya. "Uber Does Not Care about Racism, It Cares about Money." *Fusion*, July 23, 2015. http://fusion.net/story/170983/uber-racial-politics/.

Powell, Betsy. "City Councillor Asks Federal Taxman to Investigate after Email States Riders Aren't Charged HST. Uber Canada Says Its Drivers Are Responsible for Collecting and Remitting the Tax." *The Toronto Star*, July 21, 2015. http://www.thestar.com/news/city_hall/2015/07/21/uber-says-drivers-are-expected-to-collect-hst.html.

Putnam, Robert. *Bowling Alone*. Simon & Schuster, 2000.

Pyke, Alan. "California Truckers Will Get $2.2 Million In Back Pay For Being Misclassified." *ThinkProgress*, April 3, 2014. http://thinkprogress.org/economy/2014/04/03/3422713/california-truckers-misclassification-labor/.

Raman, Bhuvaneswari. "The Rhetoric of Transparency and Its Reality: Transparent Territories, Opaque Power and Empowerment." *The Journal of Community Informatics* 8, no. 2 (April 4, 2012). http://ci-journal.net/index.php/ciej/article/view/866.

Rankin, Jennifer. "Publish and Be Branded: The New Threat to Literature's Laboratory." *The Guardian*. Accessed May 17, 2015. http://www.theguardian.com/books/2014/jan/13/publish-brand-literature-hilary-mantel-jk-rowling.

Rao, Leena. "Instacart Is Asking Its Customers to Do Something New." *Fortune*, June 26, 2015. http://fortune.com/2015/06/26/instacart-grocery-stores/.

Raphel, Adrienne. "TaskRabbit Redux," July 222014. http://www.newyorker.com/business/currency/taskrabbit-redux.

Rapkin, Mickey. "Uber Cab Confessions." *GQ*, February 27, 2014. http://www.gq.com/news-politics/newsmakers/201403/uber-cab-confessions.

Raymond, Eric S. "The Cathedral and the Bazaar" 3, no. 3 (March 21998). http://www.firstmonday.org/ojs/index.php/fm/article/view/578/499.

Reader, Ruth. "Handybook Rebrands as Handy to Help Build Consumer Trust," September 162014. http://venturebeat.com/2014/09/16/handybook-rebrands-as-handy-to-help-build-consumer-trust/.

Redmond, Tim. "Does Airbnb Have an ADA Problem?" *48 Hills*, August 7, 2014. http://www.48hills.org/2014/08/07/airbnb-ada-problem/#permanently-moved.

Reynolds, Glenn H. *An Army of Davids: How Markets and Technology Empower Ordinary People to Beat Big Media, Big Government, and Other Goliaths.* Nashville, Tenn.: Nelson Current, 2006.

Riehle, Dirk, Philipp Riemer, Carsten Kolassa, and Michael Schmidt. "Paid vs. Volunteer Work in Open Source." In *Proceedings of the 47th Hawaii International Conference on System Science*, 3286–3295, 2014. http://dirkriehle.com/2013/08/22/paid-vs-volunteer-work-in-open-source/.

Robinson, Colin. "The Loneliness of the Long-Distance Reader." *The New York Times*, January 4, 2014. http://www.nytimes.com/2014/01/05/opinion/sunday/the-loneliness-of-the-long-distance-reader.html.

Robinson, Patrick. "Moving Forward in Barcelona," October 21, 2014. http://publicpolicy.airbnb.com/moving-forward-barcelona.

——. "Update from Barcelona: Airbnb Policy Blog," March 13, 2015. http://publicpolicy.airbnb.com/update-barcelona/.

Roose, Kevin. "Does Silicon Valley Have a Contract-Worker Problem?" *New York Magazine*, September 18, 2014. http://nymag.com/daily/intelligencer/2014/09/silicon-valleys-contract-worker-problem.html.

Rosen, Jody. "The Knowledge, London's Legendary Taxi-Driver Test, Puts Up a Fight in the Age of GPS." *The New York Times*, November 10, 2014. http://www.nytimes.com/2014/11/10/t-magazine/london-taxi-test-knowledge.html.

Rosenberg, Jonathan. "The Future Is Open," 2012. https://www.thinkwithgoogle.com/articles/the-future-is-open.html.

——. "The Meaning of Open," December 21, 2009. http://googleblog.blogspot.ca/2009/12/meaning-of-open.html.

Rosenblat, Alex, Karen EC Levy, Solon Barocas, and Tim Hwang. "Discriminating Tastes: Customer Ratings as Vehicles for Bias." SSRN Scholarly Paper. Rochester, NY: Social Science Research Network, October 19, 2016. https://papers.ssrn.com/abstract=2858946.

Ryssdal, Kai. "Uber's Data Makes a Creepy Point about the Company." *Marketplace*, November 18, 2014. http://www.marketplace.org/topics/business/final-note/ubers-data-makes-creepy-point-about-company.

Sadlak, Kristina. "Taxicab Deregulation." Connecticut General Assembly Office of Legislative Research, April 19, 2004. http://www.cga.ct.gov/2004/rpt/2004-R-0380.htm.

Sadowski, Jathan. "Hey, Ride-Sharing Services. Stop Greenwashing!," July 292013. http://www.slate.com/blogs/future_tense/2013/07/29/lyft_and_zipcar_climate_change_environmental_greenwashing.html.

Said, Carolyn. "Airbnb Profits Prompted S.F. Eviction, Ex-Tenant Says." *San Francisco Chronicle*. Accessed May 9, 2015. http://www.sfchronicle.com/bayarea/article/Airbnb-profits-prompted-S-F-eviction-ex-tenant-5164242.php.

——. "As Uber, Lyft, Sidecar Grow, so Do Concerns of Disabled." *SF Gate*, February 25, 2014. http://www.sfgate.com/news/article/As-Uber-Lyft-Sidecar-grow-so-do-concerns-of-5240889.php.

——. "TaskRabbit Makes Some Workers Hopping Mad," July 182014. http://www.sfgate.com/technology/article/TaskRabbit-makes-some-workers-hopping-mad-5629239.php.

Salganick, Matthew J., Peter Sheridan Dodds, and Duncan J. Watts. "Experimental Study of Inequality and Unpredictability in an Artificial Cultural Market" 311 (10 February2006): 854–856.

Salmon, Felix. "How Well uberX Pays, Part 2." *Medium*, June 8, 2014. https://medium.com/@felixsalmon/how-well-uberx-pays-part-2-cbc948eaeeaf.

——. "The Economics of 'everyone's Private Driver.'" *Medium*, May 31, 2014. https://medium.com/@felixsalmon/the-economics-of-everyones-private-driver-464bfd730b38.

——. "Why Cab Drivers Should Love Uber." *Reuters Blogs*, December 12, 2013. http://blogs.reuters.com/felix-salmon/2013/12/11/why-cab-drivers-should-love-uber/.

Sanders, Sam. "Rental Rules In California Raise Questions About Who's Using Airbnb." *NPR.org*, May 17, 2015. http://www.npr.org/2015/05/17/407529301/does-airbnb-help-folks-by-or-help-businesses-get-sly.

Satz, Debra. *Why Some Things Should Not Be for Sale*. Oxford University Press, 2010.

Sauchelli, Dana, and Bruce Golding. "Hookers Turning Airbnb Apartments into Brothels." *New York Post*, April 14, 2014. http://nypost.com/2014/04/14/hookers-using-airbnb-to-use-apartments-for-sex-sessions/.

Scassa, Teresa, and LisaM Campbell. "Data Protection, Privacy and Spatial Data." In *Spatial Data Quality*, 211–19. CRC Press, 2009. http://www.crcnetbase.com/doi/abs/10.1201/b10305-24.

Scheiber, Noam. "How Uber Uses Psychological Tricks to Push Its Drivers' Buttons." *The New York Times*, April 2, 2017. https://www.nytimes.com/interactive/2017/04/02/technology/uber-drivers-psychological-tricks.html.

Schofield, Hugh. "Short-Let Apartments Spark Paris Row as Airbnb Thrives." *BBC News*, December 26, 2014. http://www.bbc.com/news/world-europe-30580295.

Schor, Juliet. "Debating the Sharing Economy," October2014. http://www.greattransition.org/publication/debating-the-sharing-economy.

Scola, Nancy. "The Black Car Company That People Love to Hate," Features, November 11, 2013. http://nextcity.org/features/view/the-black-car-company-that-people-love-to-hate.

——. "The Very Big Thing That Uber, Lyft and Sidecar Didn't Get From California – Next City," August 6, 2013. http://nextcity.org/daily/entry/the-very-big-thing-that-uber-lyft-and-sidecar-didnt-get-from-california.

Scott, James C. *Seeing Like a State: How Certain Schemes to Improve the Human Condition Have Failed*. Yale University Press, 1998.

Shaheen, Susan. "Transportation Network Companies and Ridesourcing." Presentation, University of California Berkeley, Transportation Sustainability Research Center, November 4, 2014. http://www.cpuc.ca.gov/NR/rdonlyres/5C961222-B9C8-4E53-A54D-FC2A89C0A30C/0/RidesourcingCPUCShaheen_Final_v2.pdf.

Shieber, Jonathan. "Handy Hits $1 Million A Week In Bookings As Cleaning Economy Consolidates," October 142014. http://techcrunch.com/2014/10/14/handy-hits-1-million-a-week-in-bookings-as-cleaning-economy-consolidates/.

Shirky, Clay. *Cognitive Surplus: Creativity and Generosity in a Connected Age*. New York: Penguin Press, 2010.

Shontell, Alyson. "My Nightmare Experience As A TaskRabbit Drone," Dec 72011. http://www.businessinsider.com/confessions-of-a-task-rabbit-2011-12.

Silver, James. "The Sharing Economy: A Whole New Way of Living." *The Guardian*, August 4, 2013. http://www.theguardian.com/technology/2013/aug/04/internet-technology-fon-taskrabbit-blablacar.

Sinclair, Hugh. *Confessions of a Microfinance Heretic: How Microlending Lost Its Way and Betrayed the Poor*. 1st ed. San Francisco, Calif: Berrett-Koehler Publishers, 2012.

Skinner, Curtis. "California Prosecutors Say Uber's Background Checks Missed Convicts." *Reuters*, August 20, 2015. http://www.reuters.com/article/2015/08/20/us-usa-uber-california-idUSKCN0QP05920150820.

Slee, Tom. "Airbnb Is Facing an Existential Expansion Problem." *Harvard Business Review*, July 11, 2016. https://hbr.org/2016/07/airbnb-is-facing-an-existential-expansion-problem.

———. "Uber Drivers Earning $90K/Year? More Evidence Needed." *Whimsley*, June 2, 2014. http://tomslee.net/2014/06/uber-drivers-earning-90kyear-more-evidence-needed.html.

Smith, Ben. "Uber Executive Suggests Digging Up Dirt On Journalists." *BuzzFeed*, November 17, 2014. http://www.buzzfeed.com/bensmith/uber-executive-suggests-digging-up-dirt-on-journalists.

Smith-Spark, Laura, and Jethro Mullen. "France Tells Paris Police to Crack down on Uber - CNN.com." *CNN*, June 26, 2015. http://www.cnn.com/2015/06/26/europe/france-paris-uberpop-protests/index.html.

Snelson, A. M. Mr Y Aslam, Mr J Farrar and Others -V- Uber (2016). https://www.judiciary.gov.uk/judgments/mr-y-aslam-mr-j-farrar-and-others-v-uber/.

Soper, Taylor. "Uber Now Charging Drivers $520 per Year to Lease Company iPhone." *GeekWire*, July 25, 2014. http://www.geekwire.com/2014/uber-now-charging-drivers-520-per-year-lease-smartphone/.

Spence, A. Michael. "Job Market Signaling" 87 (1973): 355–374.

Stark, Jennifer, and Nicholas Diakopoulos. "Uber Seems to Offer Better Service in Areas with More White People. That Raises Some Tough Questions." *The Washington Post. WonkBlog*, March 10, 2016. https://www.washingtonpost.com/news/wonk/wp/2016/03/10/uber-seems-to-offer-better-service-in-areas-with-more-white-people-that-raises-some-tough-questions.

Story, Louise, and Annie Lowrey. "The Fed, Lawrence Summers, and Money." *The New York Times*, August 10, 2013. http://www.nytimes.com/2013/08/11/business/economy/the-fed-lawrence-summers-and-money.html.

Strahilevitz, Lior. "Less Regulation, More Reputation." In *The Reputation Society*, n.d.

Strochlic, Nina. "Uber: Disability Laws Don't Apply to Us." *The Daily Beast*, May 21, 2015. http://www.thedailybeast.com/articles/2015/05/21/uber-disability-laws-don-t-apply-to-us.html.

Strom, Stephanie. "Confusion on Where Money Lent via Kiva Goes." *The New York Times*, November 9, 2009, sec. Business / Global Business. http://www.nytimes.com/2009/11/09/business/global/09kiva.html.

Strom, Stephanie, and Vikas Bajaj. "Rich I.P.O. Brings Controversy to Microlender, SKS Microfinance." *The New York Times*, July 29, 2010. http://www.nytimes.com/2010/07/30/business/30micro.html.

Swisher, Kara. "Man and Uber Man." *Vanity Fair*, December 2014. http://www. vanityfair.com/news/2014/12/uber-travis-kalanick-controversy.

Tadeo, Maria. "Airbnb Wants a Truce With Barcelona." *Bloomberg.com*, February 7, 2017. https://www.bloomberg.com/news/articles/2017-02-07/ airbnb-eyes-truce-with-barcelona-as-tourist-hordes-spur-backlash.

Tam, Donna. "New York AG's Office: Airbnb Lying about User-Data Subpoena." *CNET*. Accessed May 9, 2015. http://www.cnet.com/news/new-york-ags-office-airbnb-lying-about-user-data-subpoena/.

Tam, Pui-wing, and Michael J. De La Merced. "Uber Fund-Raising Points to $50 Billion Valuation." *The New York Times*, May 9, 2015. http://www.nytimes.com/2015/05/09/ technology/uber-fund-raising-points-to-50-billion-valuation.html.

Tanz, Jason. "How Airbnb and Lyft Finally Got Americans to Trust Each Other." *Wired Magazine*, April 23, 2014. http://www.wired.com/2014/04/trust-in-the-share-economy/.

Tapscott, Don, and Anthony D. Williams. *Wikinomics: How Mass Collaboration Changes Everything*. Expanded ed., Paperback ed. New York, NY: Portfolio/ Penguin, 2010.

TaskRabbit. "TaskRabbit Announces Novel Integration with Amazon Home Services." *TaskRabbit Blog*. Accessed June 19, 2015. http://blog.taskrabbit.com/2015/03/30/ taskrabbit-announces-novel-integration-with-amazon-home-services/.

Taylor, Astra. *The People's Platform: Taking Back Power and Culture in the Digital Age*. New York: Picador, Henry Holt and Company, 2015.

The Linux Foundation. "About Us." *Linux Foundation Web Site*. Accessed August 23, 2015. http://www.linuxfoundation.org/about/about-linux.

"There's an App for That." *The Economist*, January 3, 2015. http://www.economist .com/news/briefing/21637355-freelance-workers-available-moments-notice-will-reshape-nature-companies-and?fsrc=scn/tw_ec/there_s_an_app_for_that.

Tiku, Nitasha. "Airbnb's New Office Has a Replica of the Dr. Strangelove War Room." *Valleywag*, December 3, 2013. http://valleywag.gawker.com/airbnbs-office-has-a-replica-of-the-dr-strangelove-wa-1475788543.

———. "Uber and Its Shady Partners Are Pushing Drivers into Subprime Loans." *Valleywag*. Accessed May 31, 2015. http://valleywag.gawker.com/uber-and-its-shady-partners-are-pushing-drivers-into-su-1649936785.

Titmuss, Richard M., and Ann Oakley. *The Gift Relationship: From Human Blood to Social Policy*. Orig. ed. with new chapters. New York, NY: The New Press, 1997.

Todisco, Michael. "Share and Share Alike? Considering Racial Discrimination in the Nascent Room-Sharing Economy." *Stanford Law Review Online* 67 (March 14, 2015): 121.

Toyama, Kentaro. *Ten Myths of ICT for International Development*. Accessed May 17, 2015. https://www.youtube.com/watch?v=E_mTwm5m8DM&feature=youtu.be.

Trafford, Dave. "Is John Tory Facing an Uber Battle at City Hall?" *Global News*, November 19, 2014. http://globalnews.ca/news/1681159/is-john-tory-facing-an-uber-battle-at-city-hall/.

Trautman, Ted. "Will Uber Serve Customers With Disabilities?," June 302014. http:// nextcity.org/daily/entry/wheelchair-users-ride-share-uber-lyft.

Uber. *Dynamic Pricing 101*. Accessed June 12, 2015. https://www.youtube.com/ watch?v=76q7PDnxWuE.

Underhill, Justine. "Postmates: Rise of the Anti-Amazon." *Yahoo Finance*. Accessed June 21, 2015. http://finance.yahoo.com/news/postmates-ceo-bastian-lehmann-182010837.html.

University of Chicago Press Journals. "Sharing Isn't Always Caring: Why Don't Consumers Take Care of Their Zipcars?" Accessed May 22, 2015. http://press.uchicago.edu/pressReleases/2012/July/JCR_1207_Zipcars.html.

UNWTO. "Annual Report 2013." World Tourism Organization UNWTO, 2014.

User "silentstorm2008." "My Reply to Uber's 'Low Acceptance Rate' Email." Reddit/R/Uberdrivers, November 20, 2014. http://www.reddit.com/r/uberdrivers/comments/2mykji/my_reply_to_ubers_low_acceptance_rate_email/.

Vaccaro, Adam, and Adam Adams. "8,000 Uber, Lyft, Ride-Hailing Drivers Fail New Background Checks - The Boston Globe." BostonGlobe.com, April 5, 2017. https://www.bostonglobe.com/business/2017/04/05/uber-lyft-ride-hailing-drivers-fail-new-background-checks/aX3pQy6QOpJvbtKZKw9fON/story.html.

Varian, Hal R., Joseph Farrell, and Carl Shapiro. The Economics of Information Technology: An Introduction. Cambridge University Press, 2004.

Volunteer Canada. "About Us." Volunteer Canada. Accessed June 8, 2015. http://volunteer.ca/about.

Voytek, Bradley. "Mapping the San Franciscome | Uber Blog." Uber Data Blog, January 9, 2012. http:/blog.uber.com/2012/01/09/uberdata-san-franciscomics/.

Warzel, Charlie. "Sexist French Uber Promotion Pairs Riders With 'Hot Chick' Drivers." BuzzFeed, October 21, 2014. http://www.buzzfeed.com/charliewarzel/french-uber-bird-hunting-promotion-pairs-lyon-riders-with-a.

Watters, Audrey. "The MOOC Revolution That Wasn't." The Kernel, August 23, 2015. http://kernelmag.dailydot.com/issue-sections/headline-story/14046/mooc-revolution-uber-for-education/.

Weise, Karen. "This Is How Uber Takes Over a City." Bloomberg Business, June 23, 2015. http://www.bloomberg.com/news/features/2015-06-23/this-is-how-uber-takes-over-a-city.

Weiss, Geoff. "The Median Income of an Uber Driver in NYC Is Nearly $100,000." Entrepreneur, May 28, 2014. http://www.entrepreneur.com/article/234289.

Wieczner, Jen. "Why the Disabled Are Suing Uber and Lyft." Fortune, May 22, 2015. http://fortune.com/2015/05/22/uber-lyft-disabled/.

Wilhelm, Alex. "Analyzing Postmates' Growth." TechCrunch, March 4, 2015. http://social.techcrunch.com/2015/03/04/analyzing-postmates-growth/.

Wilonsky, Robert. "On the Same Day Dallas Task Force Begins Debating Car-for-Hire Rules, Cab Industry Sues Chicago over Uber, Lyft." City Hall Blog, February 6, 2014. http://cityhallblog.dallasnews.com/2014/02/on-the-same-day-dallas-task-force-begins-debating-car-for-hire-rules-cab-industry-sues-chicago-over-uber-lyft.html/.

Wohlsen, Marcus. "Google Pours Millions Into New Tech Gold Rush: Housecleaning," December 52013. http://www.wired.com/2013/12/google-homejoy-funding/.

Zee, Renate van der. "The 'Airbnb Effect': Is It Real, and What Is It Doing to a City like Amsterdam?" The Guardian, October 6, 2016, sec. Cities. https://www.theguardian.com/cities/2016/oct/06/the-airbnb-effect-amsterdam-fairbnb-property-prices-communities.

Zervas, Georgios, Davide Proserpio, and John Byers. "A First Look at Online Reputation on Airbnb, Where Every Stay Is Above Average." SSRN Scholarly Paper. Rochester, NY: Social Science Research Network, January 28, 2015. http://papers.ssrn.com/abstract=2554500.

Zipcar. "Green Benefits," n.d. http://www.zipcar.com/universities/how/greenbenefits.

Endnotes

Chapter 1

1   Tanz, "How Airbnb and Lyft Finally Got Americans to Trust Each Other."
2   In a completely different context, I am following the example of MacQueen, *The 2001 Anthrax Deception*.
3   Barbrook and Cameron, "The Californian Ideology."

Chapter 2

1   Botsman, "Transcript of 'The Currency of the New Economy Is Trust.'"
2   Fowler and Rusli, "Don't Talk to Strangers, Unless You Plan to Share Your Mac-and-Cheese."
3   Tanz, "How Airbnb and Lyft Finally Got Americans to Trust Each Other."
4   Botsman, "The Sharing Economy Lacks a Shared Definition."
5   Owyang, "The Collaborative Sharing Economy Has Created 17 Billion-Dollar Companies (and 10 Unicorns)."
6   "From the People, for the People."
7   Lapowsky, "Believe It."
8   Schor, "Debating the Sharing Economy."
9   Johnson, *Future Perfect: The Case for Progress in a Networked Age*.
10 Tam and Merced, "Uber Fund-Raising Points to $50 Billion Valuation."
11 LeWeb, *Douglas Atkin - Airbnb - LeWeb London 2013*.
12 Leonard, "The Sharing Economy Gets Greedy."
13 Bulajewski, "The Cult of Sharing."

14   Cortese, "Loans That Avoid Banks?"

15   Clark, "A Transition at Peers to Create Greater Impact."

16   Airbnb, "Organizing in 100 Cities."

Chapter 3

1   Botsman and Rogers, *What's Mine Is Yours: The Rise of Collaborative Consumption.*

2   Chesky, "Shared City."

3   Chesky, "Who We Are, What We Stand For."

4   Baker, "Barclays: Airbnb Usage To Surpass Hotel Cos., But Not For Business Travel."

5   Robinson, "Update from Barcelona: Airbnb Policy Blog."

6   Bradshaw, "Lunch with the FT: Brian Chesky."

7   Airbnb, "Airbnb Economic Impact."

8   Airbnb, "One Way Forward."

9   Said, "Airbnb Profits Prompted S.F. Eviction, Ex-Tenant Says."

10   Marritz, *Two True Stories from the Airbnb Wars."*

11   Airbnb, "Sandy's Impact."

12   Coscarelli, "Airbnb Poster-Child Was Evicted for Airbnb-Ing a Converted Barn She Didn't Own."

13   Hantman, *New York: The next Steps.*

14   Electronic Frontier Foundation, *Airbnb, Inc. v. Schneiderman*; Internet Association, "The Internet Association Files Amicus Brief to Quash the NYAG Subpoena against Airbnb."

15   Chesky, "Who We Are, What We Stand for."

16   Tam, "New York AG's Office.""URL":"http://www.cnet.com/news/new-york-ags-office-airbnb-lying-about-user-data-subpoena/","shortTitle":"New York AG's office","author":[{"family":"Tam","given":"Donna"}],"accessed":{"date-parts":[["2015",5,9]]}}}],"schema":"https://github.com/citation-style-language/schema/raw/master/csl-citation.json"}

17   Flamm, "Strange Bedfellows in Airbnb Dispute."

18   Krueger, "On Behalf of Regular New Yorkers, Sen. Krueger Responds to Airbnb's 'Three Principles.'"

19   Tiku, "Airbnb's New Office Has a Replica of the Dr. Strangelove War Room."

20   "Airbnb in the City."

21   Airbnb, "Airbnb's Economic Impact on New York City."

22   Lecuyer, Tucker, and Chaintreau, "Improving the Transparency of the Sharing Economy."

23   Bingham, "The Sharing Economy: Q&A With Airbnb's Chip Conley."

24   UNWTO, "Annual Report 2013."

25   Kassam, "Naked Italians Spark Protests against Antics of Drunken Tourists in Barcelona."

26   Essers, "Amsterdam Using Airbnb Listing Service to Identify Illegal Rentals."

27   Haverkort, "Airbnb Is Allowed in Amsterdam."

28   Hantman, "Good News from Amsterdam."

29   News, "Amsterdammers Can Rent Their Homes to Tourists via Airbnb after All."

30   Hantman, "More Good News in Amsterdam."

31   News, "Amsterdammers Can Rent Their Homes to Tourists via Airbnb after All."

32   Daalen, "Airbnb to Collect Tourist Taxes in Amsterdam."

33   News, "Amsterdammers Break Airbnb Rules: Long Lets with Too Many People."

34   van der Zee, "The 'Airbnb Effect.'"

35   DutchNews.nl, "Amsterdam Airbnb Fines Mount Up, Top €500,000."

36   Robinson, "Moving Forward in Barcelona."

37   Robinson, "Update from Barcelona: Airbnb Policy Blog."

38   Tadeo, "Airbnb Wants a Truce With Barcelona."

39   Kuchler, "Airbnb to Collect and Remit Taxes for Hosts in Paris."

40   French, Schechner, and Verbergt, "How Airbnb Is Taking Over Paris."

41   Schofield, "Short-Let Apartments Spark Paris Row as Airbnb Thrives."

42   French, Schechner, and Verbergt, "How Airbnb Is Taking Over Paris."

43   Griswold, "Paris Is Blaming Airbnb for Population Declines in the Heart of the City."

44   Slee, "Airbnb Is Facing an Existential Expansion Problem."

45   Njus, "Portland Legalizes Airbnb-Style Short-Term Rentals."

46   Peltier, "Airbnb Faces Big Fines in Portland If Hosts Don't Get City Permits."

47   Mesh, "City Commissioner Nick Fish Berates Airbnb Lobbyist."

48   Njus, "Airbnb to Block Portland Users from Listing Multiple Properties."

49   Davies, "Activists Vow to Buy Abandoned Cinema and Save Rome's Bohemian Soul."

Chapter 4

1   Shaheen, "Transportation Network Companies and Ridesourcing."

2   Gansky, *The Mesh: Why the Future of Business Is Sharing.*

3   Bardhi and Eckhardt, "Access-Based Consumption: The Case of Car Sharing."

4   University of Chicago Press Journals, "Sharing Isn't Always Caring."

5   Kell, "Avis to Buy Car-Sharing Service Zipcar."

6   Zipcar, "Green Benefits."

7   Sadowski, "Hey, Ride-Sharing Services. Stop Greenwashing!"

8   Schor, "Debating the Sharing Economy."

9   Gannes, "Zimride Turns Regular Cars Into Taxis With New Ride-Sharing App, Lyft."

10   Gustin, "Lyft-Off: Car-Sharing Start-Up Raises $60 Million Led by Andreessen Horowitz."

11   Ibid.

12   Gannes, "Zimride Turns Regular Cars Into Taxis With New Ride-Sharing App, Lyft."

13   Gannes, "Lyft Sells Zimride Carpool Service to Rental-Car Giant Enterprise."

14   Gannes, "Competition Brings Lyft, Sidecar and Uber Closer to Cloning Each Other."

15   Carson, "Lyft Tripled Its Rides in 2016."

16   Auchard and Frost, "BlaBlaCar Changes Gear by Offering Drivers Car Leases."

17   D'Onfro, "Uber CEO Founded The Company Because He Wanted To Be A 'Baller In San Francisco.'"

18   Meelen and Frenken, "Stop Saying Uber Is Part Of The Sharing Economy."

19   Scola, "The Black Car Company That People Love to Hate."

20   Kalanick, "Uber Policy White Paper 1.0."

21   Hall and Krueger, "An Analysis of the Labor Market for Uber's Driver-Partners in the United States."

22   Geron, "California Becomes First State To Regulate Ridesharing Services Lyft, Sidecar, UberX."

23   Ferguson, "Recent Transportation Network Company Ordinances."

24   California Public Utilities Commission, "Transportation Network Companies."

25   Hirsch, "Taxi Trouble."

26   Watters, "The MOOC Revolution That Wasn't."

27   Trafford, "Is John Tory Facing an Uber Battle at City Hall?"

28   Paris, "Electric 'Boris Cars' Are Coming to London – How Do They Work in Paris?"

29   Biddle, "Here Are the Internal Documents That Prove Uber Is a Money Loser."

30   Kalanick and Swisher, "Uber CEO: We're in a Political Battle with an 'Assh*le.'"

31   Kalanick, "A Leader for the Uber Campaign."

32   Dempsey, "Taxi Industry Regulation, Deregulation, and Reregulation."

33   Rosen, "The Knowledge, London's Legendary Taxi-Driver Test, Puts Up a Fight in the Age of GPS."

34   Leisy, "TAXICAB DEREGULATION AND REREGULATION IN SEATTLE: LESSONS LEARNED."

35   Sadlak, "Taxicab Deregulation."

36   Dubinsky, Gollom, and Rieti, "Cab Driving Riskier than Police Work."

37   Dale, "Council Votes to Overhaul Toronto Taxi Industry."

38   Gans, "Is Uber Really in a Fight to the Death?"

39   Swisher, "Man and Uber Man."

40   "Craig," "An Uber Impact."

41   McFarland, "Uber's Remarkable Growth Could End the Era of Poorly Paid Cab Drivers."

42   CNBC.com staff, "Uber's $90K Salary Could Disrupt the Taxi Business."

43   Weiss, "The Median Income of an Uber Driver in NYC Is Nearly $100,000."

44   Bowles, "Tech Titans on Income Inequality and Their 'Stingy, Stingy' Industry."

45   Salmon, "Why Cab Drivers Should Love Uber"; Salmon, "The Economics of 'Everyone's Private Driver.'"

46   Salmon, "How Well uberX Pays, Part 2."

47   Slee, "Uber Drivers Earning $90K/Year?"

48   Hall and Krueger, "An Analysis of the Labor Market for Uber's Driver-Partners in the United States."

49   Bhuiyan, "What Uber Drivers Really Make (According To Their Pay Stubs)"; Griswold, "In Search of Uber's Unicorn."

50   Soper, "Uber Now Charging Drivers $520 per Year to Lease Company iPhone."

51   Huet, "Uber Now Taking Its Biggest UberX Commission Ever---25 Percent."

52   Lopez, "Billionaire Hedge-Fund Manager Says Uber Told Him It Might Cut Driver Pay 'Because We Can.'"

53   "Andrew," "Three Septembers of uberX in New York City."

54   "Andrew," "What Does a Typical New York uberX Partner Earn in a Week?"

55   Hall and Krueger, "An Analysis of the Labor Market for Uber's Driver-Partners in the United States." The report has frequently been referred to as a "paper," but given that it was paid for by Uber and was not subjected to any external review the word "report" is more accurate.

56   For example, Ellen Huet at *Forbes*, Jacob Davidson at *Time*, Andrea Peterson at the *Washington Post*.

57   Peterson, "The Missing Data Point from Uber's Driver Analysis."

58   Baker, "Ubernomics."

59   Guendelsberger, "Infographic."

60   Booth, "Uber Whistleblower Exposes Breach in Driver-Approval Process."

61   Biddle, "Uber Driver."

62   Skinner, "California Prosecutors Say Uber's Background Checks Missed Convicts."

63   Vaccaro and Adams, "8,000 Uber, Lyft, Ride-Hailing Drivers Fail New Background Checks - The Boston Globe."

64   Said, "As Uber, Lyft, Sidecar Grow, so Do Concerns of Disabled."

65   Wieczner, "Why the Disabled Are Suing Uber and Lyft."

66   Trautman, "Will Uber Serve Customers With Disabilities?"

67   Strochlic, "Uber."

68   Redmond, "Does Airbnb Have an ADA Problem?"

69   Peterson, "Uber Does Not Care about Racism, It Cares about Money."

70   Ge et al., "Racial and Gender Discrimination in Transportation Network Companies."

71   Wilonsky, "On the Same Day Dallas Task Force Begins Debating Car-for-Hire Rules, Cab Industry Sues Chicago over Uber, Lyft"; Peck, "Uber's New Delivery Service Only Caters To D.C.'s White Neighborhoods."

72   Stark and Diakopoulos, "Uber Seems to Offer Better Service in Areas with More White People. That Raises Some Tough Questions."

73   Hall and Krueger, "An Analysis of the Labor Market for Uber's Driver-Partners in the United States."

74   Edelman and Luca, *Digital Discrimination: The Case of Airbnb.com.*

75   Hannak et al., "Bias in Online Freelance Marketplaces: Evidence from TaskRabbit."

76   Rosenblat et al., "Discriminating Tastes"; Belzer and Leong, "The New Public Accommodations."

77   Todisco, "Share and Share Alike?"

78   Norris et al., "Black and Blue."

79   Norris, "The Sociological Implications of Smart Surveillance Systems."

80   Rosenblat et al., "Discriminating Tastes."

81   Tiku, "Uber and Its Shady Partners Are Pushing Drivers into Subprime Loans."

82   DeAmicis, "Uber Starts Directly Leasing Cars in Program That Could Appeal to Short-Term Drivers."

83   User "silentstorm2008, "My Reply to Uber's 'Low Acceptance Rate' Email."

84   Calo and Rosenblat, "The Taking Economy."

85   Scheiber, "How Uber Uses Psychological Tricks to Push Its Drivers' Buttons."

86   Calo and Rosenblat, "The Taking Economy."

87   Isaac, "How Uber Deceives the Authorities Worldwide."

88   Smith, "Uber Executive Suggests Digging Up Dirt On Journalists."

89   Hill, "'God View.'"

90   Voytek, "Mapping the San Franciscome | Uber Blog."

91   Bhuiyan and Warzel, "God View."

92   Cushing, "Uber Employees Warned a San Francisco Magazine Writer That Executives Might Snoop on Her."

93   Rapkin, "Uber Cab Confessions."

94   Ryssdal, "Uber's Data Makes a Creepy Point about the Company."

95   E.J. Dickson, "Gross, Sexist French Uber Campaign Features 'Sexy Girl' Drivers."

96   Warzel, "Sexist French Uber Promotion Pairs Riders With 'Hot Chick' Drivers."

97   Biddle, "Uber Calls Woman's 20-Mile Nightmare Abduction an 'Inefficient Route.'"

98   Bruce, "Uber Miami Accused of Coaching Drivers to Circumvent Airport Laws."

99   Fink, "Uber-Nasty?"

100 Fenske, "After Our Uber Exposé, Their PR Team Tried to Dupe Us."

101 Bhuiyan, "Uber Sought To Hire Opposition Researcher To 'Weaponize Facts.'"

102 Geist, "Popular yet Controversial App-Based Car Service Has No Privacy Policy Specific to Canada."

103 Powell, "City Councillor Asks Federal Taxman to Investigate after Email States Riders Aren't Charged HST. Uber Canada Says Its Drivers Are Responsible for Collecting and Remitting the Tax."

104 O'Keefe and Jones, "How Uber Plays the Tax Shell Game."

105 Fowler, "Reflecting on One Very, Very Strange Year at Uber."

106 Kalanick, "Celebrating Cities."

107 Horan, "Can Uber Ever Deliver?"

108 Newcomer, "Uber, Lifting Financial Veil, Says Sales Growth Outpaces Losses."

Chapter 5

1   Crunchbase, "TaskRabbit."

2   Silver, "The Sharing Economy: A Whole New Way of Living."

3   Carhart, "The Ten Ninety Nihilists."

4   Shontell, "My Nightmare Experience As A TaskRabbit Drone."

5   Raphel, "TaskRabbit Redux."

6   Said, "TaskRabbit Makes Some Workers Hopping Mad."

7   TaskRabbit, "TaskRabbit Announces Novel Integration with Amazon Home Services."

8   Wohlsen, "Google Pours Millions Into New Tech Gold Rush: Housecleaning."

9   Jordan, "Unpacking the Grocery Stack."

10   DePillis, "At the Uber for Home Cleaning, Workers Pay a Price for Convenience."

11   Geron, "Startup Homejoy Works With Public Sector To Find Home Cleaners."

12   Roose, "Does Silicon Valley Have a Contract-Worker Problem?"

13   Shieber, "Handy Hits $1 Million A Week In Bookings As Cleaning Economy Consolidates."

14   Handy Corporation, "About Us."

15   Reader, "Handybook Rebrands as Handy to Help Build Consumer Trust."

16   Handybook, "Handybook Raises $30 Million in Series B Led by Revolution Growth."

17   Jacobs, "Handybook Rebrands As Handy, Says It Grew 10x in Past 9 Months."

18   Handy, "Be a Professional with Handy!"

19   "There's an App for That."

20   Huet, "Apps Let Users Hire House Cleaners, Handymen without Talking."

21   Manjoo, "Grocery Deliveries in Sharing Economy."

22   DeAmicis, "On the Way to $220M in Funding, Instacart Quietly Changed Its Business Model."

23   Rao, "Instacart Is Asking Its Customers to Do Something New."

24   Erbentraut, "Here's What The People Delivering Your Instacart Groceries Really Think."

25   Manjoo, "Grocery Deliveries in Sharing Economy."

26   Wilhelm, "Analyzing Postmates' Growth."

27   Underhill, "Postmates."

28   Naughton, "Meet Tech's New Concierge Economy, Where Serfs Deliver Stuff to Rich Folk."

29   Haque, "The Servitude Bubble—Bad Words."

Chapter 6

1   Clampet, "Airbnb CEO Responds to Illegal Rentals Story."

2   Friedman, "And Now for a Bit of Good News . . ."

3   Brooks, "The Evolution of Trust."

4   Strahilevitz, "Less Regulation, More Reputation."

5   Botsman, "Welcome to the New Reputation Economy."

6   Clampet, "Airbnb CEO Responds to Illegal Rentals Story."

7   Lawler, *Mr. Kalanick Goes to Washington: How Uber Won in DC.*

8   Lieber, "Airbnb Horror Story Points to Need for Precautions."

9   Gambetta and Bacharach, "Trust in Signs."

10   Spence, "Job Market Signaling."

11   Marwick, *Status Update: Celebrity, Publicity, & Branding in the Social Media Age.*

12   Farmer and Glass, *Building Web Reputation Systems.*, p 61.

13   Salganick, Dodds, and Watts, "Experimental Study of Inequality and Unpredictability in an Artificial Cultural Market."

14   Zervas, Proserpio, and Byers, "A First Look at Online Reputation on Airbnb, Where Every Stay Is Above Average."

15   Kane, "The Big Hidden Problem With Uber?"

16   Bercovici, "Uber's Ratings Terrorize Drivers And Trick Riders. Why Not Fix Them?"

17   Dellarocas and Wood, "The Sound of Silence in Online Feedback: Estimating Trading Risks in the Presence of Reporting Bias."

18   Hutt, "The Truth About BBB and Uber"; Huet, "Uber's 'F' Rating At Better Business Bureau Isn't For Surge Pricing--Just For Unresponsiveness."

19   Tanz, "How Airbnb and Lyft Finally Got Americans to Trust Each Other."

20   Sauchelli and Golding, "Hookers Turning Airbnb Apartments into Brothels."

21   CBC News, "Airbnb Renters Who Trashed Calgary House Used Fake Credit Cards to Fuel Party."

22   McKenzie, "Airbnb Host Left Violated after Busting Fanny Pack–Clad Male Prostitutes in Her Apartment."

23   Chesters and Smith, "The Neglected Art of Hitch-Hiking: Risk, Trust and Sustainability."

24   Fradkin, "Search Frictions and the Design of Online Marketplaces."

25   Airbnb, "Building Trust with a New Review System."

26   Nosko and Tadelis, "The Limits of Reputation in Platform Markets: An Empirical Analysis and Field Experiment."

Chapter 7

1   Varian, Farrell, and Shapiro, *The Economics of Information Technology: An Introduction.*

2   Raymond, *The Cathedral and the Bazaar.*

3   Benkler, *The Wealth of Networks: How Social Production Transforms Markets and Freedom.*

4   Benkler, "Coase's Penguin, or Linux and the Nature of the Firm."

5   The Linux Foundation, "About Us."

6   Corbet, Kroah-Hartman, and McPherson, "Who Writes Linux: Linux Kernel Development: How Fast It Is Going, Who Is Doing It, What They Are Doing, and Who Is Sponsoring It."

7   Asay, "For 50 Percent of Developers, Open Source Is a 9-to-5 Job"; Riehle et al., "Paid vs. Volunteer Work in Open Source."

8   Asay, "The Effects of Commercialization on Open-Source Communities"; Berdou, "Managing the Bazaar: Commercialization and Peripheral Participation in Mature, Community-Led Free/Open Source Software Projects."

9   Rosenberg, "The Meaning of Open."

10   Pasquale, *The Black Box Society.*

11   Rosenberg, "The Future Is Open."

12   Tapscott and Williams, *Wikinomics.*

13   Many group themselves under the label of "hackers." For a perceptive study see Coleman, *Coding Freedom: The Ethics and Aesthetics of Hacking.*

14   Harris, "Under the Covers of the NSA's Big Data Effort."

15   Burkhardt and Waring, "An NSA Big Graph Experiment."

16   Gardner, "Wikipedia at 10."

17   Anderson, *The Long Tail: Why the Future of Business Is Selling Less of More.*

18   Ibid., p1.

19   Ibid., p 40.

20   Ibid., p. 16.

21   Chesky, "Shared City."

22   Elberse, *Blockbusters: Hit-Making, Risk-Taking, and the Big Business of Entertainment.* See also her earlier papers on the subject such as Elberse and Oberholzer-Gee, "Superstars and Underdogs: An Examination of the Long Tail Phenomenon in Video Sales"; Elberse, "Should You Invest in the Long Tail?"

23   Elberse, *Blockbusters: Hit-Making, Risk-Taking, and the Big Business of Entertainment.*, p. 71.

24   Ibid., p. 166.

25   Ibid., p. 159.

26   Lessig, *Remix.*, p. 29.

27   Ibid., p. 132.

28   Ibid., p. 108.

29   Lessig, *Remix.*, p. xvi.

30   Taylor, *People's Platform.*

31   Ibid., p. 47.

32   Ibid., p. 141–42.

33   Keating, "What Should I Do about Youtube?"

34   Rankin, "Publish and Be Branded." See also Robinson, "The Loneliness of the Long-Distance Reader," and Marosevic, "Is the Mid-List, 'publishing's Experimental Laboratory,' Disappearing?"

35   Clemons, "What An Antitrust Case Against Google Might Look Like."

36   Reynolds, *An Army of Davids*.

37   Hindman, *The Myth of Digital Democracy*.

38   Ibid., p. 100.

39   Open Knowledge Foundation, "What Is Open?"

40   Lathrop and Ruma, *Open Government*.

41   Open Knowledge Foundation, "What Is Open?"

42   Raman, "The Rhetoric of Transparency and Its Reality."

43   Benjamin et al., "Bhoomi: 'E-Governance', Or, An Anti-Politics Machine Necessary to Globalize Bangalore?"

44   Gurstein, "Open Data."

45   Gurstein, "Are the Open Data Warriors Fighting for Robin Hood or the Sheriff?"

46   Toyama, *Ten Myths of ICT for International Development*.

47   Scott, *Seeing Like a State: How Certain Schemes to Improve the Human Condition Have Failed*.

48   Donovan, "Seeing Like a Slum."

49   Maron, "Brain Off » We Need to Stop Google's Exploitation of Open Communities."

50   Scassa and Campbell, "Data Protection, Privacy and Spatial Data."

51   Bates, "'This Is What Modern Deregulation Looks Like': Co-Optation and Contestation in the Shaping of the UK's Open Government Data Initiative."

52   O'Neill and Townsend, "Food Security Open Data Challenge | USAID Impact."

53   Grant and Wood, *Blockbusters and Trade Wars: Popular Culture in a Globalized World*.

54   Davies, "Digital Marketplaces."

Chapter 8

1   See Lessig, *Remix*. and Linksvayer, "CC as a Hybrid Organization and a Tool for Hybrids - Creative Commons."

2   Johnson, *Future Perfect: The Case for Progress in a Networked Age*.

3   An illuminating review of all these perspectives is given in Fourcade and Healy, "Moral Views of Market Society."

4   Putnam, *Bowling Alone*.

5   Friedman, "Airbnb CEO."

6   Shirky, *Cognitive Surplus*.

7   Volunteer Canada, "About Us."

8   Satz, *Why Some Things Should Not Be for Sale.*, p. 80

9   Titmuss and Oakley, *The Gift Relationship*.

10   Uber, *Dynamic Pricing 101*; Laband, "An Economics Lesson at the Baggage Carousel."

11   "Alex," "Happy New Year!"

12   Satz, *Why Some Things Should Not Be for Sale.*

13   Cresci, "Uber Offers Free Rides after Backlash over Surge Pricing during Sydney Siege."

14   Berman, "Why Uber Will Limit Its Surge Pricing during the Snow Emergency."

15   Harvey, *Rebel Cities*.

16   The broad meaning contrasts with a narrower technical meaning of goods that are rivalrous (my use of it interferes with yours) and yet non-excludable (individuals cannot be excluded from the benefits of the common). This technical meaning contrasts with commodities (rivalrous, excludable, and so often privately owned); with public goods (non-rivalrous, non-excludable); and club goods (non-rivalrous, but excludable).

17   Harvey, *Rebel Cities*, p. 71.

18   A community may hire a commercial organization to manage a commons, but the arrangements *among members of the community* remain outside the scope of market transactions.

19   Harvey, *Rebel Cities*, p. 89.

20   Ibid., p. 90.

21   Ostrom, *Governing the Commons: The Evolution of Institutions for Collective Action*.

22   Harvey, *Rebel Cities*, p. 72.

23   Ibid., p. 73.

24   Harvey, *Rebel Cities*. p. 74.

25   Ibid.

26   Baker, "Not-for-Profit Couchsurfing Becomes a Company (with a Conscience)."

27   Coca, "The Rise and Fall of Couchsurfing."

28   Lewis, "Couchsurfing."

29   Bollier, "Lessons from the Corporatization of Couchsurfing."

30   Shirky, *Cognitive Surplus*.

31   Bruck, "Millions for Millions."

32   Sinclair, *Confessions of a Microfinance Heretic*.

33   Kiva, "Kiva - Lift Above Poverty Organization (LAPO)."

34   Strom, "Confusion on Where Money Lent via Kiva Goes."

35   Strom and Bajaj, "Rich I.P.O. Brings Controversy to Microlender, SKS Microfinance."

36   Ibid.

37   Associated Press, "SKS Under Spotlight in Suicides."

38   Sinclair, *Confessions of a Microfinance Heretic*, p. 227.

39   Ibid., p. 236.

40   Koch, "Omidyar/Hewlett Press Release - GlobalGiving."

41   Harvey, *Rebel Cities*, p. 78.

42   Ibid., p. 104.

43   Ibid., p. 105.

44   Ibid., p. 106

45   Hornig, "Darth Vader vs. Death Strip."

46   Harvey, *Rebel Cities*, pp. 107–08.

47   Ibid., p. 109.

48   Grim, "Change.org Changing: Site To Drop Progressive Litmus Test For Campaigns, Say Internal Documents."

49   Beyerstein, "Change.org Quietly Changing Course."

50   Grim, "Change.org Changing: Site To Drop Progressive Litmus Test For Campaigns, Say Internal Documents."

51   Botsman, "Collaborative Finance."

52   "From the People, for the People."

53   Cortese, "Loans That Avoid Banks?"

54   Ibid.

55   Banjo, "Wall Street Is Hogging the Peer-to-Peer Lending Market."

56   Banjo, "Citgroup Has Finally Thrown Its Lot in with Online Lending."

57   McMillan, "Peer-To-Peer Lending Is Dead."

58   Cortese, "Loans That Avoid Banks?"

59   McMillan, "Peer-To-Peer Lending Is Dead."

Chapter 9

1   Mintz, "Residents of Toronto's Kensington Market Concerned as Airbnb Moves in."

2   Ibid.

3   Fernholtz, "Is Uber Costing New Yorkers $1.2 Billion Worth of Lost Time?"

4   Bisby, "'Airbnb for Dogs.'"

5   O'Reilly, "Networks and the Nature of the Firm."

6   Legal Information Institute, "47 U.S. Code § 230 - Protection for Private Blocking and Screening of Offensive Material."

7   Electronic Frontier Foundation, "Section 230 Protections."

8   Scola, "The Very Big Thing That Uber, Lyft and Sidecar Didn't Get From California – Next City."

9   LoGiurato, "This Is The One Law Airbnb's Opponents Desperately Want To Change."

10   Weise, "This Is How Uber Takes Over a City."

11   Sanders, "Rental Rules In California Raise Questions About Who's Using Airbnb."

12   Story and Lowrey, "The Fed, Lawrence Summers, and Money."

13   Levy and Campbell, "EBay-Style Loans Lure Summers to Mack in Wall Street Asset Craze."

14   Pasquale, *The Black Box Society.*

15   Smith-Spark and Mullen, "France Tells Paris Police to Crack down on Uber - CNN.com."

16   Dyer, "Uber Says It Will Support Drivers Fined by Police in Costa Rica - "

17   Kassam, "Barcelona's Tourist Hordes Are Target for Radical New Mayor Ada Colau."

18   Lu, "Do Companies like Uber, Handy Fuel Underground Economy?"

19   Montgomery, "Handy Sued for Being a Hellscape of Labor Code Violations."

20   Huet, "Contractor or Employee? Silicon Valley's Branding Dilemma."

21   Chu, "Fedex's $228 Million Settlement Could Dent Uber, Lyft, Postmates, Homejoy, Caviar and Other San Francisco Companies Using Low-Cost Independent Contractors for Labor."

22   Pyke, "California Truckers Will Get $2.2 Million In Back Pay For Being Misclassified."

23 Hill, "Meet the Lawyer Taking on Uber and the Rest of the on-Demand Economy."

24 Isaac and Singer, "California Says Uber Driver Is Employee, Not a Contractor."

25 Paul, "Uber as For-Profit Hiring Hall."

26 Katz, "Regulating the Sharing Economy."

27 Belzer and Leong, "The New Public Accommodations."

28 Ibid.

29 Snelson, Mr Y Aslam, Mr J Farrar and Others -V- Uber.

30 Calo and Rosenblat, "The Taking Economy."

31 Gorenflo, "OuiShare Fest Finds Itself While Lost in Transition."

32 Morozov, *To Save Everything, Click Here*.

Acknowledgements

This work started to be a book in November 2014, when Trebor Scholz invited me to a conference on Digital Labor at The New School in New York City, Astra Taylor arranged a lunch with John Oakes as if it were nothing (it wasn't), and he took a chance on this project. The good people at OR Books took a manuscript and edited, designed and produced it into much more professional shape than they received.

Before that, I'd been following a pack of journalists providing critical, insightful and entertaining reporting on the emerging Sharing Economy, turning it into a beat worth covering. Pack leaders included Johana Bhuiyan, Sam Biddle, Susie Cagle, Liz Gannes, Ellen Huet, Andrew Leonard, Andrew Orlowski, Nancy Scola, and Nitasha Tiku. Meanwhile, exchanges with Frank Pasquale, James Grimmelmann, Cathy O'Neill, Karen Gregory, Tom Lee, and Denise Cheng left me wiser and with much to reflect on.

Parts of Chapter 7 and 8 appeared first in *The New Inquiry* and owed a lot to the insights and editing of Rob Horning. *The Jacobin* provided a place to work out some early ideas that are sprinkled throughout the book. Parts of Chapter 7 appeared as an invited post at the *Crooked Timber* blog as a contribution to a seminar on Open Government Data organized by Henry Farrell, who has been a source of support and inspiration.

In Waterloo, the engineering team at SAP Waterloo and my colleagues in product management continually show me how smart technology professionals can be (opinions in this book are, of course, independent of my employer). It's been a pleasure to share the progress on this work with the Friday evening seminar group.

Most close to home, I've benefited from years of helpful conversations with John, Jeff, and Liz Slee; Jamie Supeene and Simon Slee have been full of encouragement and I've been inspired by their own efforts as they shape their lives in difficult economic times. Lynne Supeene has been both a perceptive reader of this manuscript and a wonderful partner through life.

Remaining shortcomings and errors are entirely my responsibility and persist despite the efforts of those listed above.

Index

O/R C

AVAILABLE AT GOOD BOOKSTORES EVERYWHERE
FROM OR BOOKS/COUNTERPOINT PRESS

Beautiful Trouble
A Toolbox for Revolution
ASSEMBLED BY ANDREW BOYD
WITH DAVE OSWALD MITCHELL

Desperately Seeking Self-Improvement
A Year Inside the Optimization Movement
CARL CEDERSTRÖM AND ANDRÉ SPICER

Bowie
SIMON CRITCHLEY

Extinction
A Radical History
ASHLEY DAWSON

Black Ops Advertising
Native Ads, Content Marketing, and the Covert World of the Digital Sell
MARA EINSTEIN

Assuming Boycott
Resistance, Agency, and Cultural Production
EDITED BY KAREEM ESTEFAN, CARIN KUONI, AND LAURA RAICOVICH

Swords in the Hands of Children
Reflections of an American Revolutionary
JONATHAN LERNER

Folding the Red into the Black
or Developing a Viable Untopia for Human Survival in the 21st Century
WALTER MOSLEY

Inferno
(A Poet's Novel)
EILEEN MYLES

With Ash on Their Faces
Yezidi Women and the Islamic State
CATHY OTTEN

Pocket Piketty
A Handy Guide to Capital in the Twenty-first Century
JESPER ROINE

Ours to Hack and to Own
The Rise of Platform Cooperativism, A New Vision for the Future of Work and a Fairer Internet
EDITED BY TREBOR SCHOLZ AND NATHAN SCHNEIDER

Distributed to the trade by Publishers Group West